Hands-On Reinforcemen Learning with Python

CW00370576

Master reinforcement and deep reinforcement learning using OpenAI Gym and TensorFlow

Sudharsan Ravichandiran

BIRMINGHAM - MUMBAI

Hands-On Reinforcement Learning with Python

Copyright © 2018 Packt Publishing

All rights reserved. No part of this book may be reproduced, stored in a retrieval system, or transmitted in any form or by any means, without the prior written permission of the publisher, except in the case of brief quotations embedded in critical articles or reviews.

Every effort has been made in the preparation of this book to ensure the accuracy of the information presented. However, the information contained in this book is sold without warranty, either express or implied. Neither the author, nor Packt Publishing or its dealers and distributors, will be held liable for any damages caused or alleged to have been caused directly or indirectly by this book.

Packt Publishing has endeavored to provide trademark information about all of the companies and products mentioned in this book by the appropriate use of capitals. However, Packt Publishing cannot guarantee the accuracy of this information.

Commissioning Editor: Sunith Shetty
Acquisition Editor: Namrata Patil
Content Development Editor: Amrita Noronha
Technical Editor: Jovita Alva
Copy Editor: Safis Editing
Project Coordinator: Shweta H Birwatkar
Proofreader: Safis Editing
Indexer: Rekha Nair
Graphics: Jisha Chirayil
Production Coordinator: Shantanu Zagade

First published: June 2018

Production reference: 1260618

Published by Packt Publishing Ltd.
Livery Place
35 Livery Street
Birmingham
B3 2PB, UK.

ISBN 978-1-78883-652-4

www.packtpub.com

To my adorable parents, to my brother, Karthikeyan, and to my bestest friend, Nikhil Aditya.

– Sudharsan Ravichandiran

`mapt.io`

Mapt is an online digital library that gives you full access to over 5,000 books and videos, as well as industry leading tools to help you plan your personal development and advance your career. For more information, please visit our website.

Why subscribe?

- Spend less time learning and more time coding with practical eBooks and Videos from over 4,000 industry professionals

- Improve your learning with Skill Plans built especially for you

- Get a free eBook or video every month

- Mapt is fully searchable

- Copy and paste, print, and bookmark content

PacktPub.com

Did you know that Packt offers eBook versions of every book published, with PDF and ePub files available? You can upgrade to the eBook version at `www.PacktPub.com` and as a print book customer, you are entitled to a discount on the eBook copy. Get in touch with us at `service@packtpub.com` for more details.

At `www.PacktPub.com`, you can also read a collection of free technical articles, sign up for a range of free newsletters, and receive exclusive discounts and offers on Packt books and eBooks.

Contributors

About the author

Sudharsan Ravichandiran is a data scientist, researcher, artificial intelligence enthusiast, and YouTuber (search for *Sudharsan reinforcement learning*). He completed his bachelors in information technology at Anna University. His area of research focuses on practical implementations of deep learning and reinforcement learning, which includes natural language processing and computer vision. He used to be a freelance web developer and designer and has designed award-winning websites. He is an open source contributor and loves answering questions on Stack Overflow.

I would like to thank my amazing parents and my brother, Karthikeyan, for constantly inspiring and motivating me throughout this journey. My big thanks and gratitude to my bestest friend, Nikhil Aditya, who is literally the bestest, and to my editor, Amrita, and to my Soeor. Without all their support, it would have been impossible to complete this book.

About the reviewers

Sujit Pal is a Technology Research Director at Elsevier Labs, an advanced technology group within the Reed-Elsevier Group of companies. His areas of interests include semantic search, natural language processing, machine learning, and deep learning. At Elsevier, he has worked on several initiatives involving search quality measurement and improvement, image classification and duplicate detection, and annotation and ontology development for medical and scientific corpora. He has co-authored a book on deep learning with Antonio Gulli and writes about technology on his blog, *Salmon Run*.

Suriyadeepan Ramamoorthy is an AI researcher and engineer from Puducherry, India. His primary areas of research are natural language understanding and reasoning. He actively blogs about deep learning.

At SAAMA technologies, he applies advanced deep learning techniques for biomedical text analysis. He is a free software evangelist who is actively involved in community development activities at FSFTN. His other interests include community networks, data visualization and creative coding.

Packt is searching for authors like you

If you're interested in becoming an author for Packt, please visit `authors.packtpub.com` and apply today. We have worked with thousands of developers and tech professionals, just like you, to help them share their insight with the global tech community. You can make a general application, apply for a specific hot topic that we are recruiting an author for, or submit your own idea.

Table of Contents

Preface

Reinforcement learning is a self-evolving type of machine learning that takes us closer to achieving true artificial intelligence. This easy-to-follow guide explains everything from scratch using rich examples written in Python.

Who this book is for

This book is intended for machine learning developers and deep learning enthusiasts who are interested in artificial intelligence and want to learn about reinforcement learning from scratch. Read this book and become a reinforcement learning expert by implementing practical examples at work or in projects. Having some knowledge of linear algebra, calculus, and the Python programming language will help you understand the flow of the book.

What this book covers

Chapter 1, *Introduction to Reinforcement Learning*, helps us understand what reinforcement learning is and how it works. We will learn about various elements of reinforcement learning, such as agents, environments, policies, and models, and we will see different types of environments, platforms, and libraries used for reinforcement learning. Later in the chapter, we will see some of the applications of reinforcement learning.

Chapter 2, *Getting Started with OpenAI and TensorFlow*, helps us set up our machine for various reinforcement learning tasks. We will learn how to set up our machine by installing Anaconda, Docker, OpenAI Gym, Universe, and TensorFlow. Then we will learn how to simulate agents in OpenAI Gym, and we will see how to build a video game bot. We will also learn the fundamentals of TensorFlow and see how to use TensorBoard for visualizations.

Chapter 3, The *Markov Decision Process and Dynamic Programming*, starts by explaining what a Markov chain and a Markov process is, and then we will see how reinforcement learning problems can be modeled as Markov Decision Processes. We will also learn about several fundamental concepts, such as value functions, Q functions, and the Bellman equation. Then we will see what dynamic programming is and how to solve the frozen lake problem using value and policy iteration.

Chapter 4, *Gaming with Monte Carlo Methods*, explains Monte Carlo methods and different types of Monte Carlo prediction methods, such as first visit MC and every visit MC. We will also learn how to use Monte Carlo methods to play blackjack. Then we will explore different on-policy and off-policy Monte Carlo control methods.

Chapter 5, *Temporal Difference Learning*, covers temporal-difference (TD) learning, TD prediction, and TD off-policy and on-policy control methods such as Q learning and SARSA. We will also learn how to solve the taxi problem using Q learning and SARSA.

Chapter 6, *Multi-Armed Bandit Problem*, deals with one of the classic problems of reinforcement learning, the multi-armed bandit (MAB) or k-armed bandit problem. We will learn how to solve this problem using various exploration strategies, such as epsilon-greedy, softmax exploration, UCB, and Thompson sampling. Later in the chapter, we will see how to show the right ad banner to the user using MAB.

Chapter 7, *Deep Learning Fundamentals*, covers various fundamental concepts of deep learning. First, we will learn what a neural network is, and then we will see different types of neural network, such as RNN, LSTM, and CNN. We will learn by building several applications that do tasks such as generating song lyrics and classifying fashion products.

Chapter 8, *Atari Games with Deep Q Network*, covers one of the most widely used deep reinforcement learning algorithms, which is called the deep Q network (DQN). We will learn about DQN by exploring its various components, and then we will see how to build an agent to play Atari games using DQN. Then we will look at some of the upgrades to the DQN architecture, such as double DQN and dueling DQN.

Chapter 9, *Playing Doom with a Deep Recurrent Q Network*, explains the deep recurrent Q network (DRQN) and how it differs from a DQN. We will see how to build an agent to play Doom using a DRQN. Later in the chapter, we will learn about the deep attention recurrent Q network, which adds the attention mechanism to the DRQN architecture.

Chapter 10, *The Asynchronous Advantage Actor Critic Network*, explains how the Asynchronous Advantage Actor Critic (A3C) network works. We will explore the A3C architecture in detail, and then we will learn how to build an agent for driving up the mountain using A3C.

Chapter 11, *Policy Gradients and Optimization*, covers how policy gradients help us find the right policy without needing the Q function. We will also explore the deep deterministic policy gradient method. Later in the chapter, we will see state of the art policy optimization methods such as trust region policy optimization and proximal policy optimization.

Chapter 12, *Capstone Project – Car Racing Using DQN*, provides a step-by-step approach for building an agent to win a car racing game using dueling DQN.

Chapter 13, *Recent Advancements and Next Steps*, provides information about various advancements in reinforcement learning, such as imagination augmented agents, learning from human preference, deep learning from demonstrations, and hindsight experience replay, and then we will look at different types of reinforcement learning methods, such as hierarchical reinforcement learning and inverse reinforcement learning.

To get the most out of this book

You need the following software for this book:

- Anaconda
- Python
- Any web browser
- Docker

Download the example code files

You can download the example code files for this book from your account at www.packtpub.com. If you purchased this book elsewhere, you can visit www.packtpub.com/support and register to have the files emailed directly to you.

You can download the code files by following these steps:

1. Log in or register at www.packtpub.com.
2. Select the **SUPPORT** tab.
3. Click on **Code Downloads & Errata**.
4. Enter the name of the book in the **Search** box and follow the onscreen instructions.

Once the file is downloaded, please make sure that you unzip or extract the folder using the latest version of:

- WinRAR/7-Zip for Windows
- Zipeg/iZip/UnRarX for Mac
- 7-Zip/PeaZip for Linux

The code bundle for the book is also hosted on GitHub at `https://github.com/PacktPublishing/Hands-On-Reinforcement-Learning-with-Python`. In case there's an update to the code, it will be updated on the existing GitHub repository.

We also have other code bundles from our rich catalog of books and videos available at `https://github.com/PacktPublishing/`. Check them out!

Download the color images

We also provide a PDF file that has color images of the screenshots/diagrams used in this book. You can download it here: `http://www.packtpub.com/sites/default/files/downloads/HandsOnReinforcementLearningwithPython_ColorImages.pdf`.

Conventions used

There are a number of text conventions used throughout this book.

`CodeInText`: Indicates code words in text, database table names, folder names, filenames, file extensions, pathnames, dummy URLs, user input, and Twitter handles. Here is an example: "Mount the downloaded `WebStorm-10*.dmg` disk image file as another disk in your system."

A block of code is set as follows:

```
policy_iteration():
    Initialize random policy
    for i in no_of_iterations:
        Q_value = value_function(random_policy)
        new_policy = Maximum state action pair from Q value
```

Any command-line input or output is written as follows:

```
bash Anaconda3-5.0.1-Linux-x86_64.sh
```

Bold: Indicates a new term, an important word, or words that you see onscreen. For example, words in menus or dialog boxes appear in the text like this.

Warnings or important notes appear like this.

Tips and tricks appear like this.

Get in touch

Feedback from our readers is always welcome.

General feedback: Email feedback@packtpub.com and mention the book title in the subject of your message. If you have questions about any aspect of this book, please email us at questions@packtpub.com.

Errata: Although we have taken every care to ensure the accuracy of our content, mistakes do happen. If you have found a mistake in this book, we would be grateful if you would report this to us. Please visit www.packtpub.com/submit-errata, selecting your book, clicking on the Errata Submission Form link, and entering the details.

Piracy: If you come across any illegal copies of our works in any form on the Internet, we would be grateful if you would provide us with the location address or website name. Please contact us at copyright@packtpub.com with a link to the material.

If you are interested in becoming an author: If there is a topic that you have expertise in and you are interested in either writing or contributing to a book, please visit authors.packtpub.com.

Reviews

Please leave a review. Once you have read and used this book, why not leave a review on the site that you purchased it from? Potential readers can then see and use your unbiased opinion to make purchase decisions, we at Packt can understand what you think about our products, and our authors can see your feedback on their book. Thank you!

For more information about Packt, please visit packtpub.com.

Introduction to Reinforcement Learning

1

Reinforcement learning (RL) is a branch of machine learning where the learning occurs via interacting with an environment. It is goal-oriented learning where the learner is not taught what actions to take; instead, the learner learns from the consequence of its actions. It is growing rapidly with a wide variety of algorithms and it is one of the most active areas of research in **artificial intelligence (AI)**.

In this chapter, you will learn about the following:

- Fundamental concepts of RL
- RL algorithm
- Agent environment interface
- Types of RL environments
- RL platforms
- Applications of RL

What is RL?

Consider that you are teaching the dog to catch a ball, but you cannot teach the dog explicitly to catch a ball; instead, you will just throw a ball, and every time the dog catches the ball, you will give it a cookie. If it fails to catch the ball, you will not give a cookie. The dog will figure out what actions made it receive a cookie and will repeat those actions.

Similarly, in a RL environment, you will not teach the agent what to do or how to do instead, you will give a reward to the agent for each action it does. The reward may be positive or negative. Then the agent will start performing actions which made it receive a positive reward. Thus, it is a trial and error process. In the previous analogy, the dog represents the agent. Giving a cookie to the dog upon catching the ball is a positive reward, and not giving a cookie is a negative reward.

There might be delayed rewards. You may not get a reward at each step. A reward may be given only after the completion of a task. In some cases, you get a reward at each step to find out that whether you are making any mistakes.

Imagine you want to teach a robot to walk without getting stuck by hitting a mountain, but you will not explicitly teach the robot not to go in the direction of the mountain:

Instead, if the robot hits and get stuck on the mountain, you will take away ten points so that robot will understand that hitting the mountain will result in a negative reward and it will not go in that direction again:

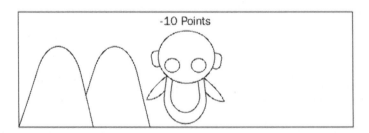

You will give 20 points to the robot when it walks in the right direction without getting stuck. So the robot will understand which is the right path and will try to maximize the rewards by going in the right direction:

The RL agent can **explore** different actions which might provide a good reward or it can **exploit** (use) the previous action which resulted in a good reward. If the RL agent explores different actions, there is a great possibility that the agent will receive a poor reward as all actions are not going to be the best one. If the RL agent exploits only the known best action, there is also a great possibility of missing out on the best action, which might provide a better reward. There is always a trade-off between exploration and exploitation. We cannot perform both exploration and exploitation at the same time. We will discuss the exploration-exploitation dilemma in detail in the upcoming chapters.

RL algorithm

The steps involved in typical RL algorithm are as follows:

1. First, the agent interacts with the environment by performing an action
2. The agent performs an action and moves from one state to another
3. And then the agent will receive a reward based on the action it performed
4. Based on the reward, the agent will understand whether the action was good or bad
5. If the action was good, that is, if the agent received a positive reward, then the agent will prefer performing that action or else the agent will try performing another action which results in a positive reward. So it is basically a trial and error learning process

How RL differs from other ML paradigms

In supervised learning, the machine (agent) learns from training data which has a labeled set of input and output. The objective is that the model extrapolates and generalizes its learning so that it can be well applied to the unseen data. There is an external supervisor who has a complete knowledge base of the environment and supervises the agent to complete a task.

Consider the dog analogy we just discussed; in supervised learning, to teach the dog to catch a ball, we will teach it explicitly by specifying turn left, go right, move forward five steps, catch the ball, and so on. But instead in RL we just throw a ball, and every time the dog catches the ball, we give it a cookie (reward). So the dog will learn to catch the ball that meant it received a cookie.

In unsupervised learning, we provide the model with training data which only has a set of inputs; the model learns to determine the hidden pattern in the input. There is a common misunderstanding that RL is a kind of unsupervised learning but it is not. In unsupervised learning, the model learns the hidden structure whereas in RL the model learns by maximizing the rewards. Say we want to suggest new movies to the user. Unsupervised learning analyses the similar movies the person has viewed and suggests movies, whereas RL constantly receives feedback from the user, understands his movie preferences, and builds a knowledge base on top of it and suggests a new movie.

There is also another kind of learning called semi-supervised learning which is basically a combination of supervised and unsupervised learning. It involves function estimation on both the labeled and unlabeled data, whereas RL is essentially an interaction between the agent and its environment. Thus, RL is completely different from all other machine learning paradigms.

Elements of RL

The elements of RL are shown in the following sections.

Agent

Agents are the software programs that make intelligent decisions and they are basically learners in RL. Agents take action by interacting with the environment and they receive rewards based on their actions, for example, Super Mario navigating in a video game.

Policy function

A policy defines the agent's behavior in an environment. The way in which the agent decides which action to perform depends on the policy. Say you want to reach your office from home; there will be different routes to reach your office, and some routes are shortcuts, while some routes are long. These routes are called policies because they represent the way in which we choose to perform an action to reach our goal. A policy is often denoted by the symbol π. A policy can be in the form of a lookup table or a complex search process.

Value function

A value function denotes how good it is for an agent to be in a particular state. It is dependent on the policy and is often denoted by $v(s)$. It is equal to the total expected reward received by the agent starting from the initial state. There can be several value functions; the optimal value function is the one that has the highest value for all the states compared to other value functions. Similarly, an optimal policy is the one that has the optimal value function.

Model

Model is the agent's representation of an environment. The learning can be of two types—model-based learning and model-free learning. In model-based learning, the agent exploits previously learned information to accomplish a task, whereas in model-free learning, the agent simply relies on a trial-and-error experience for performing the right action. Say you want to reach your office from home faster. In model-based learning, you simply use a previously learned experience (map) to reach the office faster, whereas in model-free learning you will not use a previous experience and will try all different routes and choose the faster one.

Agent environment interface

Agents are the software agents that perform actions, A_t, at a time, t, to move from one state, S_t, to another state S_{t+1}. Based on actions, agents receive a numerical reward, R, from the environment. Ultimately, RL is all about finding the optimal actions that will increase the numerical reward:

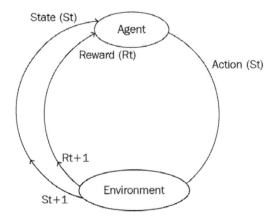

Let us understand the concept of RL with a maze game:

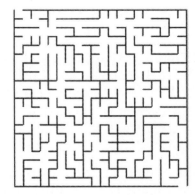

The objective of a maze is to reach the destination without getting stuck on the obstacles. Here's the workflow:

- The agent is the one who travels through the maze, which is our software program/ RL algorithm
- The environment is the maze

- The state is the position in a maze that the agent currently resides in
- An agent performs an action by moving from one state to another
- An agent receives a positive reward when its action doesn't get stuck on any obstacle and receives a negative reward when its action gets stuck on obstacles so it cannot reach the destination
- The goal is to clear the maze and reach the destination

Types of RL environment

Everything agents interact with is called an environment. The environment is the outside world. It comprises everything outside the agent. There are different types of environment, which are described in the next sections.

Deterministic environment

An environment is said to be deterministic when we know the outcome based on the current state. For instance, in a chess game, we know the exact outcome of moving any player.

Stochastic environment

An environment is said to be stochastic when we cannot determine the outcome based on the current state. There will be a greater level of uncertainty. For example, we never know what number will show up when throwing a dice.

Fully observable environment

When an agent can determine the state of the system at all times, it is called fully observable. For example, in a chess game, the state of the system, that is, the position of all the players on the chess board, is available the whole time so the player can make an optimal decision.

Partially observable environment

When an agent cannot determine the state of the system at all times, it is called partially observable. For example, in a poker game, we have no idea about the cards the opponent has.

Discrete environment

When there is only a finite state of actions available for moving from one state to another, it is called a discrete environment. For example, in a chess game, we have only a finite set of moves.

Continuous environment

When there is an infinite state of actions available for moving from one state to another, it is called a continuous environment. For example, we have multiple routes available for traveling from the source to the destination.

Episodic and non-episodic environment

The episodic environment is also called the **non-sequential** environment. In an episodic environment, an agent's current action will not affect a future action, whereas in a non-episodic environment, an agent's current action will affect a future action and is also called the **sequential** environment. That is, the agent performs the independent tasks in the episodic environment, whereas in the non-episodic environment all agents' actions are related.

Single and multi-agent environment

As the names suggest, a single-agent environment has only a single agent and the multi-agent environment has multiple agents. Multi-agent environments are extensively used while performing complex tasks. There will be different agents acting in completely different environments. Agents in a different environment will communicate with each other. A multi-agent environment will be mostly stochastic as it has a greater level of uncertainty.

RL platforms

RL platforms are used for simulating, building, rendering, and experimenting with our RL algorithms in an environment. There are many different RL platforms available, as described in the next sections.

OpenAI Gym and Universe

OpenAI Gym is a toolkit for building, evaluating, and comparing RL algorithms. It is compatible with algorithms written in any framework like TensorFlow, Theano, Keras, and so on. It is simple and easy to comprehend. It makes no assumption about the structure of our agent and provides an interface to all RL tasks.

OpenAI Universe is an extension to OpenAI Gym. It provides an ability to train and evaluate agents on a wide range of simple to real-time complex environments. It has unlimited access to many gaming environments. Using Universe, any program can be turned into a Gym environment without access to program internals, source code, or APIs as Universe works by launching the program automatically behind a virtual network computing remote desktop.

DeepMind Lab

DeepMind Lab is another amazing platform for AI agent-based research. It provides a rich simulated environment that acts as a lab for running several RL algorithms. It is highly customizable and extendable. The visuals are very rich, science fiction-style, and realistic.

RL-Glue

RL-Glue provides an interface for connecting agents, environments, and programs together even if they are written in different programming languages. It has the ability to share your agents and environments with others for building on top of your work. Because of this compatibility, reusability is greatly increased.

Project Malmo

Project Malmo is the another AI experimentation platform from Microsoft which builds on top of Minecraft. It provides good flexibility for customizing the environment. It is integrated with a sophisticated environment. It also allows overclocking, which enables programmers to play out scenarios faster than in standard Minecraft. However, Malmo currently only provides Minecraft gaming environments, unlike Open AI Universe.

ViZDoom

ViZDoom, as the name suggests, is a doom-based AI platform. It provides support for multi-agents and a competitive environment to test the agent. However, ViZDoom only supports the Doom game environment. It provides off-screen rendering and single and multiplayer support.

Applications of RL

With greater advancements and research, RL has rapidly evolved everyday applications in several fields ranging from playing computer games to automating a car. Some of the RL applications are listed in the following sections.

Education

Many online education platforms are using RL for providing personalized content for each and every student. Some students may learn better from video content, some may learn better by doing projects, and some may learn better from notes. RL is used to tune educational content personalized for each student according to their learning style and that can be changed dynamically according to the behavior of the user.

Medicine and healthcare

RL has endless applications in medicine and health care; some of them include personalized medical treatment, diagnosis based on a medical image, obtaining treatment strategies in clinical decision making, medical image segmentation, and so on.

Manufacturing

In manufacturing, intelligent robots are used to place objects in the right position. If it fails or succeeds in placing the object at the right position, it remembers the object and trains itself to do this with greater accuracy. The use of intelligent agents will reduce labor costs and result in better performance.

Inventory management

RL is extensively used in inventory management, which is a crucial business activity. Some of these activities include supply chain management, demand forecasting, and handling several warehouse operations (such as placing products in warehouses for managing space efficiently). Google researchers in DeepMind have developed RL algorithms for efficiently reducing the energy consumption in their own data center.

Finance

RL is widely used in financial portfolio management, which is the process of constant redistribution of a fund into different financial products and also in predicting and trading in commercial transactions markets. JP Morgan has successfully used RL to provide better trade execution results for large orders.

Natural Language Processing and Computer Vision

With the unified power of deep learning and RL, **Deep Reinforcement Learning (DRL)** has been greatly evolving in the fields of **Natural Language Processing** (NLP) and **Computer Vision (CV)**. DRL has been used for text summarization, information extraction, machine translation, and image recognition, providing greater accuracy than current systems.

Summary

In this chapter, we have learned the basics of RL and also some key concepts. We learned different elements of RL and different types of RL environments. We also covered the various available RL platforms and also the applications of RL in various domains.

In the next chapter, `Chapter 2`, *Getting Started with OpenAI and TensorFlow*, we will learn the basics of and how to install OpenAI and TensorFlow, followed by simulating environments and teaching the agents to learn in the environment.

Questions

The question list is as follows:

1. What is reinforcement learning?
2. How does RL differ from other ML paradigms?
3. What are agents and how do agents learn?
4. What is the difference between a policy function and a value function?
5. What is the difference between model-based and model-free learning?
6. What are all the different types of environments in RL?
7. How does OpenAI Universe differ from other RL platforms?
8. What are some of the applications of RL?

Further reading

Overview of RL: `https://www.cs.ubc.ca/~murphyk/Bayes/pomdp.html`.

Getting Started with OpenAI and TensorFlow

OpenAI is a non-profit, open source **artificial intelligence (AI)** research company founded by Elon Musk and Sam Altman that aims to build a general AI. They are sponsored by top industry leaders and top-notch companies. OpenAI comes in two flavors, Gym and Universe, using which we can simulate realistic environments, build **reinforcement learning (RL)** algorithms, and test our agents in those environments. TensorFlow is an open source machine learning library by Google that is extensively used for numerical computation. We will use OpenAI and TensorFlow for building and evaluating powerful RL algorithms in the upcoming chapters.

In this chapter, you will learn about the following:

- Setting up your machine by installing Anaconda, Docker, OpenAI Gym, and Universe and TensorFlow
- Simulating an environment using OpenAI Gym and Universe
- Training a robot to walk
- Building a video game bot
- Fundamentals of TensorFlow
- Using TensorBoard

Setting up your machine

Installing OpenAI is not a straightforward task; there are a set of steps that have to be correctly followed for setting the system up and running it. Now, let's see how to set up our machine and install OpenAI Gym and Universe.

Installing Anaconda

All the examples in the book use the Anaconda version of Python. Anaconda is an open source distribution of Python. It is widely used for scientific computing and processing a large volume of data. It provides an excellent package management environment. It provides support for Windows, macOS, and Linux. Anaconda comes with Python installed along with popular packages used for scientific computing such as NumPy, SciPy, and so on.

To download Anaconda, visit https://www.anaconda.com/download/, where you will see an option for downloading Anaconda for different platforms.

If you are using Windows or Mac, you can directly download the graphical installer according to your machine architecture and install using the graphical installer.

If you are using Linux, follow these steps:

1. Open your Terminal and type the following to download Anaconda:

```
wget
https://repo.continuum.io/archive/Anaconda3-5.0.1-Linux-x86_64.sh
```

2. Upon completion, we can install Anaconda via the following command:

```
bash Anaconda3-5.0.1-Linux-x86_64.sh
```

After successful installation of Anaconda, we need to create a new Anaconda environment that is basically a virtual environment. What is the need for a virtual environment? Say you are working on project A, which uses NumPy version 1.14, and project B, which uses NumPy version 1.13. So, to work on project B you either downgrade NumPy or reinstall Anaconda. In each project, we use different libraries with different versions which are not applicable to other projects. Instead of downgrading or upgrading versions or reinstalling Anaconda every time for a new project, we use a virtual environment. This creates an isolated environment for the current project so that each project can have its own dependencies and will not affect other projects. We will create such an environment using the following command and name our environment universe:

```
conda create --name universe python=3.6 anaconda
```

We can activate our environment using the following command:

```
source activate universe
```

Installing Docker

After installing Anaconda, we need to install Docker. Docker makes it easy to deploy applications to production. Say you built an application in your localhost that has TensorFlow and some other libraries and you want to deploy your applications into a server. You would need to install all those dependencies on the server. But with Docker, we can pack our application with its dependencies, which is called a container, and we can simply run our applications on the server without using any external dependency with our packed Docker container. OpenAI has no support for Windows, so to install OpenAI in Windows we need to use Docker. Also, the majority of OpenAI Universe's environment needs Docker to simulate the environment. Now let's see how to install Docker.

To download Docker, go to `https://docs.docker.com/` where you will see an option called **Get Docker**; if you select that, you will see options for different operating systems. If you are using either Windows or Mac, you can download Docker and install it directly using the graphical installer.

If you are using Linux, follow these steps:

Open your Terminal and type the following:

```
sudo apt-get install \
    apt-transport-https \
    ca-certificates \
    curl \
    software-properties-common
```

Then type:

```
curl -fsSL https://download.docker.com/linux/ubuntu/gpg | sudo apt-key add
-
```

And then type:

```
sudo add-apt-repository \
   "deb [arch=amd64] https://download.docker.com/linux/ubuntu \
   $(lsb_release -cs) \
   stable"
```

Finally, type:

```
sudo apt-get update
sudo apt-get install docker-ce
```

We need to be a member of the Docker user group to start using Docker. You can join the Docker user group via the following command:

```
sudo adduser $(whoami) docker
newgrp docker
groups
```

We can test the Docker installation by running the built-in `hello-world` program:

```
sudo service docker start
sudo docker run hello-world
```

In order to avoid using `sudo` to use Docker every time, we can use the following command:

```
sudo groupadd docker
sudo usermod -aG docker $USER
sudo reboot
```

Installing OpenAI Gym and Universe

Now let's see how to install OpenAI Gym and Universe. Before that, we need to install several dependencies. First, let's activate the `conda` environment we just created using the following command:

```
source activate universe
```

Then we will install the following dependencies:

```
sudo apt-get update
sudo apt-get install golang libcupti-dev libjpeg-turbo8-dev make tmux htop
chromium-browser git cmake zlib1g-dev libjpeg-dev xvfb libav-tools xorg-dev
python-opengl libboost-all-dev libsdl2-dev swig

conda install pip six libgcc swig
conda install opencv
```

Throughout this book, we will be using `gym` version `0.7.0` so you can install `gym` directly using `pip` as:

```
pip install gym==0.7.0
```

Or you can clone the `gym` repository and install the latest version by following command:

```
cd ~
git clone https://github.com/openai/gym.git
cd gym
pip install -e '.[all]'
```

The preceding commands will fetch the `gym` repository and install `gym` as a package, as shown in the following screenshot:

Common error fixes

There is a good chance that you will encounter any of the following errors while installing gym. If you get these errors, just run the following commands and try reinstalling:

- `Failed building wheel for pachi-py` or `Failed building wheel for pachi-py atari-py`:

  ```
  sudo apt-get update
  sudo apt-get install xvfb libav-tools xorg-dev libsdl2-dev swig cmake
  ```

- `Failed building wheel for mujoco-py`:

  ```
  git clone https://github.com/openai/mujoco-py.git
  cd mujoco-py
  sudo apt-get update
  sudo apt-get install libgl1-mesa-dev libgl1-mesa-glx libosmesa6-dev python3-pip python3-numpy python3-scipy
  pip3 install -r requirements.txt
  sudo python3 setup.py install
  ```

- `Error: command 'gcc' failed with exit status 1`:

  ```
  sudo apt-get update
  sudo apt-get install python-dev
  sudo apt-get install libevent-dev
  ```

Similarly, we can install OpenAI Universe by fetching the `universe` repository and installing the `universe` as a package:

```
cd ~
git clone https://github.com/openai/universe.git
cd universe
pip install -e .
```

The installation is shown in the following screenshot:

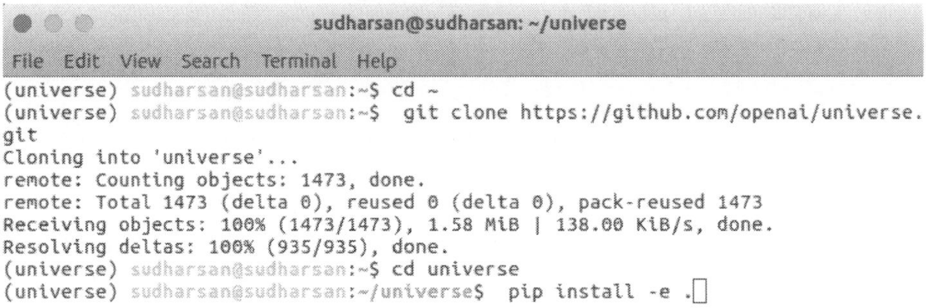

As already said, Open AI Universe needs Docker, as the majority of Universe environments run inside a Docker container.

So let's build a Docker image and name it `universe`:

```
docker build -t universe .
```

Once the Docker image is built, we run the following command, which starts a container from the Docker image:

```
docker run --privileged --rm -it -p 12345:12345 -p 5900:5900 -e
DOCKER_NET_HOST=172.17.0.1 universe /bin/bash
```

OpenAI Gym

With OpenAI Gym, we can simulate a variety of environments and develop, evaluate, and compare RL algorithms. Let's now understand how to use Gym.

Basic simulations

Let's see how to simulate a basic cart pole environment:

1. First, let's import the library:

```
import gym
```

2. The next step is to create a simulation instance using the make function:

```
env = gym.make('CartPole-v0')
```

3. Then we should initialize the environment using the reset method:

```
env.reset()
```

4. Then we can loop for some time steps and render the environment at each step:

```
for _ in range(1000):
    env.render()
    env.step(env.action_space.sample())
```

The complete code is as follows:

```
import gym
env = gym.make('CartPole-v0')
env.reset()
for _ in range(1000):
    env.render()
    env.step(env.action_space.sample())
```

If you run the preceding program, you can see the output, which shows the cart pole environment:

/home/sudharsan/anaconda/envs/universe/lib/python3.5/site-packages/i...

OpenAI Gym provides a lot of simulation environments for training, evaluating, and building our agents. We can check the available environments by either checking their website or simply typing the following, which will list the available environments:

```
from gym import envs
print(envs.registry.all())
```

Since Gym provides different interesting environments, let's simulate a car racing environment, shown as follows:

```
import gym
env = gym.make('CarRacing-v0')
env.reset()
for _ in range(1000):
    env.render()
    env.step(env.action_space.sample())
```

You will get the output as follows:

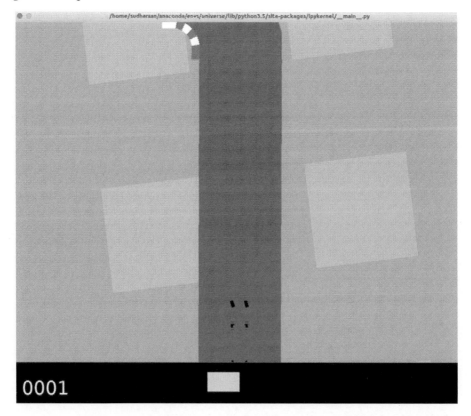

Training a robot to walk

Now let's learn how to train a robot to walk using Gym along with some fundamentals.

The strategy is that X points will be given as a reward when the robot moves forward, and if the robot fails to move then Y points will be reduced. So the robot will learn to walk in the event of maximizing the reward.

First, we will import the library, then we will create a simulation instance by the `make` function. Open AI Gym provides an environment called `BipedalWalker-v2` for training robotic agents in a simple terrain:

```
import gym
env = gym.make('BipedalWalker-v2')
```

Then, for each episode (agent-environment interaction between the initial and final state), we will initialize the environment using the `reset` method:

```
for episode in range(100):
  observation = env.reset()
```

Then we will loop and render the environment:

```
for i in range(10000):
 env.render()
```

We sample random actions from the environment's action space. Every environment has an action space which contains all possible valid actions:

```
action = env.action_space.sample()
```

For each action step, we will record `observation`, `reward`, `done`, and `info`:

```
observation, reward, done, info = env.step(action)
```

`observation` is the object representing an observation of the environment. For example, the state of the robot in the terrain.

`reward` are the rewards gained by the previous action. For example, the reward gained by a robot on successfully moving forward.

`done` is the Boolean; when it is true, it indicates that the episode has completed (that is, the robot learned to walk or failed completely). Once the episode has completed, we can initialize the environment for the next episode using `env.reset()`.

`info` is the information that is useful for debugging.

When `done` is true, we print the time steps taken for the episode and break the current episode:

```
if done:
   print("{} timesteps taken for the Episode".format(i+1))
   break
```

The complete code is as follows:

```
import gym
env = gym.make('BipedalWalker-v2')
for i_episode in range(100):
 observation = env.reset()
 for t in range(10000):
     env.render()
     print(observation)
     action = env.action_space.sample()
     observation, reward, done, info = env.step(action)
     if done:
         print("{} timesteps taken for the episode".format(t+1))
         break
```

The output is shown in the following screenshot:

OpenAI Universe

OpenAI Universe provides a wide range of realistic gaming environments. It is an extension to OpenAI Gym. It provides the ability to train and evaluate agents on a wide range of simple to real-time complex environments. It has unlimited access to many gaming environments.

Building a video game bot

Let's learn how to build a video game bot which plays a car racing game. Our objective is that the car has to move forward without getting stuck on any obstacles or hitting other cars.

First, we import the necessary libraries:

```
import gym
import universe # register universe environment
import random
```

Then we simulate our car racing environment using the make function:

```
env = gym.make('flashgames.NeonRace-v0')
env.configure(remotes=1) #automatically creates a local docker container
```

Let's create the variables for moving the car:

```
# Move left
left = [('KeyEvent', 'ArrowUp', True), ('KeyEvent', 'ArrowLeft', True),
        ('KeyEvent', 'ArrowRight', False)]

#Move right
right = [('KeyEvent', 'ArrowUp', True), ('KeyEvent', 'ArrowLeft', False),
        ('KeyEvent', 'ArrowRight', True)]

# Move forward
forward = [('KeyEvent', 'ArrowUp', True), ('KeyEvent', 'ArrowRight',
False),
        ('KeyEvent', 'ArrowLeft', False), ('KeyEvent', 'n', True)]
```

We will initialize some other variables:

```
# We use turn variable for deciding whether to turn or not
turn = 0

# We store all the rewards in rewards list
rewards = []

#we will use buffer as some threshold
buffer_size = 100

#we will initially set action as forward, which just move the car forward
#without any turn
action = forward
```

Now, let's allow our game agent to play in an infinite loop that continuously performs an action based on interaction with the environment:

```
while True:
    turn -= 1
# Let us say initially we take no turn and move forward.
# We will check value of turn, if it is less than 0
# then there is no necessity for turning and we just move forward.
    if turn <= 0:
        action = forward
        turn = 0
```

Then we use `env.step()` to perform an action (moving forward for now) for a one-time step:

```
action_n = [action for ob in observation_n]
observation_n, reward_n, done_n, info = env.step(action_n)
```

For each time step, we record the results in the `observation_n`, `reward_n`, `done_n`, and `info` variables:

- `observation _n`: State of the car
- `reward_n`: Reward gained by the previous action, if the car successfully moves forward without getting stuck on obstacles
- `done_n`: It is a Boolean; it will be set to `true` if the game is over
- `info_n`: Used for debugging purposes

Obviously, an agent (car) cannot move forward throughout the game; it needs to take a turn, avoid obstacles, and will also hit other vehicles. But it has to determine whether it should take a turn and, if yes, then in which direction it should turn.

First, we will calculate the mean of the rewards we obtained so far; if it is 0 then it is clear that we got stuck somewhere while moving forward and we need to take a turn. Then again, which direction do we need to turn? Do you recollect the **policy functions** we studied in Chapter 1, *Introduction to Reinforcement Learning*.

Referring to the same concept, we have two policies here: one is turning left and the other is turning right. We will take a random policy here and calculate a reward and improve upon that.

We will generate a random number and if it is less than 0.5, then we will take a right, otherwise we will take a left. Later, we will update our rewards and, based on our rewards, we will learn which direction is best:

```
if len(rewards) >= buffer_size:
        mean = sum(rewards)/len(rewards)

        if mean == 0:
            turn = 20
            if random.random() < 0.5:
                action = right
            else:
                action = left
        rewards = []
```

Then, for each episode (say the game is over), we reinitialize the environment (start the game from the beginning) using the env.render():

```
env.render()
```

The complete code is as follows:

```
import gym
import universe # register universe environment
import random

env = gym.make('flashgames.NeonRace-v0')
env.configure(remotes=1) # automatically creates a local docker container
observation_n = env.reset()

##Declare actions
#Move left
left = [('KeyEvent', 'ArrowUp', True), ('KeyEvent', 'ArrowLeft', True),
```

```
                ('KeyEvent', 'ArrowRight', False)]

    #move right
    right = [('KeyEvent', 'ArrowUp', True), ('KeyEvent', 'ArrowLeft', False),
            ('KeyEvent', 'ArrowRight', True)]

    # Move forward
    forward = [('KeyEvent', 'ArrowUp', True), ('KeyEvent', 'ArrowRight',
    False),
            ('KeyEvent', 'ArrowLeft', False), ('KeyEvent', 'n', True)]

    #Determine whether to turn or not
    turn = 0
    #store rewards in a list
    rewards = []
    #use buffer as a threshold
    buffer_size = 100
    #initial action as forward
    action = forward

    while True:
        turn -= 1
        if turn <= 0:
            action = forward
            turn = 0
        action_n = [action for ob in observation_n]
        observation_n, reward_n, done_n, info = env.step(action_n)
        rewards += [reward_n[0]]
        if len(rewards) >= buffer_size:
            mean = sum(rewards)/len(rewards)

            if mean == 0:
                turn = 20
                if random.random() < 0.5:
                    action = right
                else:
                    action = left
            rewards = []

        env.render()
```

If you run the program, you can see how the car learns to move without getting stuck or hitting other vehicles:

TensorFlow

TensorFlow is an open source software library from Google which is extensively used for numerical computation. It is widely used for building deep learning models and is a subset of machine learning. It uses data flow graphs that can be shared and executed on many different platforms. Tensor is nothing but a multi-dimensional array, so when we say TensorFlow, it is literally a flow of multi-dimensional arrays (tensors) in the computation graph.

With Anaconda installed, installing TensorFlow becomes very simple. Irrespective of the platform you are using, you can easily install TensorFlow by typing the following command:

```
source activate universe
conda install -c conda-forge tensorflow
```

Don't forget to activate the `universe` environment before installing TensorFlow.

We can check whether the TensorFlow installation was successful by simply running the following `Hello World` program:

```
import tensorflow as tf
hello = tf.constant("Hello World")
sess = tf.Session()
print(sess.run(hello))
```

Variables, constants, and placeholders

Variables, constants, and placeholders are the fundamental elements of TensorFlow. However, there is always confusion between these three. Let's look at each element one by one and learn the difference between them.

Variables

Variables are the containers used to store values. Variables will be used as input to several other operations in the computational graph. We can create TensorFlow variables using the `tf.Variable()` function. In the following example, we define a variable with values from a random normal distribution and name it `weights`:

```
weights = tf.Variable(tf.random_normal([3, 2], stddev=0.1), name="weights")
```

However, after defining a variable, we need to explicitly create an initialization operation using the `tf.global_variables_initializer()` method which will allocate resources for the variable.

Constants

Constants, unlike variables, cannot have their values changed. Constants are immutable; once they are assigned values they cannot be changed throughout. We can create constants using the `tf.constant()` function:

```
x = tf.constant(13)
```

Placeholders

Think of placeholders as variables where you only define the type and dimension but will not assign the value. Placeholders are defined with no values. Values for the placeholders will be fed at runtime. Placeholders have an optional argument called `shape`, which specifies the dimensions of the data. If the `shape` is set to `None` then we can feed data of any size at runtime. Placeholders can be defined using the `tf.placeholder()` function:

```
x = tf.placeholder("float", shape=None)
```

To put it in simple terms, we use `tf.Variable` to store the data and `tf.placeholder` for feeding the external data.

Computation graph

Everything in TensorFlow will be represented as a computational graph that consists of nodes and edges, where nodes are the mathematical operations, say addition, multiplication and so on, and edges are the tensors. Having a computational graph is very efficient in optimizing resources and it also promotes distributed computing.

Say we have node B, whose input is dependent on the output of node A; this type of dependency is called direct dependency.

For example:

```
A = tf.multiply(8,5)
B = tf.multiply(A,1)
```

When node B doesn't depend on node A for its input it is called indirect dependency.

For example:

```
A = tf.multiply(8,5)
B = tf.multiply(4,3)
```

So if we can understand these dependencies, we can distribute the independent computations in the available resources and reduce the computation time.

Whenever we import TensorFlow, a default graph will be created automatically and all nodes we create will get associated with the default graph.

Sessions

Computation graphs will only be defined; in order to execute the computation graph, we use TensorFlow sessions:

```
sess = tf.Session()
```

We can create the session for our computation graph using the `tf.Session()` method, which will allocate the memory for storing the current value of the variable. After creating the session, we can execute our graph with the `sess.run()` method.

In order to run anything in TensorFlow, we need to start the TensorFlow session for an instance; please refer to the code:

```
import tensorflow as tf
a = tf.multiply(2,3)
print(a)
```

It will print a TensorFlow object instead of 6. As already said, whenever we import TensorFlow a default computation graph will automatically be created and all nodes a that we created will get attached to the graph. In order to execute the graph, we need to initialize a TensorFlow session as follows:

```
#Import tensorflow
import tensorflow as tf

#Initialize variables
a = tf.multiply(2,3)

#create tensorflow session for executing the session
with tf.Session() as sess:
  #run the session
  print(sess.run(a))
```

The preceding code will print 6.

TensorBoard

TensorBoard is TensorFlow's visualization tool that can be used to visualize the computational graph. It can also be used to plot various quantitative metrics and the results of several intermediate calculations. Using TensorBoard, we can easily visualize complex models, which will be useful for debugging and also sharing.

Now, let's build a basic computation graph and visualize that in TensorBoard.

First, let's import the library:

```
import tensorflow as tf
```

Next, we initialize the variables:

```
a = tf.constant(5)
b = tf.constant(4)
c = tf.multiply(a,b)
d = tf.constant(2)
e = tf.constant(3)
f = tf.multiply(d,e)
g = tf.add(c,f)
```

Now, we will create a TensorFlow session. We will write the results of our graph to a file called event using tf.summary.FileWriter():

```
with tf.Session() as sess:
    writer = tf.summary.FileWriter("output", sess.graph)
    print(sess.run(g))
    writer.close()
```

In order to run the TensorBoard, go to your Terminal, locate the working directory, and type tensorboard --logdir=output --port=6003.

You can see the output as shown next:

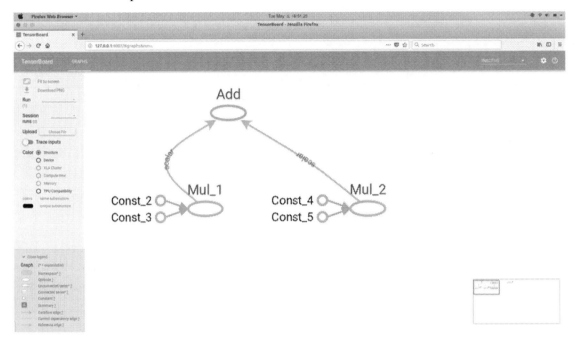

Adding scope

Scoping is used to reduce complexity and helps us to better understand the model by grouping the related nodes together. For instance, in the previous example, we can break down our graph into two different groups called computation and result. If you look at the previous example, you can see that nodes a to e perform the computation and node g calculates the result. So we can group them separately using the scope for easy understanding. Scoping can be created using the tf.name_scope() function.

Let's use the tf.name_scope() function using Computation:

```
with tf.name_scope("Computation"):
    a = tf.constant(5)
    b = tf.constant(4)
    c = tf.multiply(a,b)
    d = tf.constant(2)
    e = tf.constant(3)
    f = tf.multiply(d,e)
```

Let's use the `tf.name_scope()` function using `Result`:

```
with tf.name_scope("Result"):
    g = tf.add(c,f)
```

Look at the `Computation` scope; we can further break down into separate parts for even more understanding. We can create a scope as `Part 1`, which has nodes a to c, and a scope as `Part 2`, which has nodes d to e, as part 1 and 2 are independent of each other:

```
with tf.name_scope("Computation"):
    with tf.name_scope("Part1"):
        a = tf.constant(5)
        b = tf.constant(4)
        c = tf.multiply(a,b)
    with tf.name_scope("Part2"):
        d = tf.constant(2)
        e = tf.constant(3)
        f = tf.multiply(d,e)
```

Scoping can be better understood by visualizing them in the TensorBoard. The complete code is as follows:

```
import tensorflow as tf
with tf.name_scope("Computation"):
    with tf.name_scope("Part1"):
        a = tf.constant(5)
        b = tf.constant(4)
        c = tf.multiply(a,b)
    with tf.name_scope("Part2"):
        d = tf.constant(2)
        e = tf.constant(3)
        f = tf.multiply(d,e)

with tf.name_scope("Result"):
    g = tf.add(c,f)

with tf.Session() as sess:
  writer = tf.summary.FileWriter("output", sess.graph)
  print(sess.run(g))
  writer.close()
```

If you look at the following diagram, you can easily understand how scope helps us to reduce complexity in understanding by grouping the similar nodes together. Scoping is widely used while working on a complex project to better understand the functionality and dependencies of nodes:

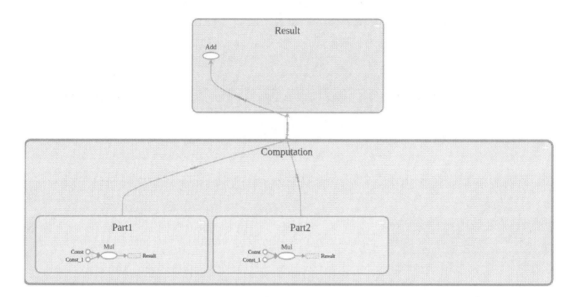

Summary

In this chapter, we learned how to set up our machine by installing Anaconda, Docker, OpenAI Gym, Universe, and TensorFlow. We also learned how to create simulations using OpenAI and how to train agents to learn in an OpenAI environment. Then we came across the fundamentals of TensorFlow followed by visualizing graphs in TensorBoard.

In the next chapter, Chapter 3, *The Markov Decision Process and Dynamic Programming* we will learn about Markov Decision Process and dynamic programming and how to solve frozen lake problem using value and policy iteration.

Questions

The question list is as follows:

1. Why and how do we create a new environment in Anaconda?
2. What is the need for using Docker?
3. How do we simulate an environment in OpenAI Gym?
4. How do we check all available environments in OpenAI Gym?
5. Are OpenAI Gym and Universe the same? If not, what is the reason?
6. How are TensorFlow variables and placeholders different from each other?
7. What is a computational graph?
8. Why do we need sessions in TensorFlow?
9. What is the purpose of TensorBoard and how do we start it?

Further reading

You can further refer to these papers:

- **OpenAI blog**: https://blog.openai.com
- **OpenAI environments**: https://gym.openai.com/envs/
- **TensorFlow official website**: https://www.tensorflow.org/

3
The Markov Decision Process and Dynamic Programming

The **Markov Decision Process (MDP)** provides a mathematical framework for solving the **reinforcement learning (RL)** problem. Almost all RL problems can be modeled as MDP. MDP is widely used for solving various optimization problems. In this chapter, we will understand what MDP is and how can we use it to solve RL problems. We will also learn about dynamic programming, which is a technique for solving complex problems in an efficient way.

In this chapter, you will learn about the following topics:

- The Markov chain and Markov process
- The Markov Decision Process
- Rewards and returns
- The Bellman equation
- Solving a Bellman equation using dynamic programming
- Solving a frozen lake problem using value and policy iteration

The Markov chain and Markov process

Before going into MDP, let us understand the Markov chain and Markov process, which form the foundation of MDP.

The Markov property states that the future depends only on the present and not on the past. The Markov chain is a probabilistic model that solely depends on the current state to predict the next state and not the previous states, that is, the future is conditionally independent of the past. The Markov chain strictly follows the Markov property.

For example, if we know that the current state is cloudy, we can predict that next state could be rainy. We came to this conclusion that the next state could be rainy only by considering the current state (cloudy) and not the past states, which might be sunny, windy, and so on. However, the Markov property does not hold true for all processes. For example, throwing a dice (the next state) has no dependency on the previous number, whatever showed up on the dice (the current state).

Moving from one state to another is called **transition** and its probability is called a **transition probability**. We can formulate the transition probabilities in the form of a table, as shown next, and it is called a **Markov table**. It shows, given the current state, what the probability of moving to the next state is:

Current state	Next state	Transition probability
Cloudy	Rainy	0.6
Rainy	Rainy	0.2
Sunny	Cloudy	0.1
Rainy	Sunny	0.1

We can also represent the Markov chain in the form a state diagram that shows the transition probability:

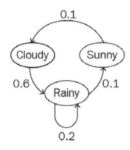

The preceding state diagram shows the probability of moving from one state to another. Still don't understand the Markov chain? Okay, let us talk.

Me: "What are you doing?"

You: "I'm reading about the Markov chain."

Me: "What is your plan after reading?"

You: "I'm going to sleep."

Me: "Are you sure you're going to sleep?"

You: "Probably. I'll watch TV if I'm not sleepy."

Me: "Cool; this is also a Markov chain."

You: "Eh?"

We can formulate our conversation into a Markov chain and draw a state diagram as follows:

The Markov chain lies in the core concept that the future depends only on the present and not on the past. A stochastic process is called a Markov process if it follows the Markov property.

Markov Decision Process

MDP is an extension of the Markov chain. It provides a mathematical framework for modeling decision-making situations. Almost all Reinforcement Learning problems can be modeled as MDP.

MDP is represented by five important elements:

- A set of states (S) the agent can actually be in.
- A set of actions (A) that can be performed by an agent, for moving from one state to another.
- A transition probability ($P^a_{ss'}$), which is the probability of moving from one state s to another s' state by performing some action a.
- A reward probability ($R^a_{ss'}$), which is the probability of a reward acquired by the agent for moving from one state s to another state s' by performing some action a.
- A discount factor (γ), which controls the importance of immediate and future rewards. We will discuss this in detail in the upcoming sections.

Rewards and returns

As we have learned, in an RL environment, an agent interacts with the environment by performing an action and moves from one state to another. Based on the action it performs, it receives a reward. A reward is nothing but a numerical value, say, +1 for a good action and -1 for a bad action. How do we decide if an action is good or bad? In a maze game, a good action is where the agent makes a move so that it doesn't hit a maze wall, whereas a bad action is where the agent moves and hits the maze wall.

An agent tries to maximize the total amount of rewards (cumulative rewards) it receives from the environment instead of immediate rewards. The total amount of rewards the agent receives from the environment is called returns. So, we can formulate total amount of rewards (returns) received by the agents as follows:

$$R_t = r_{t+1} + r_{t+2} + \dots + r_T$$

r_{t+1} is the reward received by the agent at a time step t_0 while performing an action a_0 to move from one state to another. r_{t+2} is the reward received by the agent at a time step t_1 while performing an action to move from one state to another. Similarly, r_T is the reward received by the agent at a final time step T while performing an action to move from one state to another.

Episodic and continuous tasks

Episodic tasks are the tasks that have a terminal state (end). In RL, episodes are considered agent-environment interactions from initial to final states.

For example, in a car racing video game, you start the game (initial state) and play the game until it is over (final state). This is called an episode. Once the game is over, you start the next episode by restarting the game, and you will begin from the initial state irrespective of the position you were in the previous game. So, each episode is independent of the other.

In a continuous task, there is not a terminal state. Continuous tasks will never end. For example, a personal assistance robot does not have a terminal state.

Discount factor

We have seen that an agent goal is to maximize the return. For an episodic task, we can define our return as $R_t = r_{t+1} + r_{t+2} + \dots + r_T$, where T is the final state of the episode, and we try to maximize the return R_t.

Since we don't have any final state for a continuous task, we can define our return for continuous tasks as $R_t = r_{t+1} + r_{t+2} + ...$, which sums up to infinity. But how can we maximize the return if it never stops?

That's why we introduce the notion of a discount factor. We can redefine our return with a discount factor (γ), as follows:

$$R_t = r_{t+1} + \gamma r_{t+2} + \gamma^2 r_{t+3} + \gamma^3 r_{t+4} + \cdots \quad \text{---(1)}$$

$$= \sum_{k=0}^{\infty} \gamma^k r_{t+k+1} \quad \text{---(2)}$$

The discount factor decides how much importance we give to the future rewards and immediate rewards. The value of the discount factor lies within *0* to *1*. A discount factor of *0* means that immediate rewards are more important, while a discount factor of *1* would mean that future rewards are more important than immediate rewards.

A discount factor of *0* will never learn considering only the immediate rewards; similarly, a discount factor of *1* will learn forever looking for the future reward, which may lead to infinity. So the optimal value of the discount factor lies between 0.2 to 0.8.

We give importance to immediate rewards and future rewards depending on the use case. In some cases, future rewards are more desirable than immediate rewards and vice versa. In a chess game, the goal is to defeat the opponent's king. If we give importance to the immediate reward, which is acquired by actions like our pawn defeating any opponent player and so on, the agent will learn to perform this sub-goal instead of learning to reach the actual goal. So, in this case, we give importance to future rewards, whereas in some cases, we prefer immediate rewards over future rewards. (Say, would you prefer chocolates if I gave you them today or 13 months later?)

The policy function

We have learned about the policy function in `Chapter 1`, *Introduction to Reinforcement Learning*, which maps the states to actions. It is denoted by π.

The policy function can be represented as $\pi(s) : S-> A$, indicating mapping from states to actions. So, basically, a policy function says what action to perform in each state. Our ultimate goal lies in finding the optimal policy which specifies the correct action to perform in each state, which maximizes the reward.

State value function

A state value function is also called simply a value function. It specifies how good it is for an agent to be in a particular state with a policy π. A value function is often denoted by $V(s)$. It denotes the value of a state following a policy.

We can define a state value function as follows:

$$V^{\pi}(s) = \mathbb{E}_{\pi}\left[R_t | s_t = s\right]$$

This specifies the expected return starting from state s according to policy π. We can substitute the value of R_t in the value function from (2) as follows:

$$V^{\pi}(s) = \mathbb{E}_{\pi}\left[\sum_{k=0}^{\infty} \gamma^k r_{t+k+1} | s_t = s\right]$$

Note that the state value function depends on the policy and it varies depending on the policy we choose.

We can view value functions in a table. Let us say we have two states and both of these states follow the policy π. Based on the value of these two states, we can tell how good it is for our agent to be in that state following a policy. The greater the value, the better the state is:

State	Value
State 1	0.3
State 2	0.9

Based on the preceding table, we can tell that it is good to be in state 2, as it has high value. We will see how to estimate these values intuitively in the upcoming sections.

State-action value function (Q function)

A state-action value function is also called the Q function. It specifies how good it is for an agent to perform a particular action in a state with a policy π. The Q function is denoted by $Q(s)$. It denotes the value of taking an action in a state following a policy π.

We can define Q function as follows:

$$Q^{\pi}(s, a) = \mathbb{E}_{\pi}\left[R_t | s_t = s, a_t = a\right]$$

This specifies the expected return starting from state s with the action a according to policy π. We can substitute the value of R_t in the Q function from (2) as follows:

$$Q^\pi(s,a) = \mathbb{E}_\pi\Big[\sum_{k=0}^{\infty} \gamma^k r_{t+k+1}\big|s_t = s, a_t = a\Big]$$

The difference between the value function and the Q function is that the value function specifies the goodness of a state, while a Q function specifies the goodness of an action in a state.

Like state value functions, Q functions can be viewed in a table. It is also called a Q table. Let us say we have two states and two actions; our Q table looks like the following:

State	Action	Value
State 1	Action 1	0.03
State 1	Action 2	0.02
State 2	Action 1	0.5
State 2	Action 2	0.9

Thus, the Q table shows the value of all possible state action pairs. So, by looking at this table, we can come to the conclusion that performing action 1 in state 1 and action 2 in state 2 is the better option as it has high value.

Whenever we say value function $V(S)$ or Q function $Q(S, a)$, it actually means the value table and Q table, as shown previously.

The Bellman equation and optimality

The Bellman equation, named after Richard Bellman, American mathematician, helps us to solve MDP. It is omnipresent in RL. When we say solve the MDP, it actually means finding the optimal policies and value functions. There can be many different value functions according to different policies. The optimal value function $V^*(s)$ is the one which yields maximum value compared to all the other value functions:

$$V^*(s) = max_\pi V^\pi(s)$$

Similarly, the optimal policy is the one which results in an optimal value function.

Since the optimal value function $V^*(s)$ is the one that has a higher value compared to all other value functions (that is, maximum return), it will be the maximum of the Q function. So, the optimal value function can easily be computed by taking the maximum of the Q function as follows:

$$V^*(s) = max_a Q^*(s, a) \quad \text{-- (3)}$$

The Bellman equation for the value function can be represented as, (we will see how we derived this equation in the next topic):

$$V^\pi(s) = \sum_a \pi(s, a) \sum_{s'} \mathcal{P}_{ss'}^a \left[\mathcal{R}_{ss'}^a + \gamma V^\pi(s') \right]$$

It indicates the recursive relation between a value of a state and its successor state and the average over all possibilities.

Similarly, the Bellman equation for the Q function can be represented as follows:

$$Q^\pi(s, a) = \sum_{s'} \mathcal{P}_{ss'}^a \left[\mathcal{R}_{ss'}^a + \gamma \sum_{a'} Q^\pi(s', a') \right] \quad \text{--- (4)}$$

Substituting equation (4) in (3), we get:

$$V^*(s) = max_a \sum_{s'} \mathcal{P}_{ss'}^a \left[\mathcal{R}_{ss'}^a + \gamma \sum_{a'} Q^\pi(s', a') \right]$$

The preceding equation is called a Bellman optimality equation. In the upcoming sections, we will see how to find optimal policies by solving this equation.

Deriving the Bellman equation for value and Q functions

Now let us see how to derive Bellman equations for value and Q functions.

You can skip this section if you are not interested in mathematics; however, the math will be super intriguing.

First, we define, $P_{ss'}^a$ as a transition probability of moving from state s to s' while performing an action a:

$$P_{ss'}^a = pr(s_{t+1} = s' | s_t = s, a_t = a)$$

We define $R_{ss'}^a$ as a reward probability received by moving from state s to s' while performing an action a:

$$R_{ss'}^a = \mathbb{E}(R_{t+1}|s_t = s, s_{t+1} = s', a_t = a)$$

$$= \gamma \mathbb{E}_\pi \left[\sum_{k=0}^\infty \gamma^k r_{t+k-2}|s_{t+1} = s' \right] \quad \text{from (2)} \quad \text{---(5)}$$

We know that the value function can be represented as:

$$V^\pi(s) = \mathbb{E}_\pi \left[R_t|s_t = s \right]$$

$$V^\pi(s) = \mathbb{E}_\pi \left[r_{t+1} + \gamma r_{t+2} + \gamma^2 r_{t+3} + \ldots |s_t = s \right] \text{from (1)}$$

We can rewrite our value function by taking the first reward out:

$$V^\pi(s) = \mathbb{E}_\pi \left[r_{t+1} + \gamma \sum_{k=0}^\infty \gamma^k r_{t+k+2}|s_t = s \right] \quad \text{---(6)}$$

The expectations in the value function specifies the expected return if we are in the state s, performing an action a with policy π.

So, we can rewrite our expectation explicitly by summing up all possible actions and rewards as follows:

$$\mathbb{E}_\pi[r_{t+1}|s_t = s] = \sum_a \pi(s,a) \sum_{s'} \mathcal{P}_{ss'}^a \mathcal{R}_{ss'}^a$$

In the RHS, we will substitute $R_{ss'}^a$ from equation (5) as follows:

$$\sum_a \pi(s,a) \sum_{s'} \mathcal{P}_{ss'}^a \gamma \mathbb{E}_\pi \left[\sum_{k=0}^\infty \gamma^k r_{t+k+2}|s_{t+1} = s' \right]$$

Similarly, in the LHS, we will substitute the value of r_{t+1} from equation (2) as follows:

$$\mathbb{E}_\pi \left[\gamma \sum_{k=0}^\infty \gamma^k r_{t+k+2}|s_t = s \right]$$

So, our final expectation equation becomes:

$$\mathbb{E}_\pi\left[\gamma\sum_{k=0}^\infty \gamma^k r_{t+k+2}|s_t = s\right] = \sum_a \pi(s,a)\sum_{s'}\mathcal{P}_{ss'}^a \gamma\mathbb{E}_\pi\left[\sum_{k=0}^\infty \gamma^k r_{t+k+2}|s_{t+1} = s'\right]$$
---(7)

Now we will substitute our expectation (7) in value function (6) as follows:

$$V^\pi(s) = \sum_a \pi(s,a)\sum_{s'}\mathcal{P}_{ss'}^a\left[\mathcal{R}_{ss'}^a + \gamma\mathbb{E}_\pi\left[\sum_{k=0}^\infty \gamma^k r_{t+k+2}|s_{t+1} = s'\right]\right]$$

Instead of $\mathbb{E}_\pi\left[\sum_{k=0}^\infty \gamma^k r_{t+k+2}|s_{t+1} = s'\right]$, we can substitute $V^\pi(s')$ with equation (6), and our final value function looks like the following:

$$V^\pi(s) = \sum_a \pi(s,a)\sum_{s'}\mathcal{P}_{ss'}^a\left[\mathcal{R}_{ss'}^a + \gamma V^\pi(s')\right]$$

In very similar fashion, we can derive a Bellman equation for the Q function; the final equation is as follows:

$$Q^\pi(s,a) = \sum_{s'}\mathcal{P}_{ss'}^a\left[\mathcal{R}_{ss'}^a + \gamma\sum_{a'}Q^\pi(s',a')\right]$$

Now that we have a Bellman equation for both the value and Q function, we will see how to find the optimal policies.

Solving the Bellman equation

We can find the optimal policies by solving the Bellman optimality equation. To solve the Bellman optimality equation, we use a special technique called dynamic programming.

Dynamic programming

Dynamic programming (DP) is a technique for solving complex problems. In DP, instead of solving complex problems one at a time, we break the problem into simple sub-problems, then for each sub-problem, we compute and store the solution. If the same sub-problem occurs, we will not recompute, instead, we use the already computed solution. Thus, DP helps in drastically minimizing the computation time. It has its applications in a wide variety of fields including computer science, mathematics, bioinformatics, and so on.

We solve a Bellman equation using two powerful algorithms:

- Value iteration
- Policy iteration

Value iteration

In value iteration, we start off with a random value function. Obviously, the random value function might not be an optimal one, so we look for a new improved value function in iterative fashion until we find the optimal value function. Once we find the optimal value function, we can easily derive an optimal policy from it:

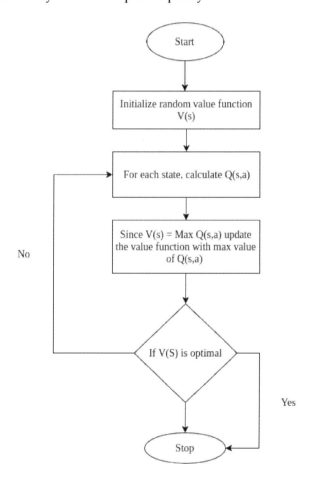

The steps involved in the value iteration are as follows:

1. First, we initialize the random value function, that is, the random value for each state.
2. Then we compute the Q function for all state action pairs of $Q(s, a)$.
3. Then we update our value function with the max value from $Q(s,a)$.
4. We repeat these steps until the change in the value function is very small.

Let us understand it intuitively by performing value iteration manually, step by step.

Consider the grid shown here. Let us say we are in state **A** and our goal is to reach state **C** without visiting state **B**, and we have two actions, 0—left/right and 1—up/down:

Can you think of what will be the optimal policy here? The optimal policy here will be the one that tells us to perform action 1 in the state **A** so that we can reach **C** without visiting **B**. How can we find this optimal policy? Let us see that now:

Initialize the random value function, that is, a random values for all the states. Let us assign **0** to all the states:

State	Value
A	0
B	0
C	0

Let's calculate the Q value for all state action pairs.

The Q value tells us the value of an action in each state. First, let us compute the Q value for state A. Recall the equation of the Q function. For calculating, we need transition and reward probabilities. Let us consider the transition and reward probability for state **A** as follows:

State (s)	Action (a)	Next State (s')	Transistion Probability $(P^a_{ss'})$	Reward Probability $(R^a_{ss'})$
A	0	A	0.1	0
A	0	B	0.4	-1.0
A	0	C	0.3	1.0
A	1	A	0.3	0
A	1	B	0.1	-2.0
A	1	C	0.5	1.0

The Q function for the state **A** can be calculated as follows:

$Q(s,a) =$ *Transition probability * (Reward probability + gamma * value_of_next_state)*

Here, *gamma* is the discount factor; we will consider it as *1*.

Q value for state *A* and action *0*:

$$Q(A,0) = (P_{AA}^0 * (R_{AA}^0 + \gamma * value\_of\_A)) + (P_{AB}^0 * (R_{AB}^0 + \gamma * value\_of\_B)) + (P_{AC}^0 * (R_{AC}^0 + \gamma * value\_of\_C))$$

$$Q(A,0) = (0.1 * (0+0)) + (0.4 * (-1.0+0)) + (0.3 * (1.0+0))$$

$$Q(A,0) = -0.1$$

Now we will compute the *Q* value for state *A* and action *1*:

$$Q(A,1) = (P_{AA}^1 * (R_{AA}^1 + \gamma * value\_of\_A)) + (P_{AB}^1 * (R_{AB}^1 + \gamma * value\_of\_B)) + (P_{AC}^1 * (R_{AC}^1 + \gamma * value\_of\_C))$$

$$Q(A,1) = (0.3 * (0+0)) + (0.1 * (-2.0 + 0)) + (0.5 * (1.0 + 0))$$

$$Q(A,1) = 0.3$$

Now we will update this in the *Q* table as follows:

State	Action	Value
A	0	-0.1
A	1	0.3
B	0	
B	1	
C	0	
C	1	

Update the value function as the max value from *Q(s,a)*.

If you look at the preceding *Q* function, *Q(A,1)* has a higher value than *Q(A,0)* so we will update the value of state *A* as *Q(A,1)*:

State	Value
A	0.3
B	
C	

Similarly, we compute the *Q* value for all state-action pairs and update the value function of each state by taking the *Q* value that has the highest state action value. Our updated value function looks like the following. This is the result of the first iteration:

State	Value
A	0.3
B	-0.2
C	0.5

We repeat this steps for several iterations. That is, we repeat step 2 to step 3 (in each iteration while calculating the Q value, we use the updated value function instead of the same randomly initialized value function).

This is the result of the second iteration:

State	Value
A	0.7
B	-0.1
C	0.5

This is the result of the third iteration:

State	Value
A	0.71
B	-0.1
C	0.53

But when do we stop this? We will stop when the change in the value between each iteration is small; if you look at iteration two and three, there is not much of a change in the value function. Given this condition, we stop iterating and consider it an optimal value function.

Okay, now that we have found the optimal value function, how can we derive the optimal policy?

It is very simple. We compute the Q function with our final optimal value function. Let us say our computed Q function looks like the following:

State	Action	Value
A	0	-0.53
A	1	0.98
B	0	-0.2
B	1	-0.3
C	0	0.2
C	1	0.01

From this Q function, we pick up actions in each state that have maximal value. At state **A**, we have a maximum value for action 1, which is our optimal policy. So if we perform action 1 in state **A** we can reach **C** without visiting **B**.

Policy iteration

Unlike value iteration, in policy iteration we start with the random policy, then we find the value function of that policy; if the value function is not optimal then we find the new improved policy. We repeat this process until we find the optimal policy.

There are two steps in policy iteration:

1. **Policy evaluation**: Evaluating the value function of a randomly estimated policy.
2. **Policy improvement**: Upon evaluating the value function, if it is not optimal, we find a new improved policy:

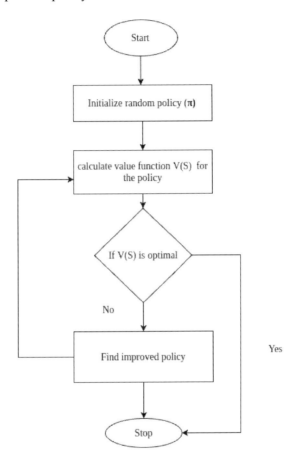

The steps involved in the policy iteration are as follows:

1. First, we initialize some random policy
2. Then we find the value function for that random policy and evaluate to check if it is optimal which is called policy evaluation
3. If it is not optimal, we find a new improved policy, which is called policy improvement
4. We repeat these steps until we find an optimal policy

Let us understand intuitively by performing policy iteration manually step by step.

Consider the same grid example we saw in the section *Value iteration*. Our goal is to find the optimal policy:

1. Initialize a random policy function.

    Let us initialize a random policy function by specifying random actions to each state:

    say $A \rightarrow 0$

    $B \rightarrow 1$

    $C \rightarrow 0$

2. Find the value function for the randomly initialized policy.

    Now we have to find the value function using our randomly initialized policy. Let us say our value function after computation looks like the following:

State	Value
A	0.3
B	-0.2
C	0.5

Now that we have a new value function according to our randomly initialized policy, let us compute a new policy using our new value function. How do we do this? It is very similar to what we did in *Value iteration*. We calculate Q value for our new value function and then take actions for each state which has a maximum value as the new policy.

Let us say the new policy results in:

A -> 0

B -> 1

C -> 1

We check our old policy, that is, the randomly initialized policy, and the new policy. If they are same, then we have attained the convergence, that is, found the optimal policy. If not, we will update our old policy (random policy) as a new policy and repeat from step 2.

Sound confusing? Look at the pseudo code:

```
policy_iteration():
    Initialize random policy
    for i in no_of_iterations:
        Q_value = value_function(random_policy)
        new_policy = Maximum state action pair from Q value
        if random_policy == new policy:
            break
        random_policy = new_policy
    return policy
```

Solving the frozen lake problem

If you haven't understood anything we have learned so far, don't worry, we will look at all the concepts along with a frozen lake problem.

Imagine there is a frozen lake stretching from your home to your office; you have to walk on the frozen lake to reach your office. But oops! There are holes in the frozen lake so you have to be careful while walking on the frozen lake to avoid getting trapped in the holes:

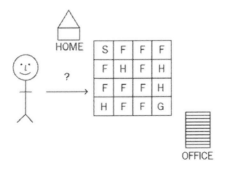

Look at the preceding diagram:

- **S** is the starting position (home)
- **F** is the frozen lake where you can walk
- **H** are the holes, which you have to be so careful about
- **G** is the goal (office)

Okay, now let us use our agent instead of you to find the correct way to reach the office. The agent's goal is to find the optimal path to go from **S** to **G** without getting trapped at **H**. How can an agent achieve this? We give +1 point as a reward to the agent if it correctly walks on the frozen lake and 0 points if it falls into a hole, so the agent can determine which is the right action. An agent will now try to find the optimal policy. Optimal policy implies taking the correct path, which maximizes the agent's reward. If the agent is maximizing the reward, apparently the agent is learning to skip the holes and reach the destination.

We can model our problem into MDP, which we studied earlier. MDP consists of the following:

- **States**: Set of states. Here we have 16 states (each little square box in the grid).
- **Actions**: Set of all possible actions (left, right, up, down; these are all the four possible actions our agent can take in our frozen lake environment).
- **Transition probabilities**: The probability of moving from one state (**F**) to another state (**H**) by performing an action *a*.
- **Rewards probabilities**: This is the probability of receiving a reward while moving from one state (**F**) to another state (**H**) by performing an action *a*.

Now our objective is to solve MDP. Solving the MDP implies finding the optimal policies. We introduce three special functions now:

- **Policy function**: Specifies what action to perform in each state
- **Value function**: Specifies how good a state is
- **Q function**: Specifies how good an action is in a particular state

When we say how good, what does that really mean? It implies how good it is to maximize the rewards.

Then, we represent the value function and *Q* function using a special equation called a Bellman Optimality equation. If we solve this equation, we can find the optimal policy. Here, solving the equation means finding the right value function and policy. If we find the right value function and policy, that will be our optimal path which yields maximum rewards.

We will use a special technique called dynamic programming to solve the Bellman optimality equation. To apply DP, the model dynamics have to be known in advance, which basically means the model environment's transition probabilities and reward probabilities have to be known in advance. Since we know the model dynamics, we can use DP here. We use two special DP algorithms to find the optimal policy:

- Value iteration
- Policy iteration

Value iteration

To put it in simple terms, in value iteration, we first initialize some random value to the value function. There is a great probability that the random value we initialize is not going to be optimal. So, we iterate over each state and find the new value function; we stop the iteration until we find the optimal value function. Once we find the optimal value function, we can easily extract the optimal policy from that.

Now we will see how to solve the frozen lake problem using value iteration.

First, we import necessary libraries:

```
import gym
import numpy as np
```

Then we make our frozen lake environment using OpenAI's Gym:

```
env = gym.make('FrozenLake-v0')
```

We will first explore the environments.

The number of states in the environment is 16 as we have a 4*4 grid:

```
print(env.observation_space.n)
```

The number of actions in the environment is four, which are up, down, left, and right:

```
print(env.observation_space.n)
```

Now we define a `value_iteration()` function which returns the optimal value function (value table). We will first see the function step by step and then look at the whole function.

First, we initialize the random value table which is 0 for all the states and numbers of iterations:

```
value_table = np.zeros(env.observation_space.n)
no_of_iterations = 100000
```

Then, upon starting each iteration, we copy the `value_table` to `updated_value_table`:

```
for i in range(no_of_iterations):
    updated_value_table = np.copy(value_table)
```

Now we calculate the Q table and pick up the maximum state-action pair which has the highest value as the value table.

We will understand the code with the example we solved previously; we computed the Q value for state A and action 1 in our previous example:

$$Q(A,1) = (0.3 * (0+0)) + (0.1 * (-1.0 + 0)) + (0.5 + (1.0 + 0))$$

$$Q(A,1) = 0.5$$

Instead of creating a Q table for each state, we create a list called `Q_value`, then for each action in the state, we create a list called `next_states_rewards`, which store the `Q_value` for the next transition state. Then we sum the `next_state_rewards` and append it to our `Q_value`.

Look at the preceding example, where the state is *A* and the action is *1*. *(0.3 * (0+0))* is the next state reward for the transition state *A* and *(0.1 * (-1.0 + 0))* is the next state reward for the transition state *B*. *(0.5 + (1.0 + 0))* is the next state reward for the transition state *C*. We sum all this as `next_state_reward` and append it to our `Q_value`, which would be 0.5.

As we calculate `next_state_rewards` for all actions of a state and append it to our *Q* value, we pick up the maximum *Q* value and update it as a value of our state:

```
for state in range(env.observation_space.n):
    Q_value = []
    for action in range(env.action_space.n):
        next_states_rewards = []
        for next_sr in env.P[state][action]:
            trans_prob, next_state, reward_prob, _ = next_sr
            next_states_rewards.append((trans_prob * (reward_prob + gamma *
updated_value_table[next_state])))
        Q_value.append(np.sum(next_states_rewards))
```

```
#Pick up the maximum Q value and update it as value of a state
value_table[state] = max(Q_value)
```

Then, we will check whether we have reached the convergence, that is, the difference between our value table and updated value table is very small. How do we know it is very small? We define a variable called `threshold` and then we will see if the difference is less than our `threshold`; if it is less, we break the loop and return the value function as the optimal value function:

```
threshold = 1e-20
if (np.sum(np.fabs(updated_value_table - value_table)) <= threshold):
    print ('Value-iteration converged at iteration# %d.' %(i+1))
    break
```

Look at the complete function of `value_iteration()` for a better understanding:

```
def value_iteration(env, gamma = 1.0):
    value_table = np.zeros(env.observation_space.n)
    no_of_iterations = 100000
    threshold = 1e-20

    for i in range(no_of_iterations):
        updated_value_table = np.copy(value_table)

        for state in range(env.observation_space.n):
            Q_value = []

            for action in range(env.action_space.n):
                next_states_rewards = []

                for next_sr in env.P[state][action]:
                    trans_prob, next_state, reward_prob, _ = next_sr
                    next_states_rewards.append((trans_prob * (reward_prob +
gamma * updated_value_table[next_state])))

                Q_value.append(np.sum(next_states_rewards))
            value_table[state] = max(Q_value)
        if (np.sum(np.fabs(updated_value_table - value_table)) <=
threshold):
            print ('Value-iteration converged at iteration# %d.' %(i+1))
            break
    return value_table, Q_value
```

Thus, we can derive `optimal_value_function` using the `value_iteration`:

```
optimal_value_function = value_iteration(env=env,gamma=1.0)
```

After finding `optimal_value_function`, how can we extract the optimal policy from the `optimal_value_function`? We calculate the Q value using our optimal value action and pick up the actions which have the highest Q value for each state as the optimal policy. We do this via a function called `extract_policy()`; we will look at this step by step now.

First, we define the random policy; we define it as 0 for all the states:

```
policy = np.zeros(env.observation_space.n)
```

Then, for each state, we build a `Q_table` and for each action in that state we compute the Q value and add it to our `Q_table`:

```
for state in range(env.observation_space.n):
        Q_table = np.zeros(env.action_space.n)
        for action in range(env.action_space.n):
            for next_sr in env.P[state][action]:
                trans_prob, next_state, reward_prob, _ = next_sr
                Q_table[action] += (trans_prob * (reward_prob + gamma *
value_table[next_state]))
```

Then we pick up the policy for the `state` as the action that has the highest Q value:

```
policy[state] = np.argmax(Q_table)
```

Look at the complete function:

```
def extract_policy(value_table, gamma = 1.0):

    policy = np.zeros(env.observation_space.n)
    for state in range(env.observation_space.n):
        Q_table = np.zeros(env.action_space.n)
        for action in range(env.action_space.n):
            for next_sr in env.P[state][action]:
                trans_prob, next_state, reward_prob, _ = next_sr
                Q_table[action] += (trans_prob * (reward_prob + gamma *
value_table[next_state]))
        policy[state] = np.argmax(Q_table)
    return policy
```

Thus, we can derive the `optimal_policy` as follows:

```
optimal_policy = extract_policy(optimal_value_function, gamma=1.0)
```

We will get an output as follows, which is the `optimal_policy`, the actions to be performed in each state:

```
array([0., 3., 3., 3., 0., 0., 0., 0., 3., 1., 0., 0., 0., 2., 1., 0.])
```

The complete program is given as follows:

```
import gym
import numpy as np
env = gym.make('FrozenLake-v0')

def value_iteration(env, gamma = 1.0):
    value_table = np.zeros(env.observation_space.n)
    no_of_iterations = 100000
    threshold = 1e-20
    for i in range(no_of_iterations):
        updated_value_table = np.copy(value_table)
        for state in range(env.observation_space.n):
            Q_value = []
            for action in range(env.action_space.n):
                next_states_rewards = []
                for next_sr in env.P[state][action]:
                    trans_prob, next_state, reward_prob, _ = next_sr
                    next_states_rewards.append((trans_prob * (reward_prob +
gamma * updated_value_table[next_state])))
                Q_value.append(np.sum(next_states_rewards))
            value_table[state] = max(Q_value)
        if (np.sum(np.fabs(updated_value_table - value_table)) <=
threshold):
            print ('Value-iteration converged at iteration# %d.' %(i+1))
            break
    return value_table


def extract_policy(value_table, gamma = 1.0):
    policy = np.zeros(env.observation_space.n)
    for state in range(env.observation_space.n):
        Q_table = np.zeros(env.action_space.n)
        for action in range(env.action_space.n):
            for next_sr in env.P[state][action]:
                trans_prob, next_state, reward_prob, _ = next_sr
                Q_table[action] += (trans_prob * (reward_prob + gamma *
value_table[next_state]))
        policy[state] = np.argmax(Q_table)
    return policy

optimal_value_function = value_iteration(env=env,gamma=1.0)
optimal_policy = extract_policy(optimal_value_function, gamma=1.0)

print(optimal_policy)
```

Policy iteration

In policy iteration, first we initialize a random policy. Then we will evaluate the random policies we initialized: are they good or not? But how can we evaluate the policies? We will evaluate our randomly initialized policies by computing value functions for them. If they are not good, then we find a new policy. We repeat this process until we find a good policy.

Now let us see how to solve the frozen lake problem using policy iteration.

Before looking at policy iteration, we will see how to compute a value function, given a policy.

We initialize `value_table` as zero with the number of states:

```
value_table = np.zeros(env.nS)
```

Then, for each state, we get the action from the policy, and we compute the value function according to that `action` and `state` as follows:

```
updated_value_table = np.copy(value_table)
for state in range(env.nS):
    action = policy[state]
    value_table[state] = sum([trans_prob * (reward_prob + gamma *
updated_value_table[next_state])
                    for trans_prob, next_state, reward_prob, _ in
env.P[state][action]])
```

We break this when the difference between `value_table` and `updated_value_table` is less than our `threshold`:

```
threshold = 1e-10
if (np.sum((np.fabs(updated_value_table - value_table))) <= threshold):
    break
```

Look at the following complete function:

```
def compute_value_function(policy, gamma=1.0):
    value_table = np.zeros(env.nS)
    threshold = 1e-10
    while True:
        updated_value_table = np.copy(value_table)
        for state in range(env.nS):
            action = policy[state]
            value_table[state] = sum([trans_prob * (reward_prob + gamma *
updated_value_table[next_state])
                    for trans_prob, next_state, reward_prob, _ in
env.P[state][action]])
```

```
        if (np.sum((np.fabs(updated_value_table - value_table))) <=
threshold):
            break
    return value_table
```

Now we will see how to perform policy iteration, step by step.

First, we initialize `random_policy` as zero NumPy array with shape as number of states:

```
    random_policy = np.zeros(env.observation_space.n)
```

Then, for each iteration, we calculate the `new_value_function` according to our random policy:

```
    new_value_function = compute_value_function(random_policy, gamma)
```

We will extract the policy using the calculated `new_value_function`. The `extract_policy` function is the same as the one we used in value iteration:

```
    new_policy = extract_policy(new_value_function, gamma)
```

Then we check whether we have reached convergence, that is, whether we found the optimal policy by comparing `random_policy` and the new policy. If they are the same, we will break the iteration; otherwise we update `random_policy` with `new_policy`:

```
if (np.all(random_policy == new_policy)):
    print ('Policy-Iteration converged at step %d.' %(i+1))
    break
random_policy = new_policy
```

Look at the complete `policy_iteration` function:

```
def policy_iteration(env,gamma = 1.0):
    random_policy = np.zeros(env.observation_space.n)
    no_of_iterations = 200000
    gamma = 1.0
    for i in range(no_of_iterations):
        new_value_function = compute_value_function(random_policy, gamma)
        new_policy = extract_policy(new_value_function, gamma)
        if (np.all(random_policy == new_policy)):
            print ('Policy-Iteration converged at step %d.' %(i+1))
            break
        random_policy = new_policy
    return new_policy
```

Thus, we can get `optimal_policy` using `policy_iteration`:

```
optimal_policy = policy_iteration(env, gamma = 1.0)
```

We will get some output, which is the `optimal_policy`, the actions to be performed in each state:

```
array([0., 3., 3., 3., 0., 0., 0., 0., 3., 1., 0., 0., 0., 2., 1., 0.])
```

The complete program is given as follows:

```python
import gym
import numpy as np

env = gym.make('FrozenLake-v0')

def compute_value_function(policy, gamma=1.0):
    value_table = np.zeros(env.nS)
    threshold = 1e-10
    while True:
        updated_value_table = np.copy(value_table)
        for state in range(env.nS):
            action = policy[state]
            value_table[state] = sum([trans_prob * (reward_prob + gamma *
updated_value_table[next_state])
                        for trans_prob, next_state, reward_prob, _ in
env.P[state][action]])
        if (np.sum((np.fabs(updated_value_table - value_table))) <=
threshold):
            break
    return value_table


def extract_policy(value_table, gamma = 1.0):
    policy = np.zeros(env.observation_space.n)
    for state in range(env.observation_space.n):
        Q_table = np.zeros(env.action_space.n)
        for action in range(env.action_space.n):
            for next_sr in env.P[state][action]:
                trans_prob, next_state, reward_prob, _ = next_sr
                Q_table[action] += (trans_prob * (reward_prob + gamma *
value_table[next_state]))
        policy[state] = np.argmax(Q_table)
    return policy

def policy_iteration(env,gamma = 1.0):
    random_policy = np.zeros(env.observation_space.n)
    no_of_iterations = 200000
```

```
gamma = 1.0
for i in range(no_of_iterations):
    new_value_function = compute_value_function(random_policy, gamma)
    new_policy = extract_policy(new_value_function, gamma)
    if (np.all(random_policy == new_policy)):
        print ('Policy-Iteration converged at step %d.' %(i+1))
        break
    random_policy = new_policy
return new_policy
```

```
print (policy_iteration(env))
```

Thus, we can derive the optimal policy, which specifies what action to perform in each state, using value and policy iteration to solve the frozen lake problem.

Summary

In this chapter, we learned what the Markov chain and Markov process are and how RL problems are represented using MDP. We have also looked at the Bellman equation, and we solved the Bellman equation to derive an optimal policy using DP. In the next chapter, `Chapter 4`, *Gaming with Monte Carlo Methods*, we will look at the Monte Carlo tree search and how to build intelligent games using it.

Questions

The question list is as follows:

1. What is the Markov property?
2. Why do we need the Markov Decision Process?
3. When do we prefer immediate rewards?
4. What is the use of the discount factor?
5. Why do we use the Bellman function?
6. How would you derive the Bellman equation for a Q function?
7. How are the value function and Q function related?
8. What is the difference between value iteration and policy iteration?

Further reading

MDP Harvard lecture materials: `http://am121.seas.harvard.edu/site/wp-content/uploads/2011/03/MarkovDecisionProcesses-HillierLieberman.pdf`

Gaming with Monte Carlo Methods

4

Monte Carlo is one of the most popular and most commonly used algorithms in various fields ranging from physics and mechanics to computer science. The Monte Carlo algorithm is used in **reinforcement learning** (**RL**) when the model of the environment is not known. In the previous chapter, Chapter 3, *Markov Decision Process and Dynamic Programming*, we looked at using **dynamic programming** (**DP**) to find an optimal policy where we know the model dynamics, which is transition and reward probabilities. But how can we determine the optimal policy when we don't know the model dynamics? In that case, we use the Monte Carlo algorithm; it is extremely powerful for finding optimal policies when we don't have knowledge of the environment.

In this chapter, you will learn about the following:

- Monte Carlo methods
- Monte Carlo prediction
- Playing Blackjack with Monte Carlo
- Model Carlo control
- Monte Carlo exploration starts
- On-policy Monte Carlo control
- Off-policy Monte Carlo control

Monte Carlo methods

The Monte Carlo method finds approximate solutions through random sampling, that is, it approximates the probability of an outcome by running multiple trails. It is a statistical technique to find an approximate answer through sampling. Let's better understand Monte Carlo intuitively with an example.

Fun fact: Monte Carlo is named after Stanislaw Ulam's uncle, who often borrowed money from his relatives to gamble in a Monte Carlo casino.

Estimating the value of pi using Monte Carlo

Imagine a quadrant of a circle is placed inside a square, as shown next, and we generate some random points inside the square. You can see that some of the points fall inside the circle while others are outside the circle:

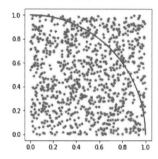

We can write:

$$\frac{Area \quad of \quad a \quad cirlce}{Area \quad of \quad a \quad square} = \frac{No \quad of \quad points \quad inside \quad the \quad circle}{No \quad of \quad points \quad inside \quad the \quad square}$$

We know that the area of a circle is πr^2 and the area of a square is a^2:

$$\frac{\pi r^2}{a^2} = \frac{No \quad of \quad points \quad inside \quad the \quad circle}{No \quad of \quad points \quad inside \quad the \quad square}$$

Let's consider that the radius of a circle is one half and the square's side is *1*, so we can substitute:

$$\frac{\pi (\frac{1}{2})^2}{1^2} = \frac{No \quad of \quad points \quad inside \quad the \quad circle}{No \quad of \quad points \quad inside \quad the \quad square}$$

Now we get the following:

$$\pi = 4 * \frac{No \quad of \quad points \quad inside \quad the \quad circle}{No \quad of \quad points \quad inside \quad the \quad square}$$

The steps to estimate π are very simple:

1. First, we generate some random points inside the square.
2. Then we can calculate the number of points that fall inside the circle by using the equation $x^2 + y^2 <= size$.
3. Then we calculate the value of π by multiplying four to the division of the number of points inside the circle to the number of points inside the square.
4. If we increase the number of samples (number of random points), the better we can approximate

Let's see how to do this in Python step by step. First, we import necessary libraries:

```
import numpy as np
import math
import random
import matplotlib.pyplot as plt
%matplotlib inline
```

Now we initialize the square size and number of points inside the circle and square. We also initialize the sample size, which denotes the number of random points to be generated. We define `arc`, which is basically the circle quadrant:

```
square_size = 1
points_inside_circle = 0
points_inside_square = 0
sample_size = 1000
arc = np.linspace(0, np.pi/2, 100)
```

Then we define a function called `generate_points()`, which generates random points inside the square:

```
def generate_points(size):
    x = random.random()*size
    y = random.random()*size
    return (x, y)
```

We define a function called `is_in_circle()`, which will check if the point we generated falls within the circle:

```
def is_in_circle(point, size):
    return math.sqrt(point[0]**2 + point[1]**2) <= size
```

Then we define a function for calculating the π value:

```
def compute_pi(points_inside_circle, points_inside_square):
    return 4 * (points_inside_circle / points_inside_square)
```

Then for the number of samples, we generate some random points inside the square and increment our `points_inside_square` variable, and then we will check if the points we generated lie inside the circle. If yes, then we increment the `points_inside_circle` variable:

```
plt.axes().set_aspect('equal')
plt.plot(1*np.cos(arc), 1*np.sin(arc))

for i in range(sample_size):
    point = generate_points(square_size)
    plt.plot(point[0], point[1], 'c.')
    points_inside_square += 1
    if is_in_circle(point, square_size):
        points_inside_circle += 1
```

Now we calculate the value of π using the `compute_pi()`, function which will print an approximate value of π:

```
print("Approximate value of pi is {}"
    .format(calculate_pi(points_inside_circle, points_inside_square)))
```

If you run the program, you will get the output shown as follows:

```
Approximate value of pi is 3.144
```

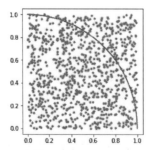

The complete program looks as follows:

```
import numpy as np
import math
import random
import matplotlib.pyplot as plt
%matplotlib inline
```

```
square_size = 1
points_inside_circle = 0
points_inside_square = 0
sample_size = 1000
arc = np.linspace(0, np.pi/2, 100)

def generate_points(size):
    x = random.random()*size
    y = random.random()*size
    return (x, y)

def is_in_circle(point, size):
    return math.sqrt(point[0]**2 + point[1]**2) <= size

def compute_pi(points_inside_circle, points_inside_square):
    return 4 * (points_inside_circle / points_inside_square)

plt.axes().set_aspect('equal')
plt.plot(1*np.cos(arc), 1*np.sin(arc))

for i in range(sample_size):
    point = generate_points(square_size)
    plt.plot(point[0], point[1], 'c.')
    points_inside_square += 1
    if is_in_circle(point, square_size):
        points_inside_circle += 1

print("Approximate value of pi is {}"
.format(calculate_pi(points_inside_circle, points_inside_square)))
```

Thus, the Monte Carlo method approximated the value of `pi` by using random sampling. We estimated the value of `pi` using the random points (samples) generated inside the square. The greater the sampling size, the better our approximation will be. Now we will see how to use Monte Carlo methods in RL.

Monte Carlo prediction

In DP, we solve the **Markov Decision Process (MDP)** by using value iteration and policy iteration. Both of these techniques require transition and reward probabilities to find the optimal policy. But how can we solve MDP when we don't know the transition and reward probabilities? In that case, we use the Monte Carlo method. The Monte Carlo method requires only sample sequences of states, actions, and rewards. the Monte Carlo methods are applied only to the episodic tasks. Since Monte Carlo doesn't require any model, it is called the model-free learning algorithm.

The basic idea of the Monte Carlo method is very simple. Do you recall how we defined the optimal value function and how we derived the optimal policy in the previous chapter, Chapter 3, *Markov Decision Process and Dynamic Programming*?

A value function is basically the expected return from a state *S* with a policy π. Here, instead of expected return, we use mean return.

 Thus, in Monte Carlo prediction, we approximate the value function by taking the mean return instead of the expected return.

Using Monte Carlo prediction, we can estimate the value function of any given policy. The steps involved in the Monte Carlo prediction are very simple and are as follows:

1. First, we initialize a random value to our value function
2. Then we initialize an empty list called a return to store our returns
3. Then for each state in the episode, we calculate the return
4. Next, we append the return to our return list
5. Finally, we take the average of return as our value function

The following flowchart makes it more simple:

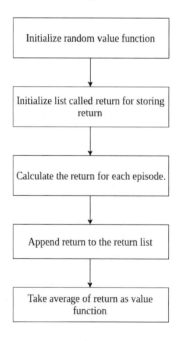

The Monte Carlo prediction algorithm is of two types:

- First visit Monte Carlo
- Every visit Monte Carlo

First visit Monte Carlo

As we have seen, in the Monte Carlo methods, we approximate the value function by taking the average return. But in the first visit MC method, we average the return only the first time the state is visited in an episode. For example, consider an agent is playing the snakes and ladder games, there is a good chance the agent will return to the state if it is bitten by a snake. When the agent revisits the state, we don't consider an average return. We consider an average return only when the agent visits the state for the first time.

Every visit Monte Carlo

In every visit Monte Carlo, we average the return every time the state is visited in an episode. Consider the same snakes and ladders game example: if the agent returns to the same state after a snake bites it, we can think of this as an average return although the agent is revisiting the state. In this case, we average return every time the agents visit the state.

Let's play Blackjack with Monte Carlo

Now let's better understand Monte Carlo with the Blackjack game. Blackjack, also called 21, is a popular card game played in casinos. The goal of the game is to have a sum of all your cards close to 21 and not exceeding 21. The value of cards J, K, and Q is 10. The value of ace can be 1 or 11; this depends on player choice. The value of the rest of the cards (1 to 10) is the same as the numbers they show.

The rules of the game are very simple:

- The game can be played with one or many players and one dealer.
- Each player competes only with the dealer and not another player.
- Initially, a player is given two cards. Both of these cards are face up, that is, visible to others.
- A dealer is also given two cards. One card is face up and the other is face down. That is, the dealer only shows one of his cards.

- If the sum of a player's cards is 21 immediately after receiving two cards (say a player has received a jack and ace which is 10+11 = 21), then it is called **natural** or **Blackjack** and the player wins.
- If the dealer's sum of cards is also 21 immediately after receiving two cards, then it is called a **draw** as both of them have 21.
- In each round, the player decides whether he needs another card or not to sum the cards close to 21.
- If a player needs a card, then it is called a **hit**.
- If a player doesn't need a card, then it is called a **stand**.
- If a player's sum of cards exceeds 21, then it is called **bust**; then the dealer will win the game.

Let's better understand Blackjack by playing. I'll let you be the player and I am the dealer:

In the preceding diagram, we have one player and a dealer. Both of them are given two cards. Both of the player's two cards are face up (visible) while the dealer has one card face up (visible) and the other face down (invisible). In the first round, you have been given two cards, say a jack and a number 7, which is (10 + 7 = 17), and I as the dealer will only show you one card which is number 2. I have another card face down. Now you have to decide to either hit (need another card) or stand (don't need another card). If you choose to hit and receive number 3 you will get 10+7+3 = 20 which is close to 21 and you win:

But if you received a card, say number 7, then 10+7+7 = 24, which exceeds 21. Then it is called bust and you lose the game. If you decide to stand with your initial cards, then you have only 10 + 7 = 17. Then we will check the dealer's sum of cards. If it is greater than 17 and does not exceed 21 then the dealer wins, otherwise you win:

The rewards here are:

- +1 if the player won the game
- -1 if the player loses the game
- 0 if the game is a draw

The possible actions are:

- **Hit**: If the player needs a card
- **Stand**: If the player doesn't need a card

The player has to decide the value of an ace. If the player's sum of cards is 10 and the player gets an ace after a hit, he can consider it as 11, and 10 + 11 = 21. But if the player's sum of cards is 15 and the player gets an ace after a hit, if he considers it as 11 and 15+11 = 26, then it's a bust. If the player has an ace we can call it a **usable ace**; the player can consider it as 11 without being bust. If the player is bust by considering the ace as 11, then it is called a **nonusable ace**.

Now we will see how to implement Blackjack using the first visit Monte Carlo algorithm.

First, we will import our necessary libraries:

```
import gym
from matplotlib import pyplot
import matplotlib.pyplot as plt
from mpl_toolkits.mplot3d import Axes3D
from collections import defaultdict
from functools import partial
```

```
%matplotlib inline
plt.style.use('ggplot')
```

Now we will create the Blackjack environment using OpenAI's Gym:

```
env = gym.make('Blackjack-v0')
```

Then we define the policy function which takes the current state and checks if the score is greater than or equal to 2o; if it is, we return 0 or else we return 1. That is, if the score is greater than or equal to 20, we stand (0) or else we hit (1):

```
def sample_policy(observation):
    score, dealer_score, usable_ace = observation
    return 0 if score >= 20 else 1
```

Now we will see how to generate an episode. An episode is a single round of a game. We will see it step by step and then look at the complete function.

We define states, actions, and rewards as a list and initiate the environment using `env.reset` and store an observation variable:

```
states, actions, rewards = [], [], []
observation = env.reset()
```

Then, until we reach the terminal state, that is, till the end of the episode, we do the following:

1. Append the observation to the states list:

    ```
    states.append(observation)
    ```

2. Now, we create an action using our `sample_policy` function and append the actions to an `action` list:

    ```
    action = sample_policy(observation)
    actions.append(action)
    ```

3. Then, for each step in the environment, we store the `state`, `reward`, and `done` (which specifies whether we reached terminal state) and we append the rewards to the `reward` list:

    ```
    observation, reward, done, info = env.step(action)
    rewards.append(reward)
    ```

4. If we reached the terminal state, then we break:

```
if done:
    break
```

5. The complete `generate_episode` function is as follows:

```
def generate_episode(policy, env):
    states, actions, rewards = [], [], []
    observation = env.reset()
    while True:
        states.append(observation)
        action = policy(observation)
        actions.append(action)
        observation, reward, done, info = env.step(action)
        rewards.append(reward)
        if done:
            break

    return states, actions, rewards
```

This is how we generate an episode. How can we play the game? For that, we need to know the value of each state. Now we will see how to get the value of each state using the first visit Monte Carlo method.

First, we initialize the empty value table as a dictionary for storing the values of each state:

```
value_table = defaultdict(float)
```

Then, for a certain number of episodes, we do the following:

1. First, we generate an episode and store the states and rewards; we initialize returns as 0 which is the sum of rewards:

```
states, _, rewards = generate_episode(policy, env)
returns = 0
```

2. Then for each step, we store the rewards to a variable *R* and states to *S*, and we calculate returns as a sum of rewards:

```
for t in range(len(states) - 1, -1, -1):
    R = rewards[t]
    S = states[t]
    returns += R
```

3. We now perform the first visit Monte Carlo; we check if the episode is being visited for the visit time. If it is, we simply take the average of returns and assign the value of the state as an average of returns:

```
if S not in states[:t]:
    N[S] += 1
    value_table[S] += (returns - V[S]) / N[S]
```

4. Look at the complete function for better understanding:

```
def first_visit_mc_prediction(policy, env, n_episodes):
    value_table = defaultdict(float)
    N = defaultdict(int)

    for _ in range(n_episodes):
        states, _, rewards = generate_episode(policy, env)
        returns = 0
        for t in range(len(states) - 1, -1, -1):
            R = rewards[t]
            S = states[t]
            returns += R
            if S not in states[:t]:
                N[S] += 1
                value_table[S] += (returns - V[S]) / N[S]
    return value_table
```

5. We can get the value of each state:

```
value = first_visit_mc_prediction(sample_policy, env,
n_episodes=500000)
```

6. Let's see the value of a few states:

```
print(value)
defaultdict(float,
            {(4, 1, False): -1.024292170184644,
             (4, 2, False): -1.8670191351012455,
             (4, 3, False): 2.211363314854649,
             (4, 4, False): 16.903201033000823,
             (4, 5, False): -5.786238030898542,
             (4, 6, False): -16.218211752577602,
```

We can also plot the value of the state to see how it is converged, as follows:

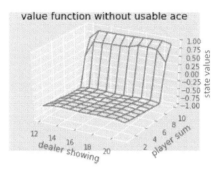

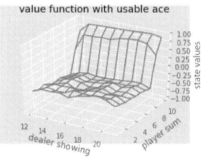

The complete code is given as follows:

```
import numpy
import gym
from matplotlib import pyplot
import matplotlib.pyplot as plt
from mpl_toolkits.mplot3d import Axes3D
from collections import defaultdict
from functools import partial
%matplotlib inline

plt.style.use('ggplot')

## Blackjack Environment

env = gym.make('Blackjack-v0')

env.action_space, env.observation_space

def sample_policy(observation):
    score, dealer_score, usable_ace = observation
    return 0 if score >= 20 else 1
```

```python
def generate_episode(policy, env):
    states, actions, rewards = [], [], []
    observation = env.reset()
    while True:
        states.append(observation)
        action = sample_policy(observation)
        actions.append(action)
        observation, reward, done, info = env.step(action)
        rewards.append(reward)
        if done:
            break

    return states, actions, rewards


def first_visit_mc_prediction(policy, env, n_episodes):
    value_table = defaultdict(float)
    N = defaultdict(int)

    for _ in range(n_episodes):
        states, _, rewards = generate_episode(policy, env)
        returns = 0
        for t in range(len(states) - 1, -1, -1):
            R = rewards[t]
            S = states[t]
            returns += R
            if S not in states[:t]:
                N[S] += 1
                value_table[S] += (returns - value_table[S]) / N[S]
    return value_table

def plot_blackjack(V, ax1, ax2):
    player_sum = numpy.arange(12, 21 + 1)
    dealer_show = numpy.arange(1, 10 + 1)
    usable_ace = numpy.array([False, True])

    state_values = numpy.zeros((len(player_sum),
                                len(dealer_show),
                                len(usable_ace)))

    for i, player in enumerate(player_sum):
        for j, dealer in enumerate(dealer_show):
            for k, ace in enumerate(usable_ace):
                state_values[i, j, k] = V[player, dealer, ace]

    X, Y = numpy.meshgrid(player_sum, dealer_show)

    ax1.plot_wireframe(X, Y, state_values[:, :, 0])
```

```
    ax2.plot_wireframe(X, Y, state_values[:, :, 1])
    for ax in ax1, ax2:
        ax.set_zlim(-1, 1)
        ax.set_ylabel('player sum')
        ax.set_xlabel('dealer showing')
        ax.set_zlabel('state-value')
fig, axes = pyplot.subplots(nrows=2, figsize=(5, 8),
subplot_kw={'projection': '3d'})
axes[0].set_title('value function without usable ace')
axes[1].set_title('value function with usable ace')
plot_blackjack(value, axes[0], axes[1])
```

Monte Carlo control

In Monte Carlo prediction, we have seen how to estimate the value function. In Monte Carlo control, we will see how to optimize the value function, that is, how to make the value function more accurate than the estimation. In the control methods, we follow a new type of iteration called generalized policy iteration, where policy evaluation and policy improvement interact with each other. It basically runs as a loop between policy evaluation and improvement, that is, the policy is always improved with respect to the value function, and the value function is always improved according to the policy. It keeps on doing this. When there is no change, then we can say that the policy and value function have attained convergence, that is, we found the optimal value function and optimal policy:

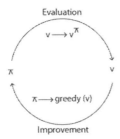

Now we will see a different Monte Carlo control algorithm as follows.

Monte Carlo exploration starts

Unlike DP methods, here we do not estimate state values. Instead, we focus on action values. State values alone are sufficient when we know the model of the environment. As we don't know about the model dynamics, it is not a good way to determine the state values alone.

Estimating an action value is more intuitive than estimating a state value because state values vary depending on the policy we choose. For example, in a Blackjack game, say we are in a state where some of the cards are 20. What is the value of this state? It solely depends on the policy. If we choose our policy as a hit, then it is not a good state to be in and the value of this state is very low. However, if we choose our policy as a stand then it is definitely a good state to be in. Thus, the value of the state depends on the policy we choose. So it is more important to estimate the value of an action instead of the value of the state.

How do we estimate the action values? Remember the Q function we learned in `Chapter 3`, *Markov Decision Process and Dynamic Programming*? The Q function denoted as $Q(s, a)$ is used for determining how good an action is in a particular state. It basically specifies the state-action pair.

But here the problem of exploration comes in. How can we know about the state-action value if we haven't been in that state? If we don't explore all the states with all possible actions, we might probably miss out the good rewards.

Say that in a Blackjack game, we are in a state where a sum of cards is 20. If we try only the action **hit** we will get a negative reward, and we learn that it is not a good state to be in. But if we try the **stand** action, we receive a positive reward and it is actually the best state to be in. So every time we come to this particular state, we stand instead of hit. For us to know which is the best action, we have to explore all possible actions in each state to find the optimal value. How can we do this?

Let me introduce a new concept called **Monte Carlo exploring starts**, which implies that for each episode we start with a random state as an initial state and perform an action. So, if we have a large number of episodes, we could possibly cover all the states with all possible actions. It is also called an **MC-ES** algorithm.

The MC-ES algorithm is very simple, as follows:

- We first initialize Q function and policy with some random values and also we initialize a return to an empty list
- Then we start the episode with our randomly initialized policy
- Then we calculate the return for all the unique state-action pairs occurring in the episode and append return to our return list
- We calculate a return only for a unique state-action pair because the same state action pair occurs in an episode multiple times and there is no point having redundant information

- Then we take an average of the returns in the return list and assign that value to our *Q* function

- Finally, we will select an optimal policy for a state, choosing an action that has the maximum *Q(s,a)* for that state

- We repeat this whole process forever or for a large number of episodes so that we can cover all different states and action pairs

Here's a flowchart of this:

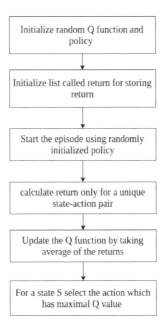

On-policy Monte Carlo control

In Monte Carlo exploration starts, we explore all state-action pairs and choose the one that gives us the maximum value. But think of a situation where we have a large number of states and actions. In that case, if we use the MC-ES algorithm, then it will take a lot of time to explore all combinations of states and actions and to choose the best one. How do we get over this? There are two different control algorithms. On policy and off policy. In on-policy Monte Carlo control, we use the ε greedy policy. Let's understand what a greedy algorithm is.

A greedy algorithm picks up the best choice available at that moment, although that choice might not be optimal when you consider the overall problem. Consider you want to find the smallest number from a list of numbers. Instead of finding the smallest number directly from the list, you will divide the list into three sublists. Then you will find the smallest number in each of the sublists (local optima). The smallest number you find in one sublist might not be the smallest number when you consider the whole list (global optima). However, if you are acting greedy then you will see the smallest number in only the current sublist (at the moment) and consider it the smallest number.

The greedy policy denotes the optimal action within the actions explored. The optimal action is the one which has the highest value.

Say we have explored some actions in the state 1, as shown in the Q table:

State	Action	Value
State 1	Action 0	0.5
State 1	Action 1	0.1
State 1	Action 2	0.8

If we are acting greedy, we would pick up the action that has maximal value out of all the actions we explored. In the preceding case, we have action 2 which has high value, so we pick up that action. But there might be other actions in the state 1 that we haven't explored and might the highest value. So we have to look for the best action or exploit the action that is best out of all explored actions. This is called an exploration-exploitation dilemma. Say you listened to Ed Sheeran and you liked him very much, so you kept on listening to Ed Sheeran only (exploiting) because you liked the music. But if you tried listening to other artists you might like someone better than Ed Sheeran (exploration). This confusion as to whether you have to listen to only Ed Sheeran (exploitation) or try listening to different artists to see if you like them (exploration) is called an exploration-exploitation dilemma.

So to avoid this dilemma, we introduce a new policy called the epsilon-greedy policy. Here, all actions are tried with a non-zero probability (epsilon). With a probability epsilon, we explore different actions randomly and with a probability 1-epsilon we choose an action that has maximum value, that is, we don't do any exploration. So instead of just exploiting the best action all the time, with probability epsilon, we explore different actions randomly. If the value of the epsilon is set to zero, then we will not do any exploration. It is simply the greedy policy, and if the value of epsilon is set to one, then it will always do only exploration. The value of the epsilon will decay over time as we don't want to explore forever. So over time our policy exploits good actions:

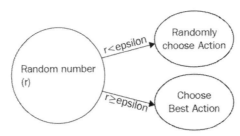

Let us say we set the value of epsilon to *0.3*. In the following code, we generate a random value from the uniform distribution and if the value is less than epsilon value, that is, 0.3, then we select a random action (in this way, we search for a different action). If the random value from the uniform distribution is greater than 0.3, then we select the action that has the best value. So, in this way, we explore actions that we haven't seen before with the probability epsilon and select the best actions out of the explored actions with the probability 1-epsilon:

```
def epsilon_greedy_policy(state, epsilon):
    if random.uniform(0,1) < epsilon:
        return env.action_space.sample()
    else:
        return max(list(range(env.action_space.n)), key = lambda x:
q[(state,x)])
```

Let us imagine that we have explored further actions in the state 1 with the epsilon-greedy policy (although not all of the actions pair) and our Q table looks as follows:

State	Action	Value
State 1	Action 0	0.5
State 1	Action 1	0.1
State 1	Action 2	0.8
State 1	Action 4	0.93

In state 1, action 4 has a higher value than the action 2 we found previously. So with the epsilon-greedy policy, we look for different actions with the probability epsilon and exploit the best action with the probability 1-epsilon.

The steps involved in the on-policy Monte Carlo method are very simple:

1. First, we initialize a random policy and a random Q function.
2. Then we initialize a list called return for storing the returns.
3. We generate an episode using the random policy π.
4. We store the return of every state action pair occurring in the episode to the return list.

5. Then we take an average of the returns in the return list and assign that value to the *Q* function.

6. Now the probability of selecting an action *a* in the state *s* will be decided by epsilon.

7. If the probability is 1-epsilon we pick up the action which has the maximal *Q* value.

8. If the probability is epsilon, we explore for different actions.

Off-policy Monte Carlo control

Off-policy Monte Carlo is another interesting Monte Carlo control method. In this method, we have two policies: one is a behavior policy and another is a target policy. In the off-policy method, agents follow one policy but in the meantime, it tries to learn and improve a different policy. The policy an agent follows is called a behavior policy and the policy an agent tries to evaluate and improve is called a target policy. The behavior and target policy are totally unrelated. The behavior policy explores all possible states and actions and that is why a behavior policy is called a soft policy, whereas a target policy is said to be a greedy policy (it selects the policy which has the maximal value).

Our goal is to estimate the *Q* function for the target policy π, but our agents behave using a completely different policy called behavior policy μ. What can we do now? We can estimate the value of π by using the common episodes that took place in μ. How can we estimate the common episodes between these two policies? We use a new technique called importance sampling. It is a technique for estimating values from one distribution given samples from another.

Importance sampling is of two types:

- Ordinary importance sampling
- Weighted importance sampling

In ordinary importance sampling, we basically take the ratio of returns obtained by the behavior policy and target policy, whereas in weighted importance sampling we take the weighted average and *C* is the cumulative sum of weights.

Let us just see this step by step:

1. First, we initialize *Q(s,a)* to random values and *C(s,a)* to *0* and weight *w* as *1*.

2. Then we choose the target policy, which is a greedy policy. This means it will pick up the policy which has a maximum value from the *Q* table.

3. We select our behavior policy. A behavior policy is not greedy and it can select any state-action pair.

4. Then we begin our episode and perform an action *a* in the state *s* according to our behavior policy and store the reward. We repeat this until the end of the episode.

5. Now, for each state in the episode, we do the following:
    1. We will calculate return *G*. We know that the return is the sum of discounted rewards: *G = discount_ factor * G + reward*.
    2. Then we update *C(s,a)* as *C(s,a) = C(s,a) + w*.
    3. We update *Q(s,a)*:
    $$Q(s, a) = Q(s, a) + \frac{w}{C(s, a)} * (G - Q(s, a))$$
    4. We update the value of *w*:
    $$w = w * \frac{1}{behaviourpolicy}$$

Summary

In this chapter, we learned about how the Monte Carlo method works and how can we use it to solve MDP when we don't know the model of the environment. We have looked at two different methods: one is Monte Carlo prediction, which is used for estimating the value function, and the other is Monte Carlo control, which is used for optimizing the value function.

We looked at two different methods in Monte Carlo prediction: first visit Monte Carlo prediction, where we average the return only the first time the state is visited in an episode, and the every visit Monte Carlo method, where we average the return every time the state is visited in an episode.

In terms of Monte Carlo control, we looked at different algorithms. We first encountered MC-ES control, which is used to cover all state-action pairs. We looked at on-policy MC control, which uses the epsilon-greedy policy, and off-policy MC control, which uses two policies at a time.

In the next chapter, Chapter 5, *Temporal Difference Learning* we will look at a different model-free learning algorithm.

Questions

The question list is as follows:

1. What is the Monte Carlo Method?
2. Estimate the value of the Golden Ratio using the Monte Carlo method.
3. What is the use of Monte Carlo prediction?
4. What is the difference between first visit MC and every visit MC?
5. Why do we estimate the state-action value?
6. What is the difference between on-policy MC control and off-policy MC control?
7. Write some Python code for playing a Blackjack game with on-policy MC control.

Further reading

Please refer to the following links:

- **David Silver's model-free prediction presentation**: `http://www0.cs.ucl.ac.uk/staff/d.silver/web/Teaching_file s/MC-TD.pdf`
- **David Silver's model-free control presentation**: `http://www0.cs.ucl.ac.uk/staff/d.silver/web/Teaching_file s/control.pdf`

Temporal Difference Learning

5

In the previous chapter, Chapter 4, *Gaming with Monte Carlo Methods*, we learned about the interesting Monte Carlo method, which is used for solving the **Markov Decision Process (MDP)** when the model dynamics of the environment are not known in advance, unlike dynamic programming. We looked at the Monte Carlo prediction method, which is used for predicting value functions and control methods for further optimizing value functions. But there are some pitfalls with the Monte Carlo method. It is applied only for episodic tasks. If an episode is very long, then we have to wait a long time for computing value functions. So, we will use another interesting algorithm called **temporal-difference (TD)** learning, which is a model-free learning algorithm: it doesn't require the model dynamics to be known in advance and it can be applied for non-episodic tasks as well.

In this chapter, you will learn about:

- TD learning
- Q learning
- SARSA
- Taxi scheduling using Q learning and SARSA
- The difference between Q learning and SARSA

TD learning

The TD learning algorithm was introduced by Sutton in 1988. The algorithm takes the benefits of both the Monte Carlo method and **dynamic programming (DP)** into account. Like the Monte Carlo method, it doesn't require model dynamics, and like DP it doesn't need to wait until the end of the episode to make an estimate of the value function. Instead, it approximates the current estimate based on the previously learned estimate, which is also called bootstrapping. If you see in Monte Carlo methods there is no bootstrapping, we made an estimate only at the end of the episode but in TD methods we can bootstrap.

TD prediction

Like we did in Monte Carlo prediction, in TD prediction we try to predict the state values. In Monte Carlo prediction, we estimate the value function by simply taking the mean return. But in TD learning, we update the value of a previous state by current state. How can we do this? TD learning using something called a TD update rule for updating the value of a state, as follows:

$$V(s) = V(s) + \alpha(r + \gamma V(s') - V(s))$$

The value of a previous state = value of previous state + learning_rate (reward + discount_factor(value of current state) - value of previous state)

What does this equation actually mean?

If you think of this equation intuitively, it is actually the difference between the actual reward $(r + \gamma V(S'))$ and the expected reward $(V(s))$ multiplied by the learning rate alpha. What does the learning rate signify? The learning rate, also called step size, is useful for convergence.

Did you notice? Since we take the difference between the actual and predicted value as $(r + \gamma V(S') - V(s)$, it is actually an error. We can call it a TD error. Over several iterations, we will try to minimize this error.

Let us understand TD prediction with the frozen lake example as we have seen in the previous chapters. The frozen lake environment is shown next. First, we will initialize the value function as *0*, as in *V(S)* as *0* for all states, as shown in the following state-value diagram:

	1	2	3	4
1	S	F	F	F
2	F	H	F	H
3	F	F	F	H
4	H	F	F	G

State	Value
(1,1)	0
(1,2)	0
(1,3)	0
⋮	⋮
(4,4)	0

Say we are in a starting state *(s)* **(1,1)** and we take an action right and move to the next state *(s')* **(1,2)** and receive a reward *(r)* as -0.3. How can we update the value of the state using this information?

Recall the TD update equation:

$$V(s) = V(s) + \alpha[r + \gamma(V(s') - V(s)]$$

Let us consider the learning rate (α) as *0.1* and the discount factor (γ) as *0.5*; we know that the value of the state **(1,1)**, as in *v(s)*, is 0 and the value of the next state **(1,2)**, as in *V(s')*, is also **0**. The reward *(r)* we obtained is -0.3. We substitute this in the TD rule as follows:

$$V(s) = 0 + 0.1 [-0.3 + 0.5 (0)-0]$$
$$v(s) = - 0.03$$

So, we update the value for the state **(1,1)** as **-0.03** in the value table, as shown in the following diagram:

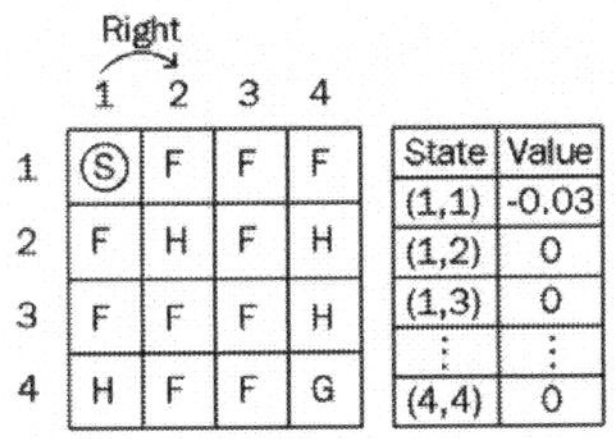

Now that we are in the state *(s)* as **(1,2)**, we take an action right and move to the next state *(s')* **(1,3)** and receive a reward *(r)* -0.3. How do we update the value of the state **(1, 2)** now?

Like we did previously, we will substitute the values in the TD update equation as:

$$V(s) = 0 + 0.1 [-0.3 + 0.5(0)-0]$$

$$V(s) = -0.03$$

So, we got the value of the state **(1,2)** as **-0.03** and we update that in the value table as shown here:

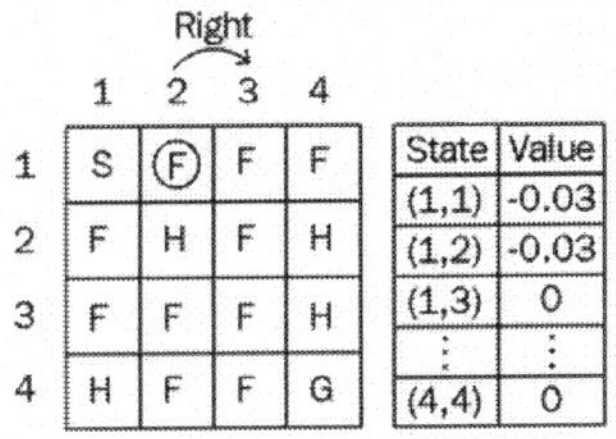

Now we are in the state *(s)* **(1,3)**; suppose we take an action left. We again go back to that state *(s')* **(1,2)** and we receive a reward *(r)* -0.3. Here, the value of the state **(1,3)** is **0** and the value of the next state **(1,2)** is **-0.03** in the value table.

Now we can update the value of state **(1,3)** as follows:

$$V(s) = 0 + 0.1 [-0.3 + 0.5 (-0.03) - 0)]$$

$$V(s) = 0.1[-0.315]$$

$$V(s) = -0.0315$$

So, we update the value of state **(1,3)** as **-0.0315** in the value table, as shown here:

In a similar way, we update the value of all the states using the TD update rule. The steps involved in the TD-prediction algorithm are as follows:

1. First, we initialize $V(S)$ to 0 or some arbitrary values
2. Then we begin the episode and for every step in the episode, we perform an action A in the state S and receive a reward R and move to the next state (s')
3. Now, we update the value of the previous state using the TD update rule
4. We repeat steps 3 and 4 until we reach the terminal state

TD control

In TD prediction, we estimated the value function. In TD control, we optimize the value function. For TD control, we use two kinds of control algorithm:

- **Off-policy learning algorithm**: Q learning
- **On-policy learning algorithm**: SARSA

Q learning

We will now look into the very popular off-policy TD control algorithm called Q learning. Q learning is a very simple and widely used TD algorithm. In control algorithms, we don't care about state value; here, in Q learning, our concern is the state-action value pair—the effect of performing an action A in the state S.

We will update the Q value based on the following equation:

$$Q(s,a) = Q(s,a) + \alpha(r + \gamma maxQ(s'a') - Q(s,a))$$

The preceding equation is similar to the TD prediction update rule with a little difference. We will see this in detail step by step. The steps involved in Q learning are as follows:

1. First, we initialize the Q function to some arbitrary values
2. We take an action from a state using epsilon-greedy policy ($\epsilon > 0$) and move it to the new state
3. We update the Q value of a previous state by following the update rule:

$$Q(s,a) = Q(s,a) + \alpha(r + \gamma maxQ(s'a) - Q(s,a))$$

4. We repeat the steps 2 and 3 till we reach the terminal state

Now, we will understand the algorithm using different steps.

Consider the same frozen lake example. Let us say we are in a state (3,2) and have two actions (left and right). Now let us refer to the figure and compare it with epsilon-greedy policy:

In Q Learning, we select an action using the epsilon-greedy policy. We either explore a new action with the probability epsilon or we select the best action with a probability 1- epsilon. Let us say we select a probability epsilon and explore a new action **Down** and we select that action:

	1	2	3	4
1	S	F	F	F
2	F	H	F	H
3	F	(F)	F	H
4	H	F	F	G

State	Action	Value
(3,2)	Left	0.1
(3,2)	Right	0.5
(3,2)	Down	0.8

Now that we have performed a downward action in the sate **(3,2)** and reached a new state **(4,2)** using the epsilon-greedy policy, how do we update the value of the previous state **(3,2)** using our update rule? It is very simple. Look at the Q table shown as following:

	1	2	3	4
1	S	F	F	F
2	F	H	F	H
3	F	(F)	F	H
4	H	F	F	G

State	Action	Value
(3,2)	Left	0.1
(3,2)	Right	0.5
(3,2)	Down	0.8
(4,2)	Up	0.3
(4,2)	Down	0.5
(4,2)	Right	0.8

Let us consider alpha as *0.1* and the discount factor as *1*:

$$Q(s,a) = Q(s,a) + \alpha(r + \gamma max Q(s'a) - Q(s,a))$$

Q((3,2) down) = Q((3,2), down) + 0.1 (0.3 + 1 max [Q((4,2) action)]- Q((3,2), down)

We can say the value of a state **(3,2)** with a downward action, as in *Q((3,2), down)*, is **0.8** in the Q table.

What is max $Q((4,2), action)$ for the state **(4,2)**? We have explored only three actions (**up**, **down**, and **right**) so we will take the maximum value only based on these actions. (Here, we will not perform epsilon greedy policy; we simply select the action that has the maximum value.)

So, based on the previous Q table, we can substitute the values as:

$$Q((3,2), down) = 0.8 + 0.1 (0.3 + 1 max [0.3, 0.5, 0.8] - 0.8)$$

$$= 0.8 + 0.1 (0.3 + 1 (0.8) - 0.8)$$

$$= 0.83$$

So, we update the value of $Q((3,2), down)$ to *0.83*.

Remember that while choosing what action to take, we perform the epsilon-greedy policy: we either explore for new actions with a probability epsilon or take an action which has a maximum value with a probability 1-epsilon. While updating the Q value, we don't perform the epsilon-greedy policy, we simply select the action that has a maximum value.

Now that we are in a state (4,2), we have to perform an action. What action should we perform? We decide that based on the epsilon-greedy policy, we either explore a new action with a probability epsilon or select the best action with a probability *1-epsilon*. Let us say we select a probability *1-epsilon* and select the best action. So, in the **(4,2)** the action **right** has a maximum value. So we will select the **right** action:

	1	2	3	4
1	S	F	F	F
2	F	H	F	H
3	F	F	F	H
4	H	(F)	F	G

Right

State	Action	Value
(4,2)	Up	0.3
(4,2)	Down	0.5
(4,2)	Right	0.8

Now we are in a state **(4,3)** as we took a **right** action on the state **(4,2)**. How do we update the value of the previous state? Like so:

Q((4,2), right) = Q((4,2), right) + 0.1 (0.3 + 1 max [Q((4,3) action)]- Q((4,2), right)

If you look at the Q table that follows, for the state **(4,3)** we have explored only two actions (**up** and **down**) so we will take a maximum value only based on these actions. (Here, we will not perform an epsilon-greedy policy; we simply select the action which has maximum value):

Q ((4,2), right) = Q((4,2),right) + 0.1 (0.3 + 1 max [(Q (4,3), up) , (Q(4,3),down)] - Q ((4,2), right)

Q ((4,2), right) = 0.8 + 0.1 (0.3 + 1 max [0.1,0.3] - 0.8)

= 0.8 + 0.1 (0.3 + 1(0.3) - 0.8)

= 0.78

Look at the following Q table:

	1	2	3	4
1	S	F	F	F
2	F	H	F	H
3	F	F	F	H
4	H	(F)	F	G

Right

State	Action	Value
(4,2)	Up	0.3
(4,2)	Down	0.5
(4,2)	Right	0.8
(4,3)	Up	0.1
(4,3)	Down	0.3

Now we update the value of the state $Q((4,2)$, *right)* as *0.78*.

So, this is how we get the state-action values in Q learning. To decide what action to take, we use the epsilon-greedy policy and while updating the Q value we simply pick up the maximum action; here's a flowchart:

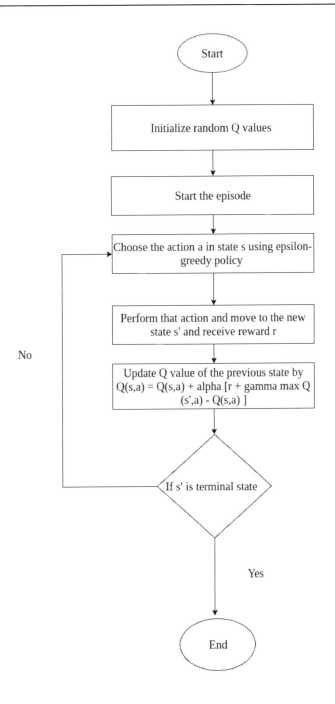

Solving the taxi problem using Q learning

To demonstrate the problem let's say our agent is the driver. There are four locations and the agent has to pick up a passenger at one location and drop them off at another. The agent will receive +20 points as a reward for successful drop off and -1 point for every time step it takes. The agent will also lose -10 points for illegal pickups and drops. So the goal of our agent is to learn to pick up and drop off passengers at the correct location in a short time without adding illegal passengers.

The environment is shown here, where the letters (**R, G, Y, B**) represent the different locations and a tiny rectangle is the agent driving the taxi:

Let's look at the coding part:

```
import gym
import random
```

Now we make our environment using a `gym`:

```
env = gym.make("Taxi-v1")
```

What does this taxi environment look like? Like so:

```
env.render()
```

Okay, first let us initialize our learning rate `alpha`, `epsilon` value, and `gamma`:

```
alpha = 0.4
gamma = 0.999
epsilon = 0.017
```

Then we initialize a Q table; it has a dictionary that stores the state-action value pair as (state, action):

```
q = {}
for s in range(env.observation_space.n):
    for a in range(env.action_space.n):
        q[(s,a)] = 0.0
```

We will define the function for updating the Q table via our Q learning update rule; if you look at the following function, you will see that we take the action that has a maximum value for the state-action pair and store it in a qa variable. Then we update the Q value of the previous state via our update rule, as in:

$$Q(s,a) = Q(s,a) + \alpha(r + \gamma max Q(s'a') - Q(s,a))$$

```
def update_q_table(prev_state, action, reward, nextstate, alpha, gamma):
    qa = max([q[(nextstate, a)] for a in range(env.action_space.n)])
    q[(prev_state,action)] += alpha * (reward + gamma * qa -
q[(prev_state,action)])
```

Then, we define a function for performing the epsilon-greedy policy where we pass the state and epsilon value. We generate some random number in uniform distribution and if the number is less than the epsilon, we explore a different action in the state, or else we exploit the action that has a maximum q value:

```
def epsilon_greedy_policy(state, epsilon):
    if random.uniform(0,1) < epsilon:
        return env.action_space.sample()
    else:
        return max(list(range(env.action_space.n)), key = lambda x:
q[(state,x)])
```

We will see how to perform Q learning, putting together all these functions:

```
# For each episode
for i in range(8000):

    r = 0
    #first we initialize the environment

    prev_state = env.reset()
    while True:
        #In each state we select action by epsilon greedy policy
        action = epsilon_greedy_policy(prev_state, epsilon)
        #then we take the selected action and move to the next state
        nextstate, reward, done, _ = env.step(action)
        #and we update the q value using the update_q_table() function
        #which updates q table according to our update rule.

        update_q_table(prev_state, action, reward, nextstate, alpha, gamma)
        #then we update the previous state as next stat
        prev_state = nextstate

        #and store the rewards in r
```

```
        r += reward
        #If done i.e if we reached the terminal state of the episode
        #if break the loop and start the next episode
        if done:
            break

    print("total reward: ", r)

env.close()
```

The complete code is given here:

```
import random
import gym

env = gym.make('Taxi-v1')

alpha = 0.4
gamma = 0.999
epsilon = 0.017

q = {}
for s in range(env.observation_space.n):
 for a in range(env.action_space.n):
 q[(s,a)] = 0


def update_q_table(prev_state, action, reward, nextstate, alpha, gamma):
 qa = max([q[(nextstate, a)] for a in range(env.action_space.n)])
 q[(prev_state,action)] += alpha * (reward + gamma * qa -
q[(prev_state,action)])

def epsilon_greedy_policy(state, epsilon):
 if random.uniform(0,1) < epsilon:
 return env.action_space.sample()
 else:
 return max(list(range(env.action_space.n)), key = lambda x: q[(state,x)])

for i in range(8000):
    r = 0
    prev_state = env.reset()
    while True:
        env.render()
        # In each state, we select the action by epsilon-greedy policy
        action = epsilon_greedy_policy(prev_state, epsilon)
        # then we perform the action and move to the next state, and
        # receive the reward
        nextstate, reward, done, _ = env.step(action)
```

```
# Next we update the Q value using our update_q_table function
# which updates the Q value by Q learning update rule
update_q_table(prev_state, action, reward, nextstate, alpha, gamma)
# Finally we update the previous state as next state
prev_state = nextstate

# Store all the rewards obtained
r += reward

#we will break the loop, if we are at the terminal
#state of the episode
if done:
    break

    print("total reward: ", r)

env.close()
```

SARSA

State-Action-Reward-State-Action (SARSA) is an on-policy TD control algorithm. Like we did in Q learning, here we also focus on state-action value instead of a state-value pair. In SARSA, we update the Q value based on the following update rule:

$$Q(s,a) = Q(s,a) + \alpha(r + \gamma Q(s'a') - Q(s,a))$$

In the preceding equation, you may notice that there is no max Q(s',a'), like there was in Q learning. Here it is simply Q(s',a'). We can understand this in detail by performing some steps. The steps involved in SARSA are as follows:

1. First, we initialize the Q values to some arbitrary values
2. We select an action by the epsilon-greedy policy ($\epsilon > 0$) and move from one state to another
3. We update the Q value previous state by following the update rule $Q(s,a) = Q(s,a) + \alpha(r + \gamma Q(s'a') - Q(s,a))$, where a' is the action selected by an epsilon-greedy policy ($\epsilon > 0$)

Now, we will understand the algorithm step by step. Let us consider the same frozen lake example. Let us say we are in state **(4,2)**. We decide the action based on the epsilon-greedy policy. Let us say we use a probability 1- epsilon and select the best action, which is **right**:

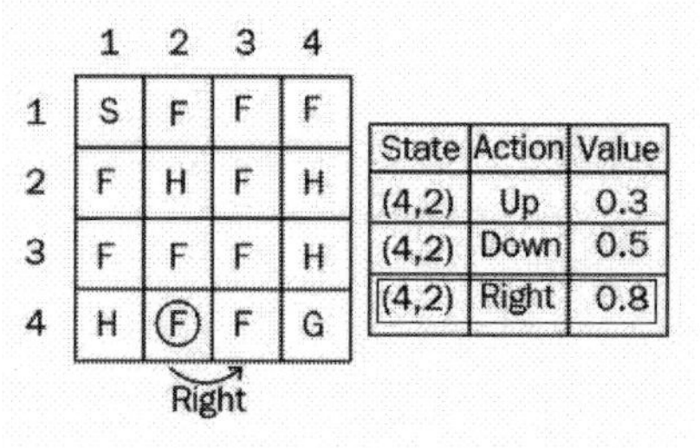

Now we are in state **(4,3)** after performing an action **right** in state **(4,2)**. How do we update a value of the previous state **(4,2)**? Let us consider the alpha as *0.1*, the reward as *0.3*, and discount factor *1*:

$$Q(s,a) = Q(s,a) + \alpha(r + \gamma Q(s'a') - Q(s,a))$$

Q((4,2), right) = Q((4,2),right) + 0.1 (0.3 + 1 Q((4,3), action)) - Q((4,2) , right)

How do we choose the value for *Q (4,3), action*)? Here, unlike in Q learning, we don't just pick up max *(Q(4,3), action)*. In SARSA, we use the epsilon-greedy policy.

Look at the Q table that follows. In state **(4,3)** we have explored two actions. Unlike Q learning, we don't select the maximum action directly as down:

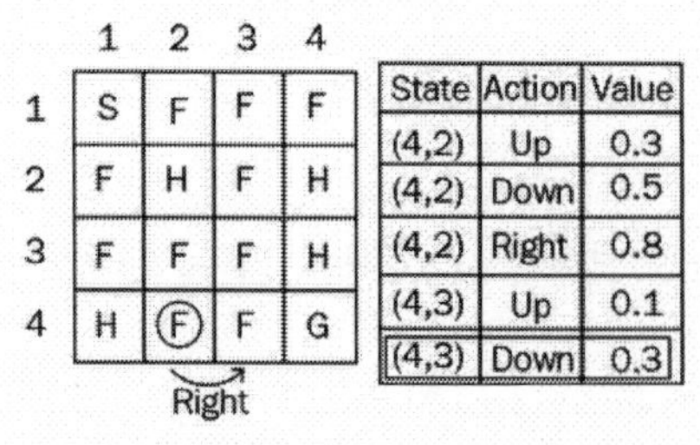

We follow the epsilon-greedy policy here as well. We either explore with a probability epsilon or exploit with a probability 1-epsilon. Let us say we select probability epsilon and explore a new action. We explore a new action, **right**, and select that action:

$$Q\,(\,(4,2),\,right) = Q((4,2),right) + 0.1\,(0.3 + 1\,(Q\,(4,3),\,right) - Q\,((4,2),\,right\,)$$

$$Q\,(\,(4,2),\,right) = 0.8 + 0.1\,(0.3 + 1(0.9) - 0.8)$$

$$= 0.8 + 0.1\,(0.3 + 1(0.9) - 0.8)$$

$$= 0.84$$

So, this is how we get the state-action values in SARSA. We take the action using the epsilon-greedy policy and also, while updating the Q value, we pick up the action using the epsilon-greedy policy.

The following diagram explains the SARSA algorithm:

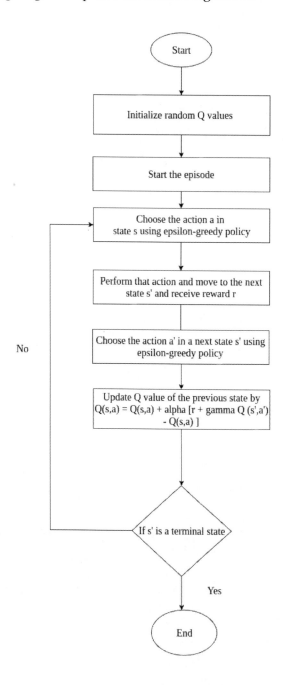

Solving the taxi problem using SARSA

Now we will solve the same taxi problem using SARSA:

```
import gym
import random
env = gym.make('Taxi-v1')
```

Also, we will initialize the learning rate, `gamma`, and `epsilon`. Q table has a dictionary:

```
alpha = 0.85
gamma = 0.90
epsilon = 0.8

Q = {}
for s in range(env.observation_space.n):
    for a in range(env.action_space.n):
        Q[(s,a)] = 0.0
```

As usual, we define an `epsilon_greedy` policy for exploration:

```
def epsilon_greedy(state, epsilon):
    if random.uniform(0,1) < epsilon:
        return env.action_space.sample()
    else:
        return max(list(range(env.action_space.n)), key = lambda x:
Q[(state,x)])
```

Now, the actual SARSA algorithm comes in:

```
for i in range(4000):
    #We store cumulative reward of each episodes in r
    r = 0
    #Then for every iterations, we initialize the state,
    state = env.reset()
    #then we pick up the action using epsilon greedy policy
    action = epsilon_greedy(state,epsilon)
    while True:
        #Then we perform the action in the state and move the next state
        nextstate, reward, done, _ = env.step(action)
        #Then we pick up the next action using epsilon greedy policy
        nextaction = epsilon_greedy(nextstate,epsilon)
        #we calculate Q value of the previous state using our update rule
        Q[(state,action)] += alpha * (reward + gamma *
Q[(nextstate,nextaction)]-Q[(state,action)])
```

```
        #finally we update our state and action with next action
        # and next state
        action = nextaction
        state = nextstate
        r += reward
        #we will break the loop, if we are at the terminal
        #state of the episode
        if done:
            break


    env.close()
```

You can run the program and see how SARSA is finding the optimal path.

The full program is given here:

```
#Like we did in Q learning, we import necessary libraries and initialize
environment

import gym
import random
env = gym.make('Taxi-v1')

alpha = 0.85
gamma = 0.90
epsilon = 0.8

#Then we initialize Q table as dictionary for storing the state-action
values
Q = {}
for s in range(env.observation_space.n):
    for a in range(env.action_space.n):
        Q[(s,a)] = 0.0

#Now, we define a function called epsilon_greedy for performing action
#according epsilon greedy policy
def epsilon_greedy(state, epsilon):
    if random.uniform(0,1) < epsilon:
        return env.action_space.sample()
    else:
        return max(list(range(env.action_space.n)), key = lambda x:
Q[(state,x)])
```

```
for i in range(4000):
    #We store cumulative reward of each episodes in
    r = 0
    #Then for every iterations, we initialize the state,
    state = env.reset()
    #then we pick up the action using epsilon greedy policy
    action = epsilon_greedy(state,epsilon)
    while True:
        #Then we perform the action in the state and move the next state
        nextstate, reward, done, _ = env.step(action)
        #Then we pick up the next action using epsilon greedy policy
        nextaction = epsilon_greedy(nextstate,epsilon)
        #we calculate Q value of the previous state using our update rule
        Q[(state,action)] += alpha * (reward + gamma *
Q[(nextstate,nextaction)]-Q[(state,action)])


        #finally we update our state and action with next action
        #and next state
        action = nextaction
        state = nextstate
        r += reward
        #we will break the loop, if we are at the terminal
        #state of the episode
        if done:
            break


env.close()
```

The difference between Q learning and SARSA

Q learning and SARSA will always be confusing for many folks. Let us break down the differences between these two. Look at the flowchart here:

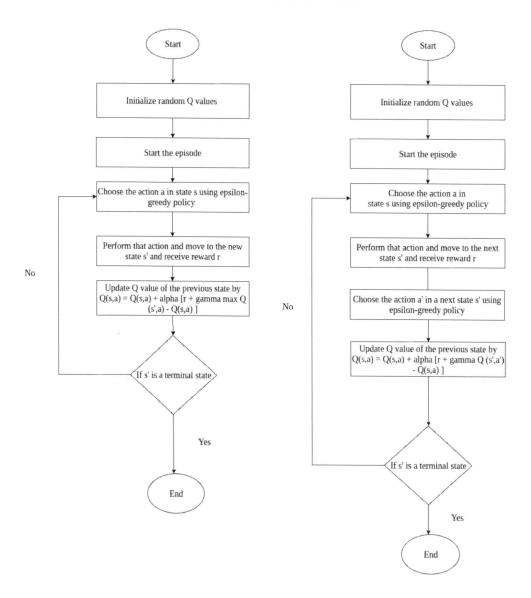

Can you spot the difference? In Q learning, we take action using an epsilon-greedy policy and, while updating the Q value, we simply pick up the maximum action. In SARSA, we take the action using the epsilon-greedy policy and also, while updating the Q value, we pick up the action using the epsilon-greedy policy.

Summary

In this chapter, we learned a different model-free learning algorithm that overcame the limitations of the Monte Carlo methods. We saw both prediction and control methods. In TD prediction, we updated the state-value of a state based on the next state. In terms of the control methods, we saw two different algorithms: Q learning and SARSA.

Questions

The question list is as follows:

1. How does TD learning differ from the Monte Carlo method?
2. What exactly is a TD error?
3. What is the difference between TD prediction and control?
4. How to build an intelligent agent using Q learning?
5. What is the difference between Q learning and SARSA?

Further reading

Sutton's original TD paper: https://pdfs.semanticscholar.org/9c06/865e912788a6a51470724e087853d72691 95.pdf

6
Multi-Armed Bandit Problem

In the previous chapters, we have learned about fundamental concepts of **reinforcement learning** (**RL**) and several RL algorithms, as well as how RL problems can be modeled as the **Markov Decision Process** (**MDP**). We have also seen different model-based and model-free algorithms that are used to solve the MDP. In this chapter, we will see one of the classical problems in RL called the **multi-armed bandit** (**MAB**) problem. We will see what the MAB problem is and how to solve the problem with different algorithms followed by how to identify the correct advertisement banner that will receive most of the clicks using MAB. We will also learn about contextual bandit that is widely used for building recommendation systems.

In the chapter, you will learn about the following:

- The MAB problem
- The epsilon-greedy algorithm
- The softmax exploration algorithm
- The upper confidence bound algorithm
- The Thompson sampling algorithm
- Applications of MAB
- Identifying the right advertisement banner using MAB
- Contextual bandits

The MAB problem

The MAB problem is one of the classical problems in RL. An MAB is actually a slot machine, a gambling game played in a casino where you pull the arm (lever) and get a payout (reward) based on a randomly generated probability distribution. A single slot machine is called a one-armed bandit and, when there are multiple slot machines it is called multi-armed bandits or k-armed bandits.

MABs are shown as follows:

As each slot machine gives us the reward from its own probability distribution, our goal is to find out which slot machine will give us the maximum cumulative reward over a sequence of time. So, at each time step t, the agent performs an action a_t, that is, pulls an arm from the slot machine and receives a reward r_t, and the goal of our agent is to maximize the cumulative reward.

We define the value of an arm $Q(a)$ as average rewards received by pulling the arm:

$$Q(a) = \frac{Sum\ of\ rewards\ received\ from\ the\ arm}{Total\ number\ of\ times\ the\ arm\ was\ pulled}$$

So the optimal arm is the one that gives us the maximum cumulative reward, that is:

$$Q(a^*) = Max\ Q(a)$$

The goal of our agent is to find the optimal arm and also to minimize the regret, which can be defined as the cost of knowing which of the k arms is optimal. Now, how do we find the best arm? Should we explore all the arms or choose the arm that already gave us a maximum cumulative reward? Here comes the exploration-exploitation dilemma. Now we will see how to solve this dilemma using various exploration strategies as follows:

- Epsilon-greedy policy
- Softmax exploration
- Upper confidence bound algorithm
- Thomson sampling technique

Before going ahead, let us install `bandit` environments in the OpenAI Gym; you can install the `bandit` environment by typing the following command in your Terminal:

```
git clone https://github.com/JKCooper2/gym-bandits.git
cd gym-bandits
pip install -e .
```

After installing, let us import `gym` and `gym_bandits`:

```
import gym_bandits
import gym
```

Now we will initialize the environment; we use an MAB with ten arms:

```
env = gym.make("BanditTenArmedGaussian-v0")
```

Our action space will be 10, as we have 10 arms:

```
env.action_space
```

The output is as follows:

```
10
```

The epsilon-greedy policy

We have already learned a lot about the epsilon-greedy policy. In the epsilon-greedy policy, either we select the best arm with a probability 1-epsilon or we select the arms at random with a probability epsilon:

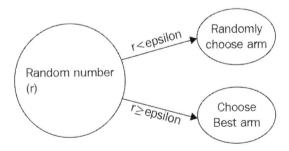

Now we will see how to select the best arm using the epsilon-greedy policy:

1. First, let us initialize all variables:

```
# number of rounds (iterations)
num_rounds = 20000

# Count of number of times an arm was pulled
count = np.zeros(10)

# Sum of rewards of each arm
sum_rewards = np.zeros(10)

# Q value which is the average reward
Q = np.zeros(10)
```

2. Now we define our `epsilon_greedy` function:

```
def epsilon_greedy(epsilon):
    rand = np.random.random()
    if rand < epsilon:
        action = env.action_space.sample()
    else:
        action = np.argmax(Q)
    return action
```

3. Start pulling the arm:

```
for i in range(num_rounds):
    # Select the arm using epsilon greedy
    arm = epsilon_greedy(0.5)
    # Get the reward
    observation, reward, done, info = env.step(arm)
    # update the count of that arm
    count[arm] += 1
    # Sum the rewards obtained from the arm
    sum_rewards[arm]+=reward
    # calculate Q value which is the average rewards of the arm
    Q[arm] = sum_rewards[arm]/count[arm]

print( 'The optimal arm is {}'.format(np.argmax(Q)))
```

The following is the output:

```
The optimal arm is 3
```

The softmax exploration algorithm

Softmax exploration, also known as Boltzmann exploration, is another strategy used for finding an optimal bandit. In the epsilon-greedy policy, we consider all of the non-best arms equivalently, but in softmax exploration, we select an arm based on a probability from the Boltzmann distribution. The probability of selecting an arm is given by:

$$P_t(a) = \frac{exp(Q_t(a)/\tau)}{\sum_{i=1}^{n} exp(Q_t(i)/\tau)}$$

τ is called a temperature factor, which specifies how many random arms we can explore. When τ is high, all arms will be explored equally, but when τ is low, high-rewarding arms will be chosen. Look at the following steps:

1. First, initialize the variables:

```
# number of rounds (iterations)
num_rounds = 20000

# Count of number of times an arm was pulled
count = np.zeros(10)

# Sum of rewards of each arm
sum_rewards = np.zeros(10)

# Q value which is the average reward
Q = np.zeros(10)
```

2. Now we define the `softmax` function:

```
def softmax(tau):
    total = sum([math.exp(val/tau) for val in Q])
    probs = [math.exp(val/tau)/total for val in Q]
    threshold = random.random()
    cumulative_prob = 0.0
    for i in range(len(probs)):
        cumulative_prob += probs[i]
        if (cumulative_prob > threshold):
            return i
    return np.argmax(probs)
```

3. Start pulling the `arm`:

```
for i in range(num_rounds):
    # Select the arm using softmax
    arm = softmax(0.5)
    # Get the reward
    observation, reward, done, info = env.step(arm)
    # update the count of that arm
    count[arm] += 1
    # Sum the rewards obtained from the arm
    sum_rewards[arm]+=reward
    # calculate Q value which is the average rewards of the arm
    Q[arm] = sum_rewards[arm]/count[arm]
print( 'The optimal arm is {}'.format(np.argmax(Q)))
```

The following is the output:

```
The optimal arm is 3
```

The upper confidence bound algorithm

With epsilon-greedy and softmax exploration, we explore random actions with a probability; the random action is useful for exploring various arms, but it might also lead us to try out actions that will not give us a good reward at all. We also don't want to miss out arms that are actually good but give poor rewards in the initial rounds. So we use a new algorithm called the **upper confidence bound** (**UCB**). It is based on the principle called optimism in the face of uncertainty.

The UCB algorithm helps us in selecting the best arm based on a confidence interval. Okay, what is a confidence interval? Let us say we have two arms. We pull both of these arms and find that arm one gives us 0.3 rewards and arm two gives us 0.8 rewards. But with one round of pulling the arms, we should not come to the conclusion that arm two will give us the best reward. We have to try pulling the arms several times and take the mean value of rewards obtained by each arm and select the arm whose mean is highest. But how can we find the correct mean value for each of these arms? Here is where the confidence interval comes into the picture. The confidence interval specifies the interval within which the mean reward value of arms lies. If the confidence interval of arm one is *[0.2, 0.9]*, it implies that the mean value of arm one lies within this interval, 0.2 to 0.9. 0.2 is called the lower confidence bound and 0.9 is called the UCB. The UCB selects a machine that has a high UCB to explore.

Let us say we have three slot machines and we have played each of the slot machines ten times. The confidence intervals of these three slot machines are shown in the following diagram:

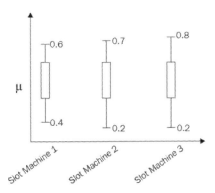

We can see that **slot machine 3** has a high UCB. But we should not come to the conclusion that **slot machine 3** will give us a good reward by just pulling ten times. Once we pull the arms several times, our confidence interval will be accurate. So, over time, the confidence interval becomes narrow and shrinks to an actual value, as shown in the next diagram. So now, we can select **slot machine 2**, which has a high UCB:

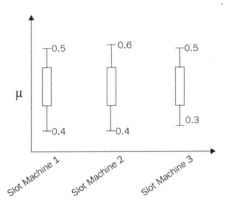

The idea behind UCB is very simple:

1. Select the action (arm) that has a high sum of average reward and upper confidence bound
2. Pull the arm and receive a reward
3. Update the arm's reward and confidence bound

But how do we calculate UCB?

We can calculate UCB using the formula $\sqrt{\dfrac{2log(t)}{N(a)}}$ where $N(a)$ is the number of times the arm was pulled and t is the total number of rounds.

So, in UCB, we select an arm with the following formula:

$$Arm = argmax_a[Q(a) + \sqrt{\dfrac{2log(t)}{N(a)}}]$$

First, initialize the variables:

```
# number of rounds (iterations)
num_rounds = 20000

# Count of number of times an arm was pulled
count = np.zeros(10)

# Sum of rewards of each arm
sum_rewards = np.zeros(10)

# Q value which is the average reward
Q = np.zeros(10)
```

Now, let us define our UCB function:

```
def UCB(iters):
    ucb = np.zeros(10)
    #explore all the arms
    if iters < 10:
        return i
    else:
        for arm in range(10):
            # calculate upper bound
            upper_bound = math.sqrt((2*math.log(sum(count))) / count[arm])
            # add upper bound to the Q value
            ucb[arm] = Q[arm] + upper_bound
        # return the arm which has maximum value
        return (np.argmax(ucb))
```

Let us start pulling the arms:

```
for i in range(num_rounds):
    # Select the arm using UCB
    arm = UCB(i)
    # Get the reward
    observation, reward, done, info = env.step(arm)
    # update the count of that arm
    count[arm] += 1
    # Sum the rewards obtained from the arm
    sum_rewards[arm]+=reward
    # calculate Q value which is the average rewards of the arm
    Q[arm] = sum_rewards[arm]/count[arm]
print( 'The optimal arm is {}'.format(np.argmax(Q)))
```

The output is as follows:

```
The optimal arm is 1
```

The Thompson sampling algorithm

Thompson sampling (**TS**) is another popularly used algorithm to overcome the exploration-exploitation dilemma. It is a probabilistic algorithm and is based on a prior distribution. The strategy behind TS is very simple: first, we calculate prior on the mean rewards for each of the *k* arms, that is, we take some *n* samples from each of the *k* arms and calculate *k* distributions. These initial distributions will not be the same as the true distribution, so we call it prior distribution:

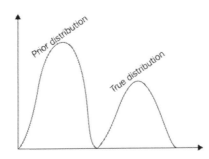

Since we have Bernoulli rewards, we use beta distribution for calculating the prior. The value of beta distribution [alpha, beta] lies within the interval [0,1]. Alpha represents the number of times we receive the positive rewards and beta represents the number of times we receive the negative rewards.

Now we will see how TS helps us in selecting the best arm. The steps involved in TS are as follows:

1. Sample a value from each of the *k* distributions and use this value as a prior mean.
2. Select the arm that has the highest prior mean and observes the reward.
3. Use the observed reward to modify the prior distribution.

So, after several rounds, a prior distribution will start resembling the true distribution:

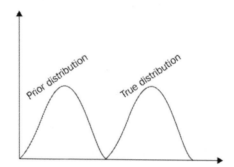

We shall better understand TS by implementing it in Python. First, let us initialize the variables:

```
# number of rounds (iterations)
num_rounds = 20000

# Count of number of times an arm was pulled
count = np.zeros(10)

# Sum of rewards of each arm
sum_rewards = np.zeros(10)

# Q value which is the average reward
Q = np.zeros(10)

# initialize alpha and beta values
alpha = np.ones(10)
beta = np.ones(10)
```

Define our `thompson_sampling` function:

```
def thompson_sampling(alpha,beta):
    samples = [np.random.beta(alpha[i]+1,beta[i]+1) for i in range(10)]

    return np.argmax(samples)
```

Start playing with the bandits using TS:

```
for i in range(num_rounds):

    # Select the arm using thompson sampling
    arm = thompson_sampling(alpha,beta)

    # Get the reward
    observation, reward, done, info = env.step(arm)

    # update the count of that arm
    count[arm] += 1

    # Sum the rewards obtained from the arm
    sum_rewards[arm]+=reward

    # calculate Q value which is the average rewards of the arm
    Q[arm] = sum_rewards[arm]/count[arm]

    # If it is a positive reward increment alpha
    if reward >0:
    alpha[arm] += 1

    # If it is a negative reward increment beta
    else:
    beta[arm] += 1

    print( 'The optimal arm is {}'.format(np.argmax(Q)))
```

The output is as follows:

```
The optimal arm is 3
```

Applications of MAB

So far, we have looked at the MAB problem and how we can solve it using various
exploration strategies. But bandits are not just used for playing slot machines; they have
many applications.

Bandits are used as a replacement for AB testing. AB testing is one of the commonly used classical methods of testing. Say you have two versions of the landing page of your website. How do you know which version is liked by most of the users? You conduct an AB test to understand which version is most liked by users.

In AB testing, we allocate a separate time for exploration and a separate time for exploitation. That is, it has two different dedicated periods only for exploration and exploitation alone. But the problem with this method is that this will incur a lot of regrets. So, we can minimize the regret using various exploration strategies that we use to solve MAB. Instead of performing complete exploration and exploitation separately with bandits, we perform both exploration and exploitation simultaneously in an adaptive fashion.

Bandits are widely used for website optimization, maximizing conversion rate, online advertisements, campaigning, and so on. Consider you are running a short-term campaign. If you perform AB testing here, then you will spend almost all of your time on exploring and exploitation alone, so in this case, using bandits would be very useful.

Identifying the right advertisement banner using MAB

Let us say you are running a website and you have five different banners for the same ad, and you want to know which banner attracts the user. We model this problem statement as a bandit problem. Let us say these five banners are the five arms of the bandit and we award one point if the user clicks the ad and award zero if the user does not click the ad.

In normal A/B testing, we will perform a complete exploration of all these five banners before deciding which banner is the best. But that will cost us a lot of energy and time. Instead, we will use a good exploration strategy for deciding which banner will give us the most rewards (most clicks).

First, let us import the necessary libraries:

```
import pandas as pd
import numpy as np
import matplotlib.pyplot as plt
import seaborn as sns
%matplotlib inline
```

Let us simulate a dataset with 5 x 10,000 as the shape, where the column is the `Banner_type` ad and the rows are either 0 or 1, that is, whether the ad has been clicked (1) or not clicked (0) by the user respectively:

```
df = pd.DataFrame()
df['Banner_type_0'] = np.random.randint(0,2,100000)
df['Banner_type_1'] = np.random.randint(0,2,100000)
df['Banner_type_2'] = np.random.randint(0,2,100000)
df['Banner_type_3'] = np.random.randint(0,2,100000)
df['Banner_type_4'] = np.random.randint(0,2,100000)
```

Let us view a few rows of our data:

```
df.head()
```

	Banner_type_0	Banner_type_1	Banner_type_2	Banner_type_3	Banner_type_4
0	1	1	0	1	1
1	0	1	1	1	0
2	1	1	0	0	1
3	0	0	0	0	1
4	0	1	1	1	1
5	0	1	1	0	1
6	1	0	0	1	1
7	0	1	1	0	1
8	0	0	1	0	1
9	0	0	0	1	0

```
num_banner = 5
no_of_iterations = 100000
banner_selected = []
count = np.zeros(num_banner)
Q = np.zeros(num_banner)
sum_rewards = np.zeros(num_banner)
```

Define an epsilon-greedy policy:

```
def epsilon_greedy(epsilon):
    random_value = np.random.random()
    choose_random = random_value < epsilon
    if choose_random:
        action = np.random.choice(num_banner)
    else:
        action = np.argmax(Q)
```

```
        return action

for i in range(no_of_iterations):
    banner = epsilon_greedy(0.5)
    reward = df.values[i, banner]
    count[banner] += 1
    sum_rewards[banner]+=reward
    Q[banner] = sum_rewards[banner]/count[banner]
    banner_selected.append(banner)
```

We can plot the results and see which banner gives us the maximum number of clicks:

```
sns.distplot(banner_selected)
```

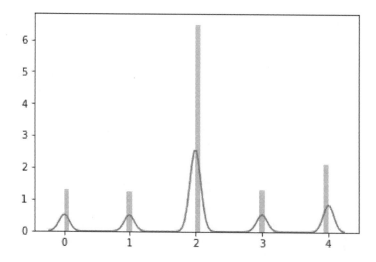

Contextual bandits

We just saw how bandits are used for recommending the correct ad banner to the user. But the banner preference varies from user to user. User A likes banner type 1, but user B might like banner type 3. So we have to personalize ad banners according to user behavior. How can we do that? We introduce a new bandit type called contextual bandits.

In a normal MABs problem, we perform the action and receive a reward. But with contextual bandits, instead of just taking the actions alone, we take the environment state as well. The state holds the context. Here, the state specifies the user behaviors, so we will take actions (show ads) according to the state (user behavior) that will result in a maximum reward (ad clicks). Thus, contextual bandits are widely used for personalizing content according to the user's preference behavior. They are used to solve cold-start problems faced in recommendation systems. Netflix uses contextual bandits for personalizing artwork for TV shows according to user behavior.

Summary

In this chapter, we have learned about the MAB problem and how it can be applied to different applications. We understood several methods to solve an explore-exploit dilemma. First, we looked at the epsilon-greedy policy, where we explored with the probability epsilon, and carried out exploration with the probability 1-epsilon. We looked at the UCB algorithm, where we picked up the best action with the maximum upper bound value, followed by the TS algorithm, where we picked up the best action via beta distribution.

In the upcoming chapters, we will learn about deep learning and how deep learning is used to solve RL problems.

Questions

The question list is as follows:

1. What is an MAB problem?
2. What is an explore-exploit dilemma?
3. What is the significance of epsilon in the epsilon-greedy policy?
4. How do we solve an explore-exploit dilemma?
5. What is a UCB algorithm?
6. How does Thompson sampling differ from the UCB algorithm?

Further reading

You can also refer to these links:

- **Contextual bandits for personalization**: `https://www.microsoft.com/en-us/research/blog/contextual-bandit-breakthrough-enables-deeper-personalization/`
- **How Netflix uses contextual bandits**: `https://medium.com/netflix-techblog/artwork-personalization-c589f074ad76`
- **Collaborative filtering using MAB**: `https://arxiv.org/pdf/1708.03058.pdf`

Deep Learning Fundamentals 7

So far, we have learned about how **reinforcement learning** (RL) works. In the upcoming chapters, we will learn about **Deep reinforcement learning** (DRL), which is a combination of deep learning and RL. DRL is creating a lot of buzz around the RL community and is making a serious impact on solving many RL tasks. To understand DRL, we need to have a strong foundation in deep learning. Deep learning is actually a subset of machine learning and it is all about neural networks. Deep learning has been around for a decade, but the reason it is so popular right now is because of the computational advancements and availability of a huge volume of data. With this huge volume of data, deep learning algorithms will outperform all classic machine learning algorithms. Therefore, in this chapter, we will learn about several deep learning algorithms like **recurrent neural network (RNN)**, **Long Short-Term Memory (LSTM)**, and **convolutional neural network (CNN)** algorithms with applications.

In this chapter, you will learn about the following:

- Artificial neurons
- **Artificial neural networks (ANNs)**
- Building a neural network to classify handwritten digits
- RNNs
- LSTMs
- Generating song lyrics using LSTMs
- CNNs
- Classifying fashion products using CNNs

Artificial neurons

Before understanding ANN, first, let's understand what neurons are and how neurons in our brain actually work. A neuron can be defined as the basic computational unit of the human brain. Our brain contains approximately 100 billion neurons. Each and every neuron is connected through synapses. Neurons receive input from the external environment, sensory organs, or from the other neurons through a branchlike structure called dendrites, as can be seen in the following diagram. These inputs are strengthened or weakened, that is, they are weighted according to their importance and then they are summed together in the soma (cell body). Then, from the cell body, these summed inputs are processed and move through the axons and are sent to the other neurons. The basic single biological neuron is shown in the following diagram:

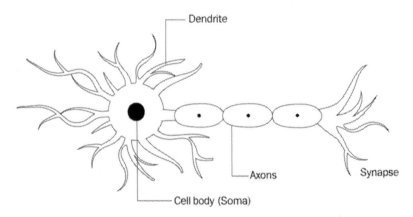

Now, how do artificial neurons work? Let's suppose we have three inputs, x_1, x_2, and x_3, to predict output y. These inputs are multiplied by weights, w_1, w_2, and w_3, and are summed together, that is, $x_1.w_1 + x_2.w_2 + x_3.w_3$. But why are we multiplying these inputs with weights? Because all of the inputs are not equally important in calculating the output y. Let's say that x_2 is more important in calculating the output compared to the other two inputs. Then, we assign a high value to w_2 rather than for the other two weights. So, upon multiplying weights with inputs, x_2 will have a higher value than the other two inputs. After multiplying inputs with the weights, we sum them up and we add a value called bias b. So, $z = (x1.w1 + x2.w2 + x3.w3) + b$, that is:

$$z = \sum (input * weights) + bias$$

Doesn't z look like the equation of linear regression? Isn't it just the equation of a straight line? $z = mx + b$.

Where m is the weights (coefficients), x is the input, and b is the bias (intercept). Well, yes. Then what is the difference between neurons and linear regression? In neurons, we introduce non-linearity to the result, z, by applying a function $f()$ called the activation or transfer function. So, our output is $y = f(z)$. A single artificial neuron is shown in the following diagram:

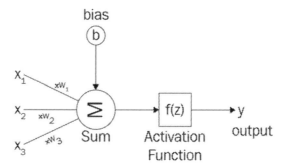

In neurons, we take the input x, multiply the input by weights w, and add bias b before applying the activation function $f(z)$ to this result and predict the output y.

ANNs

Neurons are cool, right? But single neurons cannot perform complex tasks, which is why our brain has billions of neurons, organized in layers, forming a network. Similarly, artificial neurons are arranged in layers. Each and every layer will be connected in such a way that information is passed from one layer to another. A typical ANN consists of the following layers:

- Input layer
- Hidden layer
- Output layer

Each layer has a collection of neurons, and the neurons in one layer interact with all the neurons in the other layers. However, neurons in the same layer will not interact with each other. A typical ANN is shown in the following diagram:

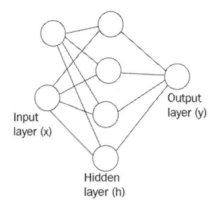

Input layer

The input layer is where we feed input to the network. The number of neurons in the input layer is the number of inputs we feed to the network. Each input will have some influence on predicting the output and this will be multiplied by weights, while bias will be added and passed to the next layer.

Hidden layer

Any layer between the input layer and the output layer is called a hidden layer. It processes the input received from the input layer. The hidden layer is responsible for deriving complex relationships between input and output. That is, the hidden layer identifies the pattern in the dataset. There can be any number of hidden layers, however we have to choose a number of hidden layers according to our problem. For a very simple problem, we can just use one hidden layer, but while performing complex tasks like image recognition, we use many hidden layers where each layer is responsible for extracting important features of the image so that we can easily recognize the image. When we use many hidden layers, the network is called a deep neural network.

Output layer

After processing the input, the hidden layer sends its result to the output layer. As the name suggests, the output layer emits the output. The number of neurons in the output layer relates to the type of problem we want our network to solve. If it is a binary classification, then the number of neurons in the output layer tells us which class the input belongs to. If it is a multi-class classification say, with five classes, and if we want to get the probability of each class being an output, then the number of neurons in the output layer is five, each emitting the probability. If it is a regression problem, then we have one neuron in the output layer.

Activation functions

Activation functions are used to introduce nonlinearity in neural networks. We apply the activation function to the input which is multiplied by weights and added to the bias, that is, *f(z)*, where *z = (input * weights) + bias*. There are different types of activation functions as follows:

- **Sigmoid function**: The sigmoid function is one of the most commonly used activation functions. It scales the value between *0* and *1*. The sigmoid function can be defined as $f(z) = \dfrac{1}{1 + e^{-z}}$. When we apply this function to z, the values will be scaled in the range of 0 to *1*. This is also called a logistic function. It is s-shaped, as shown in the following diagram:

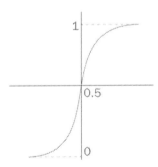

- **Hyperbolic tangent function**: Unlike the sigmoid function, the hyperbolic tangent function scales the value between *-1* and *+1*. The hyperbolic tangent function can be defined as $f(z) = \frac{e^{2z} - 1}{e^{2z} + 1}$. When we apply this function to z, the values will be scaled in the range of *-1* to *+1*. It is also s-shaped but zero centered, as shown in the following diagram:

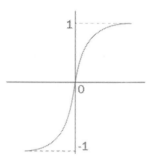

- **ReLU function**: ReLU is also known as a rectified linear unit. It is one of the most widely used activation functions. The ReLU function can be defined as $f(z) = max(0, z)$, that is, $f(z)$ is 0 when z is less than 0 and $f(z)$ is equal to z when z is greater than or equal to *0*:

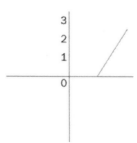

- **Softmax function**: The softmax function is actually the generalization of the sigmoid function. It is usually applied on the final layer of the network and while performing multi-class classification tasks. It gives the probabilities of each class being an output and thus the sum of softmax values will always equal to *1*. It can be defined as $\sigma(z)_i = \frac{e^{z_i}}{\sum_j e^{z_j}}$.

Deep diving into ANN

We know that in artificial neurons, we multiply the input by weights, add bias to them and apply an activation function to produce the output. Now, we will see how this happens in a neural network setting where neurons are arranged in layers. The number of layers in a network is equal to the number of hidden layers plus the number of output layers. We don't take the input layer into account. Consider a two-layer neural network with one input layer, one hidden layer, and one output layer, as shown in the following diagram:

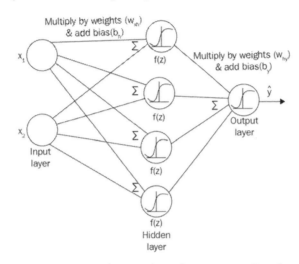

Let's say we have two inputs, x_1 and x_2, and we have to predict the output **y**. Since we have two inputs, the number of neurons in the input layer will be two. Now, these inputs will be multiplied by weights and then we add bias and propagate the resultant value to the hidden layer where the activation function will be applied. So, first we need to initialize the weight matrix. In the real world, we don't know which input is really important and needing to be weighted high to calculate the output. Therefore, we will randomly initialize weights and a bias value. We can denote the weights and bias flowing between the input layer to the hidden layer as w_{xh} and b_h, respectively. What about the dimensions of the weight matrix? The dimensions of the weight matrix must be *[number of neurons in the current layer * number of neurons in the next layer]*. Why is that? Because it is a basic matrix multiplication rule. To multiply any two matrices, AB, the number of columns in matrix A must be equal to the number of rows in matrix B. So, the dimension of weight matrix w_{xh} should be *[number of neurons in the input layer * number of neurons in the hidden layer]*, that is, *2 x 4*:

$$z_1 = xw_{xh} + b$$

That is, $z_1 = (input * weights) + bias$. Now, this is passed to the hidden layer. In the hidden layer, we apply an activation function to z_1. Let's consider the following sigmoid activation function:

$$a_1 = \sigma(z_1)$$

After applying the activation function, we again multiply result a_1 by a new weight matrix and add a new bias value which is flowing between the hidden layer and the output layer. We can denote this weight matrix and bias as w_{hy} and b_y, respectively. The dimension of this weight matrix w_{hy} will be *[number of neurons in the hidden layer * number of neurons in the output layer]*. Since we have four neurons in the hidden layer and one neuron in the output layer, the w_{hy} matrix dimension will be *4 x 1*. So, we multiply a_1 by the weight matrix w_{hy} and add bias b_y and pass the result to next layer, which is the output layer:

$$z_2 = a_1 w_{hy} + b_y$$

Now, in the output layer, we apply a sigmoid function to z_2, which will result in an output value:

$$\hat{y} = \sigma(z_2)$$

This whole process from the input layer to the output layer is known as forward propagation shown as follows:

```
def forwardProp():
        z1 = np.dot(x,wxh) + bh
        a1 = sigmoid(z1)
        z2 = np.dot(a1,why) + by
        yHat = sigmoid(z2)
```

Forward propagation is cool, isn't it? But how do we know whether the output generated by the neural network is correct? We must define a new function called the cost function (*J*), also known as the loss function, which tells us how well our neural network is performing. There are many different cost functions. We will use the mean squared error as a cost function, which can be defined as the mean of the squared difference between the actual value (y) and the predicted value $(\hat{y})$:

$$J = \frac{1}{2}(y - \hat{y})^2$$

Our objective is to minimize the cost function so that our neural network predictions will be better. How can we minimize the cost function? We can minimize the cost function by changing some values in our forward propagation. What values can we change? Obviously, we can't change input and output. We are now left with weights and bias values. We just initialized weight matrices and biases randomly, so it's not going to be perfect. Now, we will adjust these weight matrices (w_{xh} and w_{hy}) in such a way that our neural network gives a good result. How do we adjust these weight matrices? Here comes a new technique called gradient descent.

Gradient descent

As a result of forward propagation, we are in the output layer. So now, we will backpropagate the network from the output layer to the input layer and update the weights by calculating the gradient of the cost function with respect to the weights to minimize the error. Sounds confusing, right? Let's begin with an analogy. Imagine you are on top of a hill, as shown in the following diagram, and you want to reach the lowest point on the hill. You will have to make a step downwards on the hill, which leads you to the lowest point (that is, you descend from the hill towards the lowest point). There could be many regions which look like the lowest points on the hill, but we have to reach the lowest point which is actually the lowest of all. That is, you should not be stuck at a point believing it is the lowest point when the global lowest point exists:

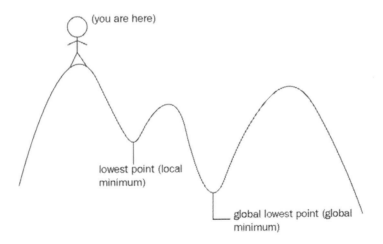

Similarly, we can represent our cost function, as follows. It is a plot of cost against weights. Our objective is to minimize the cost function. That is, we have to reach the lowest point where the cost is the minimum. The point shows our initial weights (that is where we are on the hill). If we move this point down, then we can reach the place where there is minimal error, that is, the lowest point on the cost function (the lowest point on the hill):

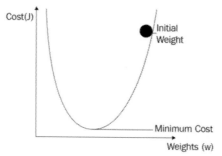

How can we move this point (initial weight) downward? How do we descend and reach the lowest point? We can move this point (initial weight) by calculating a gradient of the cost function with respect to that point. Gradients are the derivatives which are actually the slope of a tangent line, which is shown in the following diagram. So, by calculating the gradient, we descend (move downwards) and reach the lowest point:

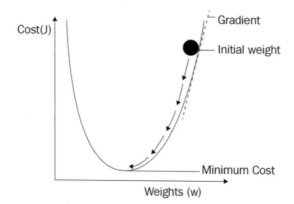

After calculating gradients, we update our old weights by our weight update rule:

$$w = w - \alpha \frac{\partial J}{\partial w}$$

What is α? It is known as the learning rate. If the learning rate is small, then we take a small step downward and our gradient descent can be slow. If the learning rate is large, then we take a large step and our gradient descent will be fast, but we might fail to reach the global minimum and become stuck at a local minimum. So, the learning rate should be chosen optimally, illustrated as follows:

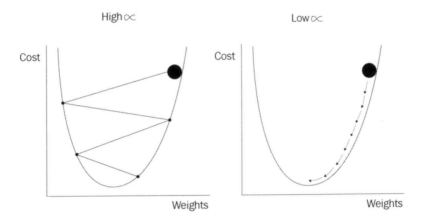

Now, let's look at this mathematically. We are going to look at a lot of interesting math now, so put on your calculus hats and follow these steps. So, we have two weights, one is w_{xh}, which is hidden to input weights and the other is w_{hy}, which is hidden to output weights. We need to update these weights according to our weight update rule. For that, first, we need to calculate the derivative of the cost function with respect to weights.

Since we are backpropagating, that is, going from the output layer to the input layer, our first weight will be w_{hy}. So, now we need to calculate the derivative of J with respect to w_{hy}.

How do we calculate the derivative? Recall our cost function $J = \frac{1}{2}(y - \hat{y})$. We cannot compute the derivative directly as there is no w_{hy} term in J.

Recall the forward propagation equations given as follows:

$$\hat{y} = \sigma(z_2)$$

$$z_2 = a_1 w_{hy} + b_y$$

First, we will calculate a partial derivative with respect to $\hat{y}$, and then from $\hat{y}$ we will calculate the partial derivative with respect to z_2. From z_2, we can directly calculate our derivative w_{hy}. It is actually the chain rule.

So, our equation becomes:

$$\frac{\partial J}{\partial w_{hy}} = \frac{\partial J}{\partial \hat{y}} \cdot \frac{\partial \hat{y}}{\partial z_2} \cdot \frac{dz_2}{dw_{hy}} \quad \text{---- (1)}$$

We will compute each of these terms:

$$\frac{\partial J}{\partial \hat{y}} = (y - \hat{y})$$

$$\frac{\partial J}{\partial z_2} = \sigma'$$

Where σ' is the derivative of our sigmoid activation function. We know that the sigmoid function is $\sigma = \frac{1}{1+e^{-z}}$, so the derivative of the sigmoid function will be $\sigma' = \frac{e^{-z}}{(1+e^{-z})^2}$.

$$\frac{dz_2}{dw_{hy}} = a_1$$

We will substitute all of these in the first equation (1).

Now, we need to compute a derivative of J with respect to our next weight w_{xh}. Similarly, we cannot calculate the derivative of w_{xh} directly from J as we don't have any w_{xh} terms in J. So, we need to use the chain rule; recall our forward propagation steps again:

$$\hat{y} = \sigma(z_2)$$

$$z_2 = a_1 w_{hy} + b_y$$

$$a_1 = \sigma(z_1)$$

$$z_1 = x w_{xh} + b$$

Now, the gradient calculation for weight w_{xh} becomes:

$$\frac{\partial J}{\partial w_{xh}} = \frac{\partial J}{\partial \hat{y}} \cdot \frac{\partial \hat{y}}{\partial z_2} \cdot \frac{\partial z_2}{\partial a_1} \cdot \frac{\partial a_1}{\partial z_1} \cdot \frac{dz_1}{dw_{xh}} \quad \text{--- (2)}$$

We will compute each of these terms:

$$\frac{\partial J}{\partial \hat{y}} = (y - \hat{y})$$

$$\frac{\partial J}{\partial z_2} = \sigma'$$

$$\frac{\partial z_2}{\partial a_1} = w_{hy}$$

$$\frac{\partial a_1}{\partial z_1} = \sigma'$$

$$\frac{dz_1}{dw_{xh}} = x$$

Once we have calculated the gradients for both weights, we will update our previous weights according to our weight update rule.

Now, let's do some coding. Look at the equations (1) and (2). We have $\frac{\partial J}{\partial \hat{y}}$ and $\frac{\partial J}{\partial z_2}$ in both equations, so we don't have to compute this again and again. We define this as `delta3`:

```
delta3 = np.multiply(-(y-yHat),sigmoidPrime(z2))
```

Now, we compute gradient for w_{hy} as:

```
dJ_dWhy = np.dot(a1.T,delta3)
```

We compute gradient for w_{xh} as:

```
delta2 = np.dot(delta3,Why.T)*sigmoidPrime(z1)
dJ_dWxh = np.dot(X.T,delta2)
```

We will update the weights according to our weight update rule as:

```
Wxh += -alpha * dJ_dWhy
Why += -alpha * dJ_dWxh
```

The complete code for this backpropagation will be as follows:

```
def backProp():

        delta3 = np.multiply(-(y-yHat),sigmoidPrime(z2))
        dJdW2 = np.dot(a1.T, delta3)
        delta2 = np.dot(delta3,Why.T)*sigmoidPrime(z1)
        dJdW1 = np.dot(X.T, delta2)
        Wxh += -alpha * dJdW1
        Why += -alpha * dJdW2
```

Before going ahead, let's familiarize ourselves with some of the frequently used terminologies in neural networks:

- **Forward pass**: Forward pass implies forward propagating from the input layer to the output layer.
- **Backward pass**: Backward pass implies backpropagating from the output layer to the input layer.
- **Epoch**: Epoch specifies the number of times the neural network sees our whole training data. So, we can say one epoch is equal to one forward pass and one backward pass for all training samples.
- **Batch size**: The batch size specifies the number of training samples we use in one forward pass and one backward pass.
- **No. of iterations**: The number of iterations implies the number of passes where *one pass = one forward pass + one backward pass*.

Say that we have 12,000 training samples and that our batch size is 6,000. It will take us two iterations to complete one epoch. That is, in the first iteration, we pass the first 6,000 samples and perform a forward pass and a backward pass; in the second iteration, we pass the next 6,000 samples and perform a forward pass and a backward pass. After two iterations, our neural network will see the whole 12,000 training samples, which makes it one epoch.

Neural networks in TensorFlow

Now, we will see how to build a basic neural network using TensorFlow, which predicts handwritten digits. We will use the popular MNIST dataset which has a collection of labeled handwritten images for training.

First, we must import TensorFlow and load the dataset from
`tensorflow.examples.tutorial.mnist`:

```
import tensorflow as tf
from tensorflow.examples.tutorials.mnist import input_data
mnist = input_data.read_data_sets("/tmp/data/", one_hot=True)
```

Now, we will see what we have in our data:

```
print("No of images in training set {}".format(mnist.train.images.shape))
print("No of labels in training set {}".format(mnist.train.labels.shape))

print("No of images in test set {}".format(mnist.test.images.shape))
print("No of labels in test set {}".format(mnist.test.labels.shape))
```

It will print the following:

```
No of images in training set (55000, 784)
No of labels in training set (55000, 10)
No of images in test set (10000, 784)
No of labels in test set (10000, 10)
```

We have `55000` images in the `training set` and each image is of size `784`. We also have
`10` labels which are actually `0` to `9`. Similarly, we have `10000` images in the `test set`.

Now, we plot an input image to see what it looks like:

```
img1 = mnist.train.images[41].reshape(28,28)
plt.imshow(img1, cmap='Greys')
```

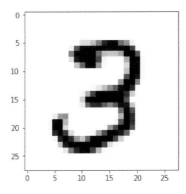

Let's start building our network. We will build the two-layer neural network with one input
layer, one hidden layer, and one output layer which predicts a handwritten digit.

First, we define the placeholders for our input and output. As our input data shape is 784, we can define the input placeholder as:

```
x = tf.placeholder(tf.float32, [None, 784])
```

What does `None` imply? None specifies the number of samples (batch size) passed, which will be decided dynamically at runtime.

Since we have 10 classes as output, we can define the `placeholder` output as:

```
y = tf.placeholder(tf.float32, [None, 10]
```

Next, we initialize our hyperparameters:

```
learning_rate = 0.1
epochs = 10
batch_size = 100
```

We then define the weight and biases between an input to the hidden layer as `w_xh` and `b_h`, respectively. We initialize the weight matrix with values, randomly drawing from a normal distribution with a standard deviation of 0.03:

```
w_xh = tf.Variable(tf.random_normal([784, 300], stddev=0.03), name='w_xh')
b_h = tf.Variable(tf.random_normal([300]), name='b_h')
```

Next, we define the weights and bias between our hidden layer to the output layer as `w_hy` and `b_y`, respectively:

```
w_hy = tf.Variable(tf.random_normal([300, 10], stddev=0.03), name='w_hy')
b_y = tf.Variable(tf.random_normal([10]), name='b_y')
```

Let's perform the forward propagation now. Recall the steps we performed in forward propagation:

```
z1 = tf.add(tf.matmul(x, w_xh), b_h)
a1 = tf.nn.relu(z1)
z2 = tf.add(tf.matmul(a1, w_hy), b_y)
yhat = tf.nn.softmax(z2)
```

We define our cost function as a cross-entropy loss. Cross-entropy loss is also known as log loss and it can be defined as follows:

$$-\sum_i y_i \log(\hat{y}_i)$$

Where y_i is the actual value and $\hat{y}_i$ is the predicted value:

```
cross_entropy = tf.reduce_mean(-tf.reduce_sum(y * tf.log(yhat),
reduction_indices=[1]))
```

Our objective is to minimize the cost function. We can minimize the cost function by propagating the network backward and perform a gradient descent. With TensorFlow, we don't have to manually calculate the gradients; we can use TensorFlow's built-in gradient descent optimizer function as follows:

```
optimiser =
tf.train.GradientDescentOptimizer(learning_rate=learning_rate).minimize(cro
ss_entropy)
```

To evaluate our model, we will calculate the accuracy as follows:

```
correct_prediction = tf.equal(tf.argmax(y, 1), tf.argmax(yhat, 1))
accuracy = tf.reduce_mean(tf.cast(correct_prediction, tf.float32))
```

As we know that TensorFlow runs by building the computation graph, whatever we have written so far will actually only run if we start the TensorFlow session. So, let's do that.

First, initialize the TensorFlow variables:

```
init_op = tf.global_variables_initializer()
```

Now, start the TensorFlow session and start training the model:

```
with tf.Session() as sess:
    sess.run(init_op)
    total_batch = int(len(mnist.train.labels) / batch_size)
    for epoch in range(epochs):
        avg_cost = 0
        for i in range(total_batch):
            batch_x, batch_y =
mnist.train.next_batch(batch_size=batch_size)
            _, c = sess.run([optimiser, cross_entropy],
                    feed_dict={x: batch_x, y: batch_y})
            avg_cost += c / total_batch
        print("Epoch:", (epoch + 1), "cost =""{:.3f}".format(avg_cost))
    print(sess.run(accuracy, feed_dict={x: mnist.test.images, y:
mnist.test.labels}))
```

RNN

The birds are flying in the ____. If I ask you to predict the blank, you might predict *sky*. How did you predict that the word *sky* would be a good fit to fill this blank? Because you read the whole sentence and predicted *sky* would be the right word based on understanding the context of the sentence. If we ask our normal neural network to predict the right word for this blank, it will not predict the correct word. This is because a normal neural network's output is based on only the current input. So, the input to the neural network will be just the previous word, *the*. That is, in normal neural networks, each input is independent of the others. So, it will not perform well in a case where we have to remember the sequence of input to predict the next sequence.

How do we make our network remember the whole sentence to predict the next word correctly? Here is where RNN comes into play. RNN predicts the output not only based on the current input but also on the previous hidden state. You might be wondering why RNN has to predict the output based on the current input and the previous hidden state and why it can't just use the current input and the previous input instead of the current input and the previous hidden state to predict the output. This is because the previous input will store information about the previous word, while the previous hidden state captures information about the whole sentence, that is, the previous hidden states stores the context. So, it is useful to predict the output based on the current input and the previous hidden state instead of just the current input and previous input.

RNN is a special type of neural network that is widely applied over sequential data. In other words, it is applied over the data where ordering matters. In a nutshell, RNN has a memory which holds previous information. It is widely applied over various **Natural Language Processing** (**NLP**) tasks such as machine translation, sentiment analysis, and so on. It is also applied over time series data such as stock market data. Still not clear what RNN is exactly? Look at the following diagram showing the comparison of normal neural networks and RNN:

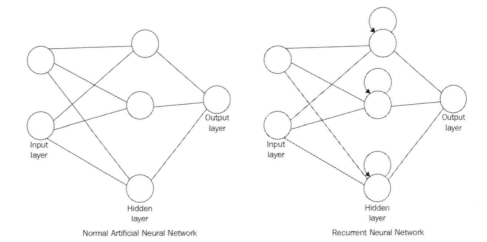

Did you notice how RNN differs from the normal neural networks we saw in the previous topic? Yes. The difference is that there is a loop in the hidden states which implies how previous hidden states are used to calculate the output.

Still confusing? Look at the following unrolled version of an RNN:

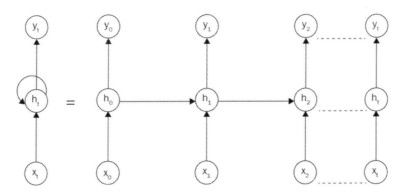

As you can see, the output y_1 is predicted based on the current input x_1, the current hidden state h_1, and also the previous hidden state h_0. Similarly, look at how output y_2 is computed. It takes the current input x_2 and the current hidden state h_2 as well as the previous hidden state h_1. This is how RNN works; it takes the current input and previous hidden state to predict the output. We can call these hidden states a memory as they hold information that has been seen so far.

Now, we will see a little bit of math:

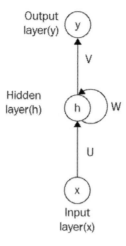

In the preceding diagram:

- **U** represents the input to the hidden state weight matrix
- **W** represents the hidden to the hidden state weight matrix
- **V** represents the hidden to the output state weight matrix

So, in the forward pass, we compute the following:

$$h_t = \phi(Ux_t + Wh_{t-1})$$

That is, *hidden state at a time t = tanh([input to hidden weight matrix * input] + [hidden to hidden weight matrix * previous hidden state at a time t-1]):*

$$\hat{y}_t = \sigma(vh_t)$$

That is, *output at a time t = Sigmoid (hidden to output weight matrix * hidden state at a time t).*

We can also define our loss function as a cross-entropy loss, like so:

$$Loss = -y_t \log \hat{y}_t$$

$$Total\ loss = -\sum_t y_t \log \hat{y}_t$$

In the preceding example, y_t is the actual word at time t and $\hat{y}_t$ is the predicted word at time t. Since we take the whole sequence as a training sample, the total loss will be the sum of loss at each time step.

Backpropagation through time

Now, how do we train RNNs? Just like we have trained our normal neural networks, we can use backpropagation for training RNNs. But in RNNs, since there is a dependency on all the time steps, gradients at each output will not depend only on the current time step but also on the previous time step. We call this **backpropagation through time (BPTT)**. It is basically the same as backpropagation except that it is applied an RNN. To see how it occurs in an RNN, let's consider the unrolled version of an RNN, as shown in the following diagram:

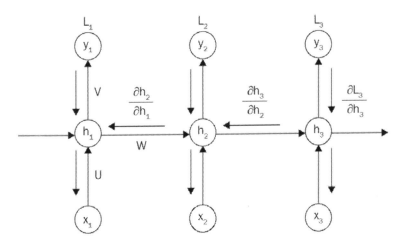

In the preceding diagram, L_1, L_2, and L_3 are the losses at each time step. Now, we need to compute the gradients of this loss with respect to our weight matrices **U**, **V**, and **W** at each time step. Like we previously calculated the total loss by summing up a loss at each time step, we update the weight matrices with a sum of the gradients at each time step:

$$\frac{\partial L}{\partial V} = \sum_t \frac{\partial L_t}{\partial V}$$

However, we have a problem with this method. The gradient calculation involves calculating the gradient with respect to the activation function. When we calculate the gradient with respect to the sigmoid/tanh function, the gradient will become very small. When we further backpropagate the network over many time steps and multiply the gradients, the gradients will tend to get smaller and smaller. This is called a vanishing gradient problem. So, what would happen because of this problem? Because of the gradients vanishing over time, we cannot learn information about long-term dependencies, that is, RNNs cannot retain information for a longer time in the memory.

The vanishing gradient occurs not only in RNNs but also in other deep networks where we have many hidden layers when we use sigmoid/tanh functions. There is also a problem called exploding gradients where the gradient values become greater than one, and when we multiply these gradients, it will lead to a very big number.

One solution is to use ReLU as an activation function. However, we have a variant of the RNN called LSTM, which can solve the vanishing gradient problem effectively. We will see how it works in the upcoming section.

Long Short-Term Memory RNN

RNNs are pretty cool, right? But we have seen a problem in training the RNNs called the vanishing gradient problem. Let's explore that a bit. The sky is __. An RNN can easily predict the last word as *blue* based on the information it has seen. But an RNN cannot cover long-term dependencies. What does that mean? Let's say Archie lived in China for 20 years. He loves listening to good music. He is a very big comic fan. He is fluent in _. Now, you would predict the blank as Chinese. How did you predict that? Because you understood that Archie lived for 20 years in China, you thought he might be fluent in Chinese. But an RNN cannot retain all of this information in memory to say that Archie is fluent in Chinese. Due to the vanishing gradient problem, it cannot recollect/remember the information for a long time in memory. How do we solve that?

Here comes LSTM to the rescue!!!!

LSTM is a variant of the RNN that resolves the vanishing gradient problem. LSTM retains information in the memory as long as it is required. So basically, RNN cells are replaced with LSTM. How does LSTM achieve this?

A typical LSTM cell is shown in the following diagram:

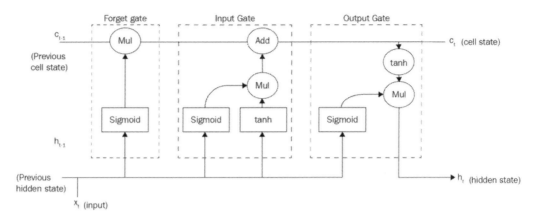

LSTM cells are called memory and they are responsible for storing information. But how long does the information have to be in the memory? When can we delete the old information and update the cell with the new one? All of these decisions will be made by three special gates as follows:

- Forget gate
- Input gate
- Output gate

If you look at the LSTM cell, the top horizontal line C_t is called the cell state. It is where the information flows. Information on the cell state will be constantly updated by LSTM gates. Now, we will see the function of these gates:

- **Forget gate**: The forget gate is responsible for deciding what information should not be in the cell state. Look at the following statement:
  Harry is a good singer. He lives in New York. Zayn is also a good singer.
  As soon as we start talking about Zayn, the network will understand that the subject has been changed from Harry to Zayn and the information about Harry is no longer required. Now, the forget gate will remove/forget information about Harry from the cell state.

- **Input gate**: The input gate is responsible for deciding what information should be stored in the memory. Let's consider the same example:
Harry is a good singer. He lives in New York. Zayn is also a good singer.
So, after the forget gate removes information from the cell state, the input gate decides what information has to be in the memory. Here, since the information about Harry is removed from the cell state by the forget gate, the input gate decides to update the cell state with the information about Zayn.

- **Output gate**: The output gate is responsible for deciding what information should be shown from the cell state at a time, *t*. Now, consider the following sentence:
Zayn's debut album was a huge success. Congrats ____.
Here, *congrats* is an adjective which is used to describe a noun. The output layer will predict *Zayn* (noun), to fill in the blank.

Generating song lyrics using LSTM RNN

Now, we will see how to use the LSTM network to generate Zayn Malik's song lyrics. The dataset can be downloaded from here (`https://github.com/sudharsan13296/Hands-On-Reinforcement-Learning-With-Python/blob/master/07.%20Deep%20Learning%20Fundamentals/data/ZaynLyrics.txt`) ,which has a collection of Zayn's song lyrics.

First, we will import the necessary libraries:

```
import tensorflow as tf
import numpy as np
```

Now, we will read our file containing the song lyrics:

```
with open("Zayn_Lyrics.txt","r") as f:
    data=f.read()
    data=data.replace('\n','')
    data = data.lower()
```

Let's see what we have in our data:

```
data[:50]
"now i'm on the edge can't find my way it's inside "
```

Then, we store all the characters in the `all_chars` variable:

```
all_chars=list(set(data))
```

We store the number of unique characters in `unique_chars`:

```
unique_chars = len(all_chars)
```

We also store the total number of characters in `total_chars`:

```
total_chars =len(data)
```

Now, we will create a mapping between each character to their index. `char_to_ix` will have a character to index mapping, while `ix_to_char` will have an index to character mapping:

```
char_to_ix = { ch:i for i,ch in enumerate(all_chars) }
ix_to_char = { i:ch for i,ch in enumerate(all_chars) }
```

That is, for example:

```
char_to_ix['e']
9

ix_to_char[9]
e
```

Next, we define a `generate_batch` function which will generate input and target values. Target values are just the `i` times the shift of the input value.

For example: if `input = [12,13,24]` with a shift value of 1, the target will be `[13,24]`:

```
def generate_batch(seq_length,i):
    inputs = [char_to_ix[ch] for ch in data[i:i+seq_length]]
    targets = [char_to_ix[ch] for ch in data[i+1:i+seq_length+1]]
    inputs=np.array(inputs).reshape(seq_length,1)
    targets=np.array(targets).reshape(seq_length,1)
    return inputs,targets
```

We will define the sequence length, learning rate, and the number of nodes, which is the number of neurons:

```
seq_length = 25
learning_rate = 0.1
num_nodes = 300
```

Let's build our LSTM RNN. TensorFlow provides us with a `BasicLSTMCell()` function for building the LSTM cell and we need to specify the number of units in the LSTM cell and the type of activation function we wish to use.

So, we will create an LSTM cell and then build the RNN with that cell using the `tf.nn.dynamic_rnn()` function, which will return the output and the state value:

```
def build_rnn(x):
        cell= tf.contrib.rnn.BasicLSTMCell(num_units=num_nodes,
activation=tf.nn.relu)
        outputs, states = tf.nn.dynamic_rnn(cell, x, dtype=tf.float32)
        return outputs,states
```

Now, we will create a placeholder for our input X and the target Y:

```
X=tf.placeholder(tf.float32,[None,1])
Y=tf.placeholder(tf.float32,[None,1])
```

Convert the X and Y to `int`:

```
X=tf.cast(X,tf.int32)
Y=tf.cast(Y,tf.int32)
```

We will also create `onehot` representations for X and Y as follows:

```
X_onehot=tf.one_hot(X,unique_chars)
Y_onehot=tf.one_hot(Y,unique_chars)
```

Get the outputs and states from the RNN by calling the `build_rnn` function:

```
outputs,states=build_rnn(X_onehot)
```

Transpose the output:

```
outputs=tf.transpose(outputs,perm=[1,0,2])
```

Initialize the weights and biases:

```
W=tf.Variable(tf.random_normal((num_nodes,unique_chars),stddev=0.001))
B=tf.Variable(tf.zeros((1,unique_chars)))
```

We will calculate our output by multiplying the output with weights and add bias:

```
Ys=tf.matmul(outputs[0],W)+B
```

Next, perform softmax activation and get the probabilities:

```
prediction = tf.nn.softmax(Ys)
```

We will calculate the `cross_entropy` loss as:

```
cross_entropy=tf.reduce_mean(tf.nn.softmax_cross_entropy_with_logits(labels
=Y_onehot,logits=Ys))
```

Our objective is to minimize the loss, so we will backpropagate the network and perform gradient descent:

```
optimiser =
tf.train.GradientDescentOptimizer(learning_rate=learning_rate).minimize(cro
ss_entropy)
```

Now, we will define the helper function called `predict`, which results in the indices of the next predicted character according to our RNN model:

```
def predict(seed,i):
    x=np.zeros((1,1))
    x[0][0]= seed
    indices=[]
    for t in range(i):
        p=sess.run(prediction,{X:x})
        index = np.random.choice(range(unique_chars), p=p.ravel())
        x[0][0]=index
        indices.append(index)
    return indices
```

We set our `batch_size`, number of batches, and number of `epochs` along with the `shift` value for generating a batch:

```
batch_size=100
total_batch=int(total_chars//batch_size)
epochs=1000
shift=0
```

Finally, we will start the TensorFlow session and build the model:

```
init=tf.global_variables_initializer()

with tf.Session() as sess:
    sess.run(init)
    for epoch in range(epoch):
        print("Epoch {}:".format(epoch))
        if shift + batch_size+1 >= len(data):
            shift =0
         ## get the input and target for each batch by generate_batch
         #function which shifts the input by shift value
         ## and form target
```

```
        for i in range(total_batch):
            inputs,targets=generate_batch(batch_size,shift)
            shift += batch_size
            # calculate loss
            if(i%100==0):
                loss=sess.run(cross_entropy,feed_dict={X:inputs,
Y:targets})
                # We get index of next predicted character by
                # the predict function
                index =predict(inputs[0],200)
                # pass the index to our ix_to_char dictionary and
                #get the char
                txt = ''.join(ix_to_char[ix] for ix in index)
                print('Iteration %i: '%(i))
                print ('\n %s \n' % (txt, ))
            sess.run(optimiser,feed_dict={X:inputs,Y:targets})
```

We can see that the outputs are some random characters in the initial epoch, but as the training steps increase, we get better results:

```
Epoch 0:
Iteration 0:

 wsadrpud,kpswkypeqawnlfyweudkgt,khdi nmgof' u vnvlmbis .
snsblp,podwjqehb,e;g-
'fyqjsyeg,byjgyotsrdf;;u,h.a;ik'sfc;dvtauofd.,q.;npsw'wjy-quw'quspfqw-
 .
 .
 .
Epoch 113:
Iteration 0:
i wanna see you, yes, and she said yes!
```

Convolutional neural networks

CNN, also known as ConvNet, is a special type of neural network and it is extensively used in Computer Vision. The application of a CNN ranges from enabling vision in self-driving cars to the automatic tagging of friends in your Facebook pictures. CNNs make use of spatial information to recognize the image. But how do they really work? How can the neural networks recognize these images? Let's go through this step by step.

A CNN typically consists of three major layers:

- Convolutional layer
- Pooling layer
- Fully connected layer

Convolutional layer

When we feed an image as input, it will actually be converted to a matrix of pixel values. These pixel values range from 0 to 255 and the dimensions of this matrix will be *[image height * image width * number of channels]*. If the input image is 64 x 64 in size, then the pixel matrix dimension would be 64 x 64 x 3, where the 3 refers to the channel number. A grayscale image has 1 channel and color images have 3 channels (RGB). Look at the following photograph. When this image is fed as an input, it will be converted into a matrix of pixel values, which we will see in a moment. For better understanding, we will consider the grayscale image since grayscale images have 1 channel and so we will get the 2D matrix.

The input image is as follows:

Now, let's see the matrix value in the following graphic:

13	8	18	63	7
5	3	1	2	33
1	9	0	7	16
3	16	5	8	18
5	7	81	36	9

So, this is how the image is represented by a matrix. What happens next? How does the network identify the image from this pixel's values? Now, we introduce an operation called convolution. It is used to extract important features from the image so that we can understand what the image is all about. Let's say we have the image of a dog; what do you think the features of this image are, which will help us to understand that this is an image of a dog? We can say body structure, face, legs, tail, and so on. Convolution operations will help the network to learn those features which characterize the dog. Now, we will see how exactly the convolution operation is performed to extract features from the image.

As we know, every image is represented by a matrix. Let's suppose we have a pixel matrix of the dog image, and let's call this matrix an input matrix. We will also consider another *n x n* matrix called filter, as shown in the following diagram:

13	8	18	63	7
5	3	1	2	33
1	9	0	7	16
3	16	5	8	18
5	7	81	36	9

Input Matrix

0	1	0
1	1	0
0	0	1

Filter Matrix

Now, this filter will slide over our input matrix by one pixel and will perform element-wise multiplication, producing a single number. Confused? Look at the following diagram:

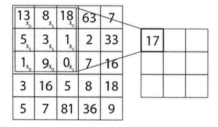

That is, *(13*0) + (8*1) + (18*0) + (5*1) + (3*1) + (1*1) + (1*0) + (9*0) + (0*1) = 17.*

Similarly, we move our filter matrix over the input matrix by one pixel and perform element-wise multiplication:

13	8	18	63	7
5	3	1	2	33
1	9	0	7	16
3	16	5	8	18
5	7	81	36	9

17	31	

That is, *(8*0) + (18*1) + (63*0) + (3*1) + (1*1) + (2*1) + (9*0) + (0*0) + (7*1) = 31.*

The filter matrix will slide over the entire input matrix, perform element-wise multiplication, and produce a new matrix called a feature map or activation map. This operation is known as convolution as shown in the following diagram:

13	8	18	63	7
5	3	1	2	33
1	9	0	7	16
3	16	5	8	18
5	7	81	36	9

17	31	115
18	25	43
114	65	47

The following output shows an actual and convolved image:

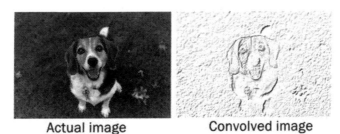

Actual image   Convolved image

You can see that our filter has detected an edge in the actual image and produced a convolved image. Similarly, different filters are used to extract different features from the image.

For example, if we use a filter matrix, say a sharpen filter $\begin{bmatrix} 0 & -1 & 0 \\ -1 & 5 & -1 \\ 0 & -1 & 0 \end{bmatrix}$, then our convolved image will look as follows:

Thus, filters are responsible for extracting features from the actual image by performing a convolutional operation. There will be more than one filter for extracting different features of the image that produces the feature maps. The depth of the feature map is the number of the filters we use. If we use 5 filters to extract features and produce 5 feature maps, then the depth of the feature map is **5** shown as follows:

Feature Map of depth 5

When we have many filters, our network will better understand the image by extracting many features. While building our CNN, we don't have to specify the values for this filter matrix. The optimal values for this filter will be learned during the training process. However, we have to specify the number of filters and dimensions of the filters we want to use.

We can slide over the input matrix by one pixel with the filter and performed convolution operation. Not only can we slide by one pixel; we can also slide over an input matrix by any number of pixels. The number of pixels we slide over the input matrix by in the filter matrix is called strides.

But what happens when the sliding window (filter matrix) reaches the border of the image? In that case, we pad the input matrix with zero so that we can apply a filter on the image's edges. Padding with zeros on the image is called same padding, or wide convolutional or zero padding illustrated as follows:

13	8	18	63	7	0
5	3	1	2	33	0
1	9	0	7	16	0
3	16	5	8	18	
5	7	81	36	9	

Instead of padding them with zeros, we can also simply discard that region. This is known as valid padding or narrow convolution illustrated as follows:

13	8	18	63	7	0
5	3	1	2	33	0
1	9	0	7	16	0
3	16	5	8	18	
5	7	81	36	9	

After performing the convolution operation, we apply the ReLU activation function to introduce nonlinearity.

Pooling layer

After the convolution layer, we have the pooling layer. The pooling layer is used to reduce the dimensions of the feature maps and keeps only necessary details so that the amount of computation can be reduced. For example, to identify whether there is a dog in the image, we don't want to understand at which location the dog is in the image, we just want the features of the dog. So, the pooling layer reduces spatial dimensions by keeping only the important features. There are different types of pooling operations. Max pooling is one of the most commonly used pooling operations where we just take the maximum value from the feature map within the window.

Max pooling with a 2 x 2 filter and a stride of 2 is shown as follows:

40	8	13	9
10	16	11	20
9	8	6	11
1	0	12	18

Max Pooling with 2x2 filter & stride of 2 →

40	13
9	18

In average pooling, we just take the average of elements in the feature map within the window and in sum pooling, we take the sum of elements of a feature map in the window.

 The pooling operation will not change the depth of the feature maps, it will only affect the height and width.

Fully connected layer

We can have multiple convolutional layers followed by pooling layers. However, these layers will only extract features from the input image and produce the activation maps. How do we classify whether there is a dog in the image with the activation maps alone? We have to introduce a new layer called a fully connected layer. It receives input as the activation maps (which are now basically the features of the image) apply the activation function and it produces the output. A fully connected layer is actually the normal neural network where we have an input layer, hidden layer, and output layer. Here, instead of an input layer, we use convolution and pooling layers, which together produce the activation maps as an input.

CNN architecture

Now, let's just see how all of these layers are organized in the CNN architecture, as follows:

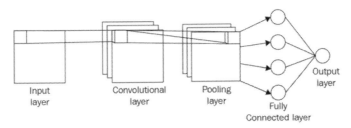

First, the image is passed to the convolutional layer, where we apply the convolution operation to extract features, and then feature maps are passed to the pooling layer where the dimensions are reduced. We can add any number of convolution and pooling layers depending on the use case. After this, we can add a neural network with one hidden layer at the end, which is known as a fully connected layer, which classifies the image.

Classifying fashion products using CNN

We will now see how to use CNN for classifying fashion products.

First, we will import our required libraries as usual:

```
import tensorflow as tf
import numpy as np
import matplotlib.pyplot as plt
%matplotlib inline
```

Now, we will read the data. The dataset is available in `tensorflow.examples`, so we can directly extract the data as follows:

```
from tensorflow.examples.tutorials.mnist import input_data
fashion_mnist = input_data.read_data_sets('data/fashion/', one_hot=True)
```

We will check what we have in our data:

```
print("No of images in training set
{}".format(fashion_mnist.train.images.shape))
print("No of labels in training set
{}".format(fashion_mnist.train.labels.shape))

print("No of images in test set
{}".format(fashion_mnist.test.images.shape))
print("No of labels in test set
{}".format(fashion_mnist.test.labels.shape))

No of images in training set (55000, 784)
```

```
No of labels in training set (55000, 10)
No of images in test set (10000, 784)
No of labels in test set (10000, 10)
```

So, we have `55000` data points in a `training set` and `10000` data points in a `test set`. We also have `10` labels, which means we have `10` categories.

We have `10` categories of products and we will label all of them:

```
labels = {
0: 'T-shirt/top',
1: 'Trouser',
2: 'Pullover',
3: 'Dress',
4: 'Coat',
5: 'Sandal',
6: 'Shirt',
7: 'Sneaker',
8: 'Bag',
9: 'Ankle boot'
}
```

Now, we will look at some of our images:

```
img1 = fashion_mnist.train.images[41].reshape(28,28)
# Get corresponding integer label from one-hot encoded data
label1 = np.where(fashion_mnist.train.labels[41] == 1)[0][0]
# Plot sample
print("y = {} ({})".format(label1, labels[label1]))
plt.imshow(img1, cmap='Greys')
```

The output and visual are as follows:

```
y = 6 (Shirt)
```

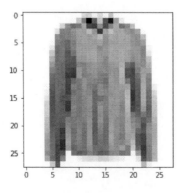

That's a pretty good shirt, isn't it? We will look at one more image:

```
img1 = fashion_mnist.train.images[19].reshape(28,28)
# Get corresponding integer label from one-hot encoded data
label1 = np.where(fashion_mnist.train.labels[19] == 1)[0][0]
# Plot sample
print("y = {} ({})".format(label1, labels[label1]))
plt.imshow(img1, cmap='Greys')
```

The output and visual are as follows:

```
y = 8 (Bag)
```

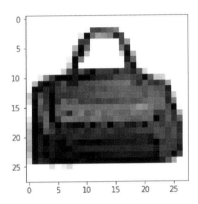

That's a good bag to hold!!

So now, we have to build a convolutional neural network that actually classifies all of these images into their respective categories. We define the placeholders for input images and output labels. As our input image is of size 784, we define a placeholder for input x as follows:

```
x = tf.placeholder(tf.float32, [None, 784])
```

We need to reshape the input to the format [p, q, r, s], where q and r are the actual size of an input image, which is 28 x 28, and s is the channel number. As we have only grayscale images, the value of s is 1. p implies the number of training samples, that is, the batch size. Since we don't know the batch size, we can set that as −1 and it will be dynamically changed during training:

```
x_shaped = tf.reshape(x, [-1, 28, 28, 1])
```

As we have 10 different labels, we define placeholders for the output as follows:

```
y = tf.placeholder(tf.float32, [None, 10])
```

Now, we need to define a function called `conv2d` which actually performs the convolutional operation, that is, element-wise multiplication of the input matrix (x) by the filter (w) with a stride of 1 and `SAME` padding.

We set `strides = [1, 1, 1, 1]`. The first and last values of strides are set to 1, which implies we don't want to move between training samples and different channels. The second and third values of strides are also set to 1, which implies that we move the filter by 1 pixel in both height and width direction:

```
def conv2d(x, w):
    return tf.nn.conv2d(x, w, strides=[1, 1, 1, 1], padding='SAME')
```

We define a function called `maxpool2d` to perform the pooling operation. We perform max pooling with a stride of 2 and `SAME` padding. `ksize` implies our pooling window shape:

```
def maxpool2d(x):
    return tf.nn.max_pool(x, ksize=[1, 2, 2, 1], strides=[1, 2, 2, 1],
    padding='SAME')
```

Next, we define weights and biases. We will build a convolutional network with two convolutional layers followed by a fully connected layer and an output layer, so we will define the weights for all of these layers. The weights are actually the filters in the convolutional layers.

So, the weight matrix will be initialized as `[filter_shape[0],filter_shape[1], number_of_input_channel, filter_size]`.

We will use a 5 x 5 filter and we will set our filter size to 32. Since we use grayscale images, our input channel number will 1. So, our weight matrix will be `[5,5,1,32]`:

```
w_c1 = tf.Variable(tf.random_normal([5,5,1,32]))
```

As the second convolutional layer takes the input from the first convolutional layer which has 32 as its channel output, the number of input channels to the next layer becomes 32:

```
w_c2 = tf.Variable(tf.random_normal([5,5,32,64]))
```

Next, we initialize the biases:

```
b_c1 = tf.Variable(tf.random_normal([32]))
b_c2 = tf.Variable(tf.random_normal([64]))
```

Now, we perform operations on the first convolution layer, that is, the convolution operation on the input x with ReLU activations followed by a max pooling:

```
conv1 = tf.nn.relu(conv2d(x, w_c1) + b_c1)
conv1 = maxpool2d(conv1)
```

Now, the result of the first convolutional layer will be passed to the next convolutional layer where we perform the convolutional operation on the result of a first convolutional layer with ReLU activations, followed by max pooling:

```
conv2 = tf.nn.relu(conv2d(conv1, w_c2) + b_c2)
conv2 = maxpool2d(conv2)
```

After two convolution layers with convolution and pooling operations, our input image will be downsampled from 28*28*1 to 7*7*1. We need to flatten this output before feeding it to the fully connected layer. Then, the result of the second convolutional layer will be fed into the fully connected layer and we multiply this with weights, add bias, and apply ReLU activations:

```
x_flattened = tf.reshape(conv2, [-1, 7*7*64])
w_fc = tf.Variable(tf.random_normal([7*7*64,1024]))
b_fc = tf.Variable(tf.random_normal([1024]))
fc = tf.nn.relu(tf.matmul(x_flattened,w_fc)+ b_fc)
```

Now, we need to define the weights and bias for the output layer, which is [number of neurons in the current layer, number of neurons layer in the next layer]:

```
w_out = tf.Variable(tf.random_normal([1024, 10]))
b_out = tf.Variable(tf.random_normal([10]))
```

We can get the output by multiplying the result of a fully connected layer with the weight matrix and add bias. We will get the probabilities of the output by using the softmax activation function:

```
output = tf.matmul(fc, w_out)+ b_out
yhat = tf.nn.softmax(output)
```

We can define our loss function as a cross-entropy loss. We will minimize our loss function using a new type of optimizer called the Adam optimizer (https://www.tensorflow.org/api_docs/python/tf/train/AdamOptimizer) instead of using the gradient descent optimizer:

```
cross_entropy =
tf.reduce_mean(tf.nn.softmax_cross_entropy_with_logits(logits=output,
labels=y))optimiser =
tf.train.AdamOptimizer(learning_rate=learning_rate).minimize(cross_entropy)
```

Next, we will calculate the `accuracy` as follows:

```
correct_prediction = tf.equal(tf.argmax(y, 1), tf.argmax(yhat, 1))
accuracy = tf.reduce_mean(tf.cast(correct_prediction, tf.float32))
```

And define the hyperparameters:

```
epochs = 10
batch_size = 100
```

Now, we will start the TensorFlow session and build the model:

```
init_op = tf.global_variables_initializer()

with tf.Session() as sess:
   sess.run(init_op)
   total_batch = int(len(fashion_mnist.train.labels) / batch_size)
    # For each epoch
   for epoch in range(epochs):
        avg_cost = 0
        for i in range(total_batch):
            batch_x, batch_y =
fashion_mnist.train.next_batch(batch_size=batch_size)
            _, c = sess.run([optimiser, cross_entropy],
                     feed_dict={x: batch_x, y: batch_y})
            avg_cost += c / total_batch
        print("Epoch:", (epoch + 1), "cost =""{:.3f}".format(avg_cost))
   print(sess.run(accuracy, feed_dict={x: mnist.test.images, y:
mnist.test.labels}))
```

Summary

In this chapter, we learned how neural networks actually work followed by building a neural network to classify handwritten digits using TensorFlow. We also saw different types of neural networks such as an RNN, which can remember information in the memory. Then, we saw the LSTM network, which is used to overcome the vanishing gradient problem by keeping several gates to retain information in the memory as long as it is required. We also saw another interesting neural network for recognizing images called CNN. We saw how CNN use different layers to understand the image. Following this, we learned how to build a CNN to recognize fashion products using TensorFlow.

In the next chapter, Chapter 8, *Atari Games With Deep Q Network*, we will see how neural networks will actually help our RL agents to learn more efficiently.

Questions

The question list is as follows:

1. What is the difference between linear regression and neural networks?
2. What is the use of the activation function?
3. Why do we need to calculate the gradient in gradient descent?
4. What is the advantage of an RNN?
5. What are vanishing and exploding gradient problems?
6. What are gates in LSTM?
7. What is the use of the pooling layer?

Further reading

Deep learning is a vast topic. To explore more about deep learning and other related algorithms check out the following very useful links:

- **More about CNNs is on this awesome Stanford course**: https://www.youtube.com/watch?v=NfnWJUyUJYUlist=PLkt2uSq6rBVctENoVBg1TpCC7OQi31AlC
- **Dive into RNNs with this awesome blog post**: http://www.wildml.com/2015/09/recurrent-neural-networks-tutorial-part-1-introduction-to-rnns/

8
Atari Games with Deep Q Network

Deep Q Network (DQN) is one of the very popular and widely used **deep reinforcement learning (DRL)** algorithms. In fact, it created a lot of buzz around the **reinforcement learning (RL)** community after its release. The algorithm was proposed by researchers at Google's DeepMind and achieved human-level results when playing any Atari game by just taking the game screen as input.

In this chapter, we will explore how DQN works and also learn how to build a DQN that plays any Atari game by taking only the game screen as input. We will look at some of the improvements made to DQN architecture, such as double DQN and dueling network architecture.

In this chapter, you will learn about:

- **Deep Q Networks (DQNs)**
- Architecture of DQN
- Building an agent to play Atari games
- Double DQN
- Prioritized experience replay

What is a Deep Q Network?

Before going ahead, first, let us just recap the Q function. What is a Q function? A Q function, also called a state-action value function, specifies how good an action *a* is in the state *s*. So, we store the value of all possible actions in each state in a table called a Q table and we pick the action that has the maximum value in a state as the optimal action. Remember how we learned this Q function? We used Q learning, which is an off-policy temporal difference learning algorithm for estimating the Q function. We looked at this in Chapter 5, *Temporal Difference Learning*.

So far, we have seen environments with a finite number of states with limited actions, and we did an exhaustive search through all possible state-action pairs for finding the optimal Q value. Think of an environment where we have a very large number of states and, in each state, we have a lot of actions to try. It would be time-consuming to go through all the actions in each state. A better approach would be to approximate the Q function with some parameter θ as $Q(s, a; \theta) \approx Q^*(s, a)$. We can use a neural network with weights θ to approximate the Q value for all possible actions in each state. As we are using neural networks to approximate the Q function, we can call it a Q network. Okay, but how do we train the network and what will be our objective function? Recall our Q learning update rule:

$$Q(s, a) = Q(s, a) + \alpha(r + \gamma max Q(s'a') - Q(s, a)).$$

$r + \gamma max Q(s'a)$ is the target value and $Q(s, a)$ is the predicted value; we tried to minimize this value by learning a right policy.

Similarly, in DQN, we can define the loss function as the squared difference between the target and predicted value, and we will also try to minimize the loss by updating the weights θ:

$$Loss = (y_i - Q(s, a; \theta))^2$$

Where $y_i = r + \gamma max_{a'} Q(s', a'; \theta)$.

We update the weights and minimize the loss through gradient descent. In a nutshell, in DQN, we use neural networks as function approximators for approximating a Q function, and we minimize errors through gradient descent.

Architecture of DQN

Now that we have a basic understanding of DQN, we will go into detail about how DQN works and the architecture of DQN for playing Atari games. We will look at each component and then we will view the algorithm as a whole.

Convolutional network

The first layer of DQN is the convolutional network, and the input to the network will be a raw frame of the game screen. So, we take a raw frame and pass that to the convolutional layers to understand the game state. But the raw frames will have 210 x 160 pixels with a 128 color palette and it will clearly take a lot of computation and memory if we feed the raw pixels directly. So, we downsample the pixel to 84 x 84 and convert the RGB values to grayscale values and we feed this pre-processed game screen as the input to the convolutional layers. The convolutional layer understands the game screen by identifying the spatial relationship between different objects in the image. We use two convolutional layers followed by a fully connected layer with ReLU as the activation function. Here, we don't use a pooling layer.

A pooling layer is useful when we perform tasks such as object detection or classification, where we don't consider the position of the object in the image and we just want to know whether the desired object is in the image. For example, if we want to classify whether there is a dog in an image, we only look at whether a dog is there in an image and we don't check where the dog is. In that case, a pooling layer is used to classify the image irrespective of the position of the dog. But for us to understand the game screen, the position is important as it depicts the game status. For example, in a Pong game, we don't just want to classify if there is a ball on the game screen. We want to know the position of the ball so that we can make our next move. That's why we don't use a pooling layer in our architecture.

Okay, how can we compute the Q value? If we pass one game screen and one action as an input to the DQN, it will give us the Q value. But it will require one complete forward pass, as there will be many actions in a state. Also, there will be many states in a game with one forward pass for each action, which will be computationally expensive. So, we simply pass the game screen alone as an input and get the Q values for all possible actions in the state by setting the number of units in the output layer to the number of actions in the game state.

The architecture of DQN is shown in the following diagram, where we feed a game screen and it provides the Q value for all actions in that game state:

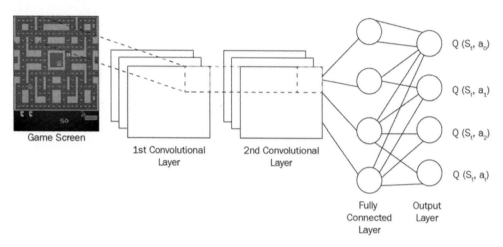

To predict the Q values of the game state, we don't use only the current game screen; we also consider the past four game screens. Why is that? Consider the Pac-Man game where the goal of the Pac-Man is to move and eat all the dots. By just looking at the current game screen, we cannot know in which direction Pac-Man is moving. But if we have past game screens, we can understand in which direction Pac-Man is moving. We use the past four game screens along with the current game screen as input.

Experience replay

We know that in RL environments, we make a transition from one state s to the next state s' by performing some action a and receive a reward r. We save this transition information as $< s, a, r, s' >$ in a buffer called a replay buffer or experience replay. These transitions are called the agent's experience.

The key idea of experience replay is that we train our deep Q network with transitions sampled from the replay buffer instead of training with the last transitions. Agent's experiences are correlated one at a time, so selecting a random batch of training samples from the replay buffer will reduce the correlation between the agent's experience and helps the agent to learn better from a wide range of experiences.

Also, neural networks will overfit with correlated experience, so by selecting a random batch of experiences from reply buffer we will reduce the overfitting. We can use uniform sampling for sampling the experience. We can think of experience replay as a queue rather than a list. A replay buffer will store only a fixed number of recent experiences, so when the new information comes in, we delete the old:

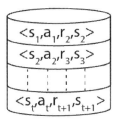

Target network

In our loss function, we calculate the squared difference between a target and predicted value:

$$Loss = (r + \gamma max_{a'} Q(s', a'; \theta) - Q(s, a; \theta))^2$$

We are using the same Q function for calculating the target value and the predicted value. In the preceding equation, you can see the same weights θ are used for both target Q and predicted Q. Since the same network is calculating the predicted value and target value, there could be a lot of divergence between these two.

To avoid this problem, we use a separate network called a target network for calculating the target value. So, our loss function becomes:

$$Loss = (r + \gamma max_{a'} Q(s', a'; \theta') - Q(s, a; \theta))^2$$

You may notice that the parameter of target Q is θ' instead of θ. Our actual Q network, which is used for predicting Q values, learns the correct weights of θ by using gradient descent. The target network is frozen for several time steps and then the target network weights are updated by copying the weights from the actual Q network. Freezing the target network for a while and then updating its weights with the actual Q network weights stabilizes the training.

Clipping rewards

How do we assign rewards? Reward assignment varies for each game. In some games, we can assign rewards such as +1 for winning, -1 for loss, and 0 for nothing, but in some other games, we have to assign rewards such as + 100 for doing an action and +50 for doing another action. To avoid this problem, we clip all the rewards to -1 and +1.

Understanding the algorithm

Now, we will see how DQN works overall. The steps involved in DQN are as follows:

1. First, we preprocess and feed the game screen (state s) to our DQN, which will return the Q values of all possible actions in the state.

2. Now we select an action using the epsilon-greedy policy: with the probability epsilon, we select a random action a and with probability 1-epsilon, we select an action that has a maximum Q value, such as $a = argmax(Q(s,a;\theta))$.

3. After selecting the action a, we perform this action in a state s and move to a new state s' and receive a reward. The next state, s', is the preprocessed image of the next game screen.

4. We store this transition in our replay buffer as `<s,a,r,s'>`.

5. Next, we sample some random batches of transitions from the replay buffer and calculate the loss.

6. We know that $Loss = (r + \gamma max_{a'} Q(s',a';\theta') - Q(s,a;\theta))^2$, as in the squared difference between target Q and predicted Q.

7. We perform gradient descent with respect to our actual network parameters θ in order to minimize this loss.

8. After every k steps, we copy our actual network weights θ to the target network weights θ'.

9. We repeat these steps for M number of episodes.

Building an agent to play Atari games

Now we will see how to build an agent to play any Atari game. You can get the complete code as a Jupyter notebook with the explanation here (`https://github.com/ sudharsan13296/Hands-On-Reinforcement-Learning-With-Python/blob/master/08. %20Atari%20Games%20with%20DQN/8. 8%20Building%20an%20Agent%20to%20Play%20Atari%20Games.ipynb`).

First, we import all the necessary libraries:

```
import numpy as np
import gym
import tensorflow as tf
from tensorflow.contrib.layers import flatten, conv2d, fully_connected
from collections import deque, Counter
import random
from datetime import datetime
```

We can use any of the Atari gaming environments given here: `http://gym.openai.com/ envs/#atari`.

In this example, we use the Pac-Man game environment:

```
env = gym.make("MsPacman-v0")
n_outputs = env.action_space.n
```

The Pac-Man environment is shown here:

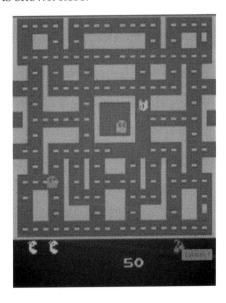

Now we define a `preprocess_observation` function for preprocessing our input game screen. We reduce the image size and convert the image to grayscale:

```
color = np.array([210, 164, 74]).mean()

def preprocess_observation(obs):

    # Crop and resize the image
    img = obs[1:176:2, ::2]

    # Convert the image to greyscale
    img = img.mean(axis=2)

    # Improve image contrast
    img[img==color] = 0

    # Next we normalize the image from -1 to +1
    img = (img - 128) / 128 - 1

    return img.reshape(88,80,1)
```

Okay, now we define a `q_network` function for building our Q network. The input to our Q network will be the game state X.

We build a Q network with three convolutional layers with the same padding, followed by a fully connected layer:

```
tf.reset_default_graph()

def q_network(X, name_scope):
    # Initialize layers
    initializer = tf.contrib.layers.variance_scaling_initializer()

    with tf.variable_scope(name_scope) as scope:

        # initialize the convolutional layers
        layer_1 = conv2d(X, num_outputs=32, kernel_size=(8,8), stride=4,
padding='SAME', weights_initializer=initializer)
        tf.summary.histogram('layer_1',layer_1)
        layer_2 = conv2d(layer_1, num_outputs=64, kernel_size=(4,4),
stride=2, padding='SAME', weights_initializer=initializer)
        tf.summary.histogram('layer_2',layer_2)
        layer_3 = conv2d(layer_2, num_outputs=64, kernel_size=(3,3),
stride=1, padding='SAME', weights_initializer=initializer)
        tf.summary.histogram('layer_3',layer_3)
        # Flatten the result of layer_3 before feeding to the
        # fully connected layer
```

```
        flat = flatten(layer_3)

        fc = fully_connected(flat, num_outputs=128,
weights_initializer=initializer)
        tf.summary.histogram('fc',fc)
        output = fully_connected(fc, num_outputs=n_outputs,
activation_fn=None, weights_initializer=initializer)
        tf.summary.histogram('output',output)

        # Vars will store the parameters of the network such as weights
        vars = {v.name[len(scope.name):]: v for v in
tf.get_collection(key=tf.GraphKeys.TRAINABLE_VARIABLES, scope=scope.name)}
        return vars, output
```

Next, we define an `epsilon_greedy` function for performing the epsilon-greedy policy. In the epsilon-greedy policy, we either select the best action with the probability 1-epsilon or a random action with the probability epsilon.

We use a decaying epsilon-greedy policy where the value of epsilon will be decaying over time as we don't want to explore forever. So, over time, our policy will be exploiting only good actions:

```
epsilon = 0.5
eps_min = 0.05
eps_max = 1.0
eps_decay_steps = 500000
def epsilon_greedy(action, step):
    p = np.random.random(1).squeeze()
    epsilon = max(eps_min, eps_max - (eps_max-eps_min) *
step/eps_decay_steps)
    if np.random.rand() < epsilon:
        return np.random.randint(n_outputs)
    else:
        return action
```

Now, we initialize our experience replay buffer of length 20000, which holds the experience.

We store all the agent's experiences (state, action, rewards) in the experience replay buffer and we sample this mini batch of experiences for training the network:

```
def sample_memories(batch_size):
    perm_batch = np.random.permutation(len(exp_buffer))[:batch_size]
    mem = np.array(exp_buffer)[perm_batch]
    return mem[:,0], mem[:,1], mem[:,2], mem[:,3], mem[:,4]
```

Next, we define all our hyperparameters:

```
num_episodes = 800
batch_size = 48
input_shape = (None, 88, 80, 1)
learning_rate = 0.001
X_shape = (None, 88, 80, 1)
discount_factor = 0.97

global_step = 0
copy_steps = 100
steps_train = 4
start_steps = 2000
logdir = 'logs'
```

Now we define the `placeholder` for our input, such as the game state:

```
X = tf.placeholder(tf.float32, shape=X_shape)
```

We define a boolean called `in_training_mode` to toggle the training:

```
in_training_mode = tf.placeholder(tf.bool)
```

We build our Q network, which takes the input X and generates Q values for all the actions in the state:

```
mainQ, mainQ_outputs = q_network(X, 'mainQ')
```

Similarly, we build our target Q network:

```
targetQ, targetQ_outputs = q_network(X, 'targetQ')
```

Define the `placeholder` for our action values:

```
X_action = tf.placeholder(tf.int32, shape=(None,))
Q_action = tf.reduce_sum(targetQ_outputs * tf.one_hot(X_action, n_outputs),
axis=-1, keep_dims=True)
```

Copy the main Q network parameters to the target Q network:

```
copy_op = [tf.assign(main_name, targetQ[var_name]) for var_name, main_name
in mainQ.items()]
copy_target_to_main = tf.group(*copy_op)
```

Define a `placeholder` for our output, such as action:

```
y = tf.placeholder(tf.float32, shape=(None,1))
```

Now we calculate the loss, which is the difference between the actual value and predicted value:

```
loss = tf.reduce_mean(tf.square(y - Q_action))
```

We use `AdamOptimizer` for minimizing the loss:

```
optimizer = tf.train.AdamOptimizer(learning_rate)
training_op = optimizer.minimize(loss)
```

Set up the log files for visualization in TensorBoard:

```
loss_summary = tf.summary.scalar('LOSS', loss)
merge_summary = tf.summary.merge_all()
file_writer = tf.summary.FileWriter(logdir, tf.get_default_graph())
```

Next, we start the TensorFlow session and run the model:

```
init = tf.global_variables_initializer()
with tf.Session() as sess:
    init.run()
    # for each episode
    for i in range(num_episodes):
        done = False
        obs = env.reset()
        epoch = 0
        episodic_reward = 0
        actions_counter = Counter()
        episodic_loss = []

        # while the state is not the terminal state
        while not done:

           #env.render()
            # get the preprocessed game screen
            obs = preprocess_observation(obs)

            # feed the game screen and get the Q values for each action
```

```
        actions = mainQ_outputs.eval(feed_dict={X:[obs],
in_training_mode:False})

        # get the action
        action = np.argmax(actions, axis=-1)
        actions_counter[str(action)] += 1

        # select the action using epsilon greedy policy
        action = epsilon_greedy(action, global_step)
        # now perform the action and move to the next state,
        # next_obs, receive reward
        next_obs, reward, done, _ = env.step(action)

        # Store this transition as an experience in the replay buffer
        exp_buffer.append([obs, action,
preprocess_observation(next_obs), reward, done])
        # After certain steps, we train our Q network with samples from
the experience replay buffer
        if global_step % steps_train == 0 and global_step >
start_steps:
            # sample experience
            o_obs, o_act, o_next_obs, o_rew, o_done =
sample_memories(batch_size)

            # states
            o_obs = [x for x in o_obs]

            # next states
            o_next_obs = [x for x in o_next_obs]

            # next actions
            next_act = mainQ_outputs.eval(feed_dict={X:o_next_obs,
in_training_mode:False})


            # reward
            y_batch = o_rew + discount_factor * np.max(next_act,
axis=-1) * (1-o_done)

            # merge all summaries and write to the file
            mrg_summary = merge_summary.eval(feed_dict={X:o_obs,
y:np.expand_dims(y_batch, axis=-1), X_action:o_act,
in_training_mode:False})
            file_writer.add_summary(mrg_summary, global_step)
```

```
            # now we train the network and calculate loss
            train_loss, _ = sess.run([loss, training_op],
feed_dict={X:o_obs, y:np.expand_dims(y_batch, axis=-1), X_action:o_act,
in_training_mode:True})
            episodic_loss.append(train_loss)
        # after some interval we copy our main Q network weights to
target Q network
        if (global_step+1) % copy_steps == 0 and global_step >
start_steps:
            copy_target_to_main.run()
        obs = next_obs
        epoch += 1
        global_step += 1
        episodic_reward += reward
    print('Epoch', epoch, 'Reward', episodic_reward,)
```

You can see the output as follows:

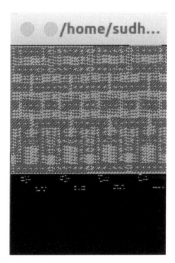

We can see the computation graph of the DQN in TensorBoard as follows:

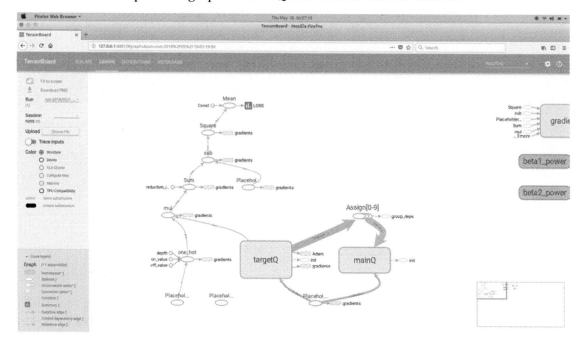

We can visualize the distribution of weights in both our main and target networks:

We can also see the loss:

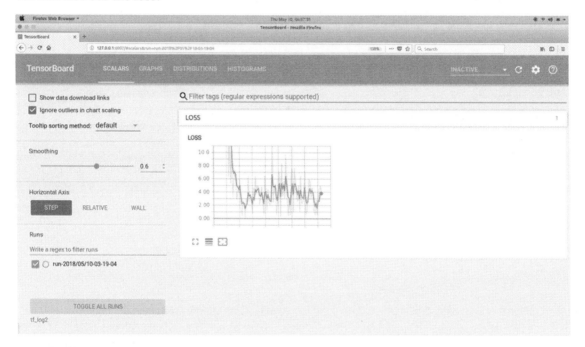

Double DQN

Deep Q learning is pretty cool, right? It has generalized its learning to play any Atari game. But the problem with DQN is that it tends to overestimate Q values. This is because of the max operator in the Q learning equation. The max operator uses the same value for both selecting and evaluating an action. What do I mean by that? Let's suppose we are in a state s and we have five actions a_1 to a_5. Let's say a_3 is the best action. When we estimate Q values for all these actions in the state s, the estimated Q values will have some noise and differ from the actual value. Due to this noise, action a_2 will get a higher value than the optimal action a_3. Now, if we select the best action as the one that has maximum value, we will end up selecting a suboptimal action a_2 instead of optimal action a_3.

We can solve this problem by having two separate Q functions, each learning independently. One Q function is used to select an action and the other Q function is used to evaluate an action. We can implement this by just tweaking the target function of DQN. Recall the target function of DQN:

$$y_i^{DQN} = r + \gamma max_{a'} Q(s', a'; \theta')$$

We can modify our target function as follows:

$$y_i^{DoubleDQN} = r + \gamma Q(s, argmax Q(s, a; \theta^-); \theta')$$

In the preceding equation, we have two Q functions each with different weights. So a Q function with weights θ' is used to select the action and the other Q function with weights θ^- is used to evaluate the action. We can also switch the roles of these two Q functions.

Prioritized experience replay

In DQN architecture, we use experience replay to remove correlations between the training samples. However, uniformly sampling transitions from the replay memory is not an optimal method. Instead, we can prioritize transitions and sample according to priority. Prioritizing transitions helps the network to learn swiftly and effectively. How do we prioritize the transitions? We prioritize the transitions that have a high TD error. We know that a TD error specifies the difference between the estimated Q value and the actual Q value. So, transitions with a high TD error are the transition we have to focus on and learn from because those are the transitions that deviate from our estimation. Intuitively, let us say you try to solve a set of problems, but you fail in solving two of these problems. You then give priority to those two problems alone to focus on what went wrong and try to fix that:

We use two types of prioritization—proportional prioritization and rank-based prioritization.

In **proportional prioritization**, we define the priority as:

$$p_i = (\delta_i + \epsilon)^\alpha$$

p_i is the priority of the transition i, δ_i is the TD error of transition i, and ϵ is simply some positive constant value that makes sure that every transition has non-zero priority. When δ is zero, adding ϵ makes the transition have a priority instead of zero priority. However, the transition will have lower priority than the transitions whose δ is not zero. The α exponent denotes the amount of prioritization being used. When α is zero, then it is simply the uniform case.

Now, we can translate this priority into a probability using the following formula:

$$P_i = \frac{p_i}{\sum_k p_k}$$

In rank-based prioritization, we define the priority as:

$$p_i = \left(\frac{1}{rank(i)}\right)^\alpha$$

rank(i) specifies the location of the transition i in the replay buffer where the transitions are sorted from high TD error to low TD error. After calculating the priority, we can convert the priority into a probability using the same formula, $P_i = \frac{p_i}{\sum_k p_k}$.

Dueling network architecture

We know that the Q function specifies how good it is for an agent to perform an action a in the state s and the value function specifies how good it is for an agent to be in a state s. Now we introduce a new function called an advantage function which can be defined as the difference between the value function and the advantage function. The advantage function specifies how good it is for an agent to perform an action a compared to other actions.

Thus, the value function specifies the goodness of a state and the advantage function specifies the goodness of an action. What would happen if we were to combine the value function and advantage function? It would tell us how good it is for an agent to perform an action *a* in a state *s* that is actually our *Q* function. So we can define our *Q* function as a sum of a value function and an advantage function, as in $Q(s, a) = V(s) + A(a)$.

Now we will see how the dueling network architecture works. The following diagram shows the architecture of dueling DQN:

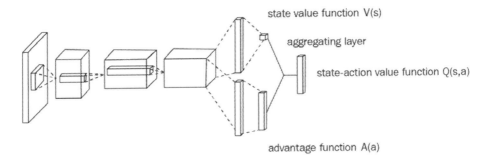

The architecture of dueling DQN is essentially the same as DQN, except that the fully connected layer at the end is divided into two streams. One stream computes the value function, and the other stream computes the advantage function. Finally, we combine these two streams using the aggregate layer and get the Q function.

Why do we have to break our Q function computation into two streams? In many states, it is not important to compute value estimates of all the actions, especially when we have a large action space in a state; then most of the actions will not have any effect on the state. Also, there could be many actions with redundant effects. In these cases, dueling DQN estimates the Q values more precisely than the existing DQN architecture:

- The first stream, as in value function stream, is useful when we have a large number of actions in the state and when estimating a value of each action is not really important
- The second stream, as in advantage function stream, is useful when the network has to decide which action is preferred over the other

The aggregator layer combines the value of these two streams and produces the *Q* function. Thus, a dueling network is more effective and robust than the standard DQN architecture.

Summary

In this chapter, we have learned about one of the very popular deep reinforcement learning algorithms called DQN. We saw how deep neural networks are used to approximate the Q function. We also learned how to build an agent to play Atari games. Later, we looked at several advancements to the DQN, such as double DQN, which is used to avoid overestimating Q values. We then looked at prioritized experience replay, for prioritizing the experience, and dueling network architecture, which breaks down the Q function computation into two streams, called value stream and advantage stream.

In the next chapter, Chapter 9, *Playing Doom with Deep Recurrent Q Network*, we will look at a really cool variant of DQNs called DRQN, which makes use of an RNN for approximating a Q function.

Questions

The question list is as follows:

1. What is DQN?
2. What is the need for experience replay?
3. Why do we keep a separate target network?
4. Why is DQN overestimating?
5. How does double DQN avoid overestimating the Q value?
6. How are experiences prioritized in prioritized experience replay?
7. What is the need for duel architecture?

Further reading

- **DQN paper**: https://storage.googleapis.com/deepmind-media/dqn/DQNNaturePaper.pdf
- **Double DQN paper**: https://arxiv.org/pdf/1509.06461.pdf
- **Dueling network architecture**: https://arxiv.org/pdf/1511.06581.pdf

9
Playing Doom with a Deep Recurrent Q Network

In the last chapter, we saw how to build an agent using a **Deep Q Network (DQN)** in order to play Atari games. We have taken advantage of neural networks for approximating the Q function, used the **convolutional neural network (CNN)** to understand the input game screen, and taken the past four game screens to better understand the current game state. In this chapter, we will learn how to improve the performance of our DQN by taking advantage of the **recurrent neural network (RNN)**. We will also look at what is partially observable with the **Markov Decision Process (MDP)** and how we can solve that using a **Deep Recurrent Q Network (DRQN)**. Following this, we will learn how to build an agent to play the game Doom using a DRQN. Finally, we will see a variant of DRQN called **Deep Attention Recurrent Q Network (DARQN)**, which augments the attention mechanism to the DRQN architecture.

In this chapter, you will learn the following topics:

- DRQN
- Partially observable MDP
- The architecture of DRQN
- How to build an agent to play the game Doom using a DRQN
- DARQN

DRQN

So, why do we need DRQN when our DQN performed at a human level at Atari games? To answer this question, let us understand the problem of the **partially observable Markov Decision Process (POMDP)**. An environment is called a partially observable MDP when we have a limited set of information available about the environment. So far, in the previous chapters, we have seen a fully observable MDP where we know all possible actions and states—although the agent might be unaware of transition and reward probabilities, it had complete knowledge of the environment, for example, a frozen lake environment, where we clearly know about all the states and actions of the environment; we easily modeled that environment as a fully observable MDP. But most of the real-world environments are only partially observable; we cannot see all the states. Consider the agent learning to walk in the real-world environment; obviously, the agent will not have complete knowledge of the environment, it will have no information outside its view. In POMDP, states provide only partial information, but keeping the information about past states in the memory might help the agent better understand the nature of the environment and improve the policy. Thus, in POMDP, we need to retain the information about previous states in order to take the optimal action.

To recollect what we learned in previous chapters, consider the game Pong, shown in the following. By just looking at the current game screen, we can tell the position of the ball, but we also need to know the direction in which the ball is moving and the velocity of the ball, so that we can take the optimal action. Just looking at the current game screen, however, does not give us the direction and velocity of the ball:

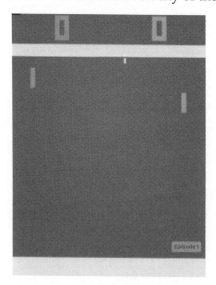

To overcome this, instead of considering only the current game screen, we will take the past four game screens to understand the direction and velocity of the ball. This is what we have seen in DQN. We feed the past four game screens as the input to the convolutional layer, along with the current game screen, and received the Q values for all possible actions in the state. But, do you think using only the past four screens will help us in understanding different environments? There will be some environments where we might even require the past 100 game screens to better understand the current game state. But, stacking the past *n* game screens will slow down our training process, and it will also increase the size of our experience replay buffer.

So, we can take the advantage of the RNN here to understand and retain information about the previous states as long as it is required. In `Chapter 7`, *Deep Learning Fundamentals*, we learned how **Long Short-Term Memory recurrent neural networks (LSTM RNN)** are used for text generation and how they understand the context of words by retaining, forgetting, and updating the information as required. We will modify the DQN architecture by augmenting with the LSTM layer to understand the previous information. In DQN architecture, we replace the first post convolutional fully connected layer with the LSTM RNN. In this way, we can also solve the problem of partial observability, as now our agent has the ability to remember the past states and can improve the policy.

Architecture of DRQN

The architecture of DRQN is shown next. It is similar to DQN, but we replace the first post convolutional fully connected layer with the LSTM RNN, shown as follows:

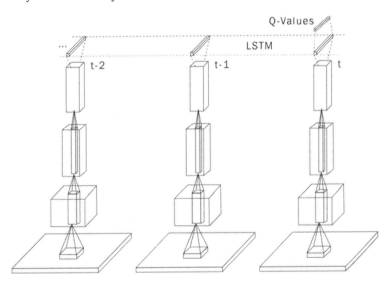

Thus, we pass the game screen as an input to the convolutional layer. The convolutional layer convolves the image and produces feature maps. The resulting feature map is then passed to the LSTM layer. The LSTM layer has the memory for holding information. The LSTM layer retains the information about important previous game states and updates its memory over time steps as required. It outputs Q values after passing through a fully connected layer. Therefore, unlike DQN, we don't estimate $Q(s_t, a_t)$ directly. Instead, we estimate $Q(h_t, a_t)$ where h_t is the input returned by the network at the previous time step. That is, $h_t = LSTM(h_{t-1}, o_t)$. As we are using RNN, we train our network by backpropagation through time.

Wait. What about the experience replay buffer? In DQN, to avoid correlated experience, we used an experience replay, which stores the game transition, and we used a random batch of experience to train the network. In the case of DRQN, we store an entire episode in an experience buffer and we randomly sample n steps from a random batch of episodes. So, in this way, we can accommodate both randomization and also an experience that actually follows another.

Training an agent to play Doom

Doom is a very popular first-person shooter game. The goal of the game is to kill monsters. Doom is another example of a partially observable MDP as the agent's (player) view is limited to 90 degrees. The agent has no idea about the rest of the environment. Now, we will see how can we use DRQN to train our agent to play Doom.

Instead of OpenAI Gym, we will use the ViZDoom package to simulate the Doom environment to train our agent. To learn more about the ViZDoom package, check out its official website at http://vizdoom.cs.put.edu.pl/. We can install ViZDoom simply by using the following command:

```
pip install vizdoom
```

ViZDoom provides a lot of Doom scenarios and those scenarios can be found in the package folder vizdoom/scenarios.

Basic Doom game

Before diving in, let us familiarize ourselves with a `vizdoom` environment by seeing a basic example:

1. Let's load the necessary libraries:

    ```
    from vizdoom import *
    import random
    import time
    ```

2. Create an instance to the `DoomGame`:

    ```
    game = DoomGame()
    ```

3. As we know ViZDoom provides a lot of Doom scenarios, let us load the basic scenario:

    ```
    game.load_config("basic.cfg")
    ```

4. The `init()` method initializes the game with the scenario:

    ```
    game.init()
    ```

5. Now, let's define the one with hot encoded `actions`:

    ```
    shoot = [0, 0, 1]
    left = [1, 0, 0]
    right = [0, 1, 0]
    actions = [shoot, left, right]
    ```

6. Now, let us start playing the game:

    ```
    no_of_episodes = 10

    for i in range(no_of_episodes):
        # for each episode start the game
        game.new_episode()
        # loop until the episode is over
        while not game.is_episode_finished():
            # get the game state
            state = game.get_state()
            img = state.screen_buffer
            # get the game variables
            misc = state.game_variables
    ```

```
# perform some action randomly and receive reward
reward = game.make_action(random.choice(actions))
print(reward)
# we will set some time before starting the next episode
time.sleep(2)
```

Once you run the program, you can see the output as follows:

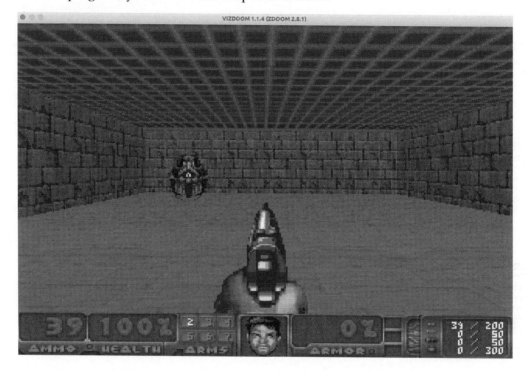

Doom with DRQN

Now, let us see how to make use of the DRQN algorithm to train our agent to play Doom. We assign positive rewards for successfully killing the monsters and negative rewards for losing life, suicide, and losing ammo (bullets). You can get the complete code as a Jupyter notebook with the explanation at `https://github.com/sudharsan13296/Hands-On-Reinforcement-Learning-With-Python/blob/master/09.` `%20Playing%20Doom%20Game%20using%20DRQN/9.5%20Doom%20Game%20Using%20DRQN.ipynb.` The credits for the code used in this section go to **Luthanicus** (`https://github.com/Luthanicus/losaltoshackathon-drqn`).

First, let us import all the necessary libraries:

```
import tensorflow as tf
import numpy as np
import matplotlib.pyplot as plt
from vizdoom import *
import timeit
import math
import os
import sys
```

Now, let us define the `get_input_shape` function to compute the final shape of the input image after it gets convolved after the convolutional layer:

```
def get_input_shape(Image,Filter,Stride):
    layer1 = math.ceil(((Image - Filter + 1) / Stride))
    o1 = math.ceil((layer1 / Stride))
    layer2 = math.ceil(((o1 - Filter + 1) / Stride))
    o2 = math.ceil((layer2 / Stride))
    layer3 = math.ceil(((o2 - Filter + 1) / Stride))
    o3 = math.ceil((layer3 / Stride))
    return int(o3)
```

We will now define the DRQN class, which implements the DRQN algorithm. Check the comments that precede each line of code to understand it:

```
class DRQN():
    def __init__(self, input_shape, num_actions, initial_learning_rate):
        # first, we initialize all the hyperparameters

        self.tfcast_type = tf.float32
        # shape of our input, which would be (length, width, channels)
        self.input_shape = input_shape
        # number of actions in the environment
        self.num_actions = num_actions
        # learning rate for the neural network
        self.learning_rate = initial_learning_rate
        # now we will define the hyperparameters of the convolutional
neural network

        # filter size
        self.filter_size = 5
        # number of filters
        self.num_filters = [16, 32, 64]
        # stride size
        self.stride = 2
        # pool size
```

```
        self.poolsize = 2
        # shape of our convolutional layer
        self.convolution_shape = get_input_shape(input_shape[0],
self.filter_size, self.stride) * get_input_shape(input_shape[1],
self.filter_size, self.stride) * self.num_filters[2]
        # now, we define the hyperparameters of our recurrent neural
network and the final feed forward layer
        # number of neurons
        self.cell_size = 100
        # number of hidden layers
        self.hidden_layer = 50
        # drop out probability
        self.dropout_probability = [0.3, 0.2]

        # hyperparameters for optimization
        self.loss_decay_rate = 0.96
        self.loss_decay_steps = 180

        # initialize all the variables for the CNN

        # we initialize the placeholder for input whose shape would be
(length, width, channel)
        self.input = tf.placeholder(shape = (self.input_shape[0],
self.input_shape[1], self.input_shape[2]), dtype = self.tfcast_type)
        # we will also initialize the shape of the target vector whose
shape is equal to the number of actions
        self.target_vector = tf.placeholder(shape = (self.num_actions, 1),
dtype = self.tfcast_type)

        # initialize feature maps for our corresponding 3 filters
        self.features1 = tf.Variable(initial_value =
np.random.rand(self.filter_size, self.filter_size, input_shape[2],
self.num_filters[0]),
                                        dtype = self.tfcast_type)
        self.features2 = tf.Variable(initial_value =
np.random.rand(self.filter_size, self.filter_size, self.num_filters[0],
self.num_filters[1]),
                                        dtype = self.tfcast_type)
        self.features3 = tf.Variable(initial_value =
np.random.rand(self.filter_size, self.filter_size, self.num_filters[1],
self.num_filters[2]),
                                        dtype = self.tfcast_type)

        # initialize variables for RNN
        # recall how RNN works from chapter 7
        self.h = tf.Variable(initial_value = np.zeros((1, self.cell_size)),
dtype = self.tfcast_type)
        # hidden to hidden weight matrix
```

```
        self.rW = tf.Variable(initial_value = np.random.uniform(
                                               low = -np.sqrt(6. /
(self.convolution_shape + self.cell_size)),
                                               high = np.sqrt(6. /
(self.convolution_shape + self.cell_size)),
                                               size = (self.convolution_shape,
self.cell_size)),
                                dtype = self.tfcast_type)
        # input to hidden weight matrix
        self.rU = tf.Variable(initial_value = np.random.uniform(
                                               low = -np.sqrt(6. / (2 *
self.cell_size)),
                                               high = np.sqrt(6. / (2 *
self.cell_size)),
                                               size = (self.cell_size,
self.cell_size)),
                                dtype = self.tfcast_type)
        # hidden to output weight matrix
        self.rV = tf.Variable(initial_value = np.random.uniform(
                                               low = -np.sqrt(6. / (2 *
self.cell_size)),
                                               high = np.sqrt(6. / (2 *
self.cell_size)),
                                               size = (self.cell_size,
self.cell_size)),
                                dtype = self.tfcast_type)
        # bias
        self.rb = tf.Variable(initial_value = np.zeros(self.cell_size),
dtype = self.tfcast_type)
        self.rc = tf.Variable(initial_value = np.zeros(self.cell_size),
dtype = self.tfcast_type)

        # initialize weights and bias of feed forward network
        # weights
        self.fW = tf.Variable(initial_value = np.random.uniform(
                                               low = -np.sqrt(6. /
(self.cell_size + self.num_actions)),
                                               high = np.sqrt(6. /
(self.cell_size + self.num_actions)),
                                               size = (self.cell_size,
self.num_actions)),
                                dtype = self.tfcast_type)
        # bias
        self.fb = tf.Variable(initial_value = np.zeros(self.num_actions),
dtype = self.tfcast_type)

        # learning rate
        self.step_count = tf.Variable(initial_value = 0, dtype =
```

```
self.tfcast_type)
        self.learning_rate = tf.train.exponential_decay(self.learning_rate,
                                        self.step_count,
                                        self.loss_decay_steps,
                                        self.loss_decay_steps,
                                        staircase = False)
        # now let us build the network

        # first convolutional layer
        self.conv1 = tf.nn.conv2d(input = tf.reshape(self.input, shape =
(1, self.input_shape[0], self.input_shape[1], self.input_shape[2])), filter
= self.features1, strides = [1, self.stride, self.stride, 1], padding =
"VALID")
        self.relu1 = tf.nn.relu(self.conv1)
        self.pool1 = tf.nn.max_pool(self.relu1, ksize = [1, self.poolsize,
self.poolsize, 1], strides = [1, self.stride, self.stride, 1], padding =
"SAME")

        # second convolutional layer
        self.conv2 = tf.nn.conv2d(input = self.pool1, filter =
self.features2, strides = [1, self.stride, self.stride, 1], padding =
"VALID")
        self.relu2 = tf.nn.relu(self.conv2)
        self.pool2 = tf.nn.max_pool(self.relu2, ksize = [1, self.poolsize,
self.poolsize, 1], strides = [1, self.stride, self.stride, 1], padding =
"SAME")

        # third convolutional layer
        self.conv3 = tf.nn.conv2d(input = self.pool2, filter =
self.features3, strides = [1, self.stride, self.stride, 1], padding =
"VALID")
        self.relu3 = tf.nn.relu(self.conv3)
        self.pool3 = tf.nn.max_pool(self.relu3, ksize = [1, self.poolsize,
self.poolsize, 1], strides = [1, self.stride, self.stride, 1], padding =
"SAME")

        # add dropout and reshape the input
        self.drop1 = tf.nn.dropout(self.pool3, self.dropout_probability[0])
        self.reshaped_input = tf.reshape(self.drop1, shape = [1, -1])


        # now we build the recurrent neural network, which takes the input
from the last layer of the convolutional network
        self.h = tf.tanh(tf.matmul(self.reshaped_input, self.rW) +
tf.matmul(self.h, self.rU) + self.rb)
        self.o = tf.nn.softmax(tf.matmul(self.h, self.rV) + self.rc)

        # add drop out to RNN
```

```
            self.drop2 = tf.nn.dropout(self.o, self.dropout_probability[1])
            # we feed the result of RNN to the feed forward layer
            self.output = tf.reshape(tf.matmul(self.drop2, self.fW) + self.fb,
    shape = [-1, 1])
            self.prediction = tf.argmax(self.output)

            # compute loss
            self.loss = tf.reduce_mean(tf.square(self.target_vector -
    self.output))
            # we use Adam optimizer for minimizing the error
            self.optimizer = tf.train.AdamOptimizer(self.learning_rate)
            # compute gradients of the loss and update the gradients
            self.gradients = self.optimizer.compute_gradients(self.loss)
            self.update = self.optimizer.apply_gradients(self.gradients)

            self.parameters = (self.features1, self.features2, self.features3,
                               self.rW, self.rU, self.rV, self.rb, self.rc,
                               self.fW, self.fb)
```

Now we define the `ExperienceReplay` class to implement the experience replay buffer. We store all the agent's experience, that is, state, action, and rewards in the experience replay buffer, and we sample this minibatch of experience for training the network:

```
class ExperienceReplay():
    def __init__(self, buffer_size):
        # buffer for holding the transition
        self.buffer = []
        # size of the buffer
        self.buffer_size = buffer_size
    # we remove the old transition if the buffer size has reached it's
    limit. Think off the buffer as a queue, when the new
    # one comes, the old one goes off
    def appendToBuffer(self, memory_tuplet):
        if len(self.buffer) > self.buffer_size:
            for i in range(len(self.buffer) - self.buffer_size):
                self.buffer.remove(self.buffer[0])
        self.buffer.append(memory_tuplet)
    # define a function called sample for sampling some random n number of
    transitions
    def sample(self, n):
        memories = []
        for i in range(n):
            memory_index = np.random.randint(0, len(self.buffer))
            memories.append(self.buffer[memory_index])
        return memories
```

Now, we define the `train` function for training our network:

```
def train(num_episodes, episode_length, learning_rate, scenario =
"deathmatch.cfg", map_path = 'map02', render = False):
    # discount parameter for Q-value computation
    discount_factor = .99
    # frequency for updating the experience in the buffer
    update_frequency = 5
    store_frequency = 50
    # for printing the output
    print_frequency = 1000

    # initialize variables for storing total rewards and total loss
    total_reward = 0
    total_loss = 0
    old_q_value = 0

    # initialize lists for storing the episodic rewards and losses
    rewards = []
    losses = []

    # okay, now let us get to the action!
    # first, we initialize our doomgame environment
    game = DoomGame()
    # specify the path where our scenario file is located
    game.set_doom_scenario_path(scenario)
    # specify the path of map file
    game.set_doom_map(map_path)

    # then we set screen resolution and screen format
    game.set_screen_resolution(ScreenResolution.RES_256X160)
    game.set_screen_format(ScreenFormat.RGB24)

    # we can add particles and effects we needed by simply setting them to
true or false
    game.set_render_hud(False)
    game.set_render_minimal_hud(False)
    game.set_render_crosshair(False)
    game.set_render_weapon(True)
    game.set_render_decals(False)
    game.set_render_particles(False)
    game.set_render_effects_sprites(False)
    game.set_render_messages(False)
    game.set_render_corpses(False)
    game.set_render_screen_flashes(True)

    # now we will specify buttons that should be available to the agent
```

```python
    game.add_available_button(Button.MOVE_LEFT)
    game.add_available_button(Button.MOVE_RIGHT)
    game.add_available_button(Button.TURN_LEFT)
    game.add_available_button(Button.TURN_RIGHT)
    game.add_available_button(Button.MOVE_FORWARD)
    game.add_available_button(Button.MOVE_BACKWARD)
    game.add_available_button(Button.ATTACK)
    # okay, now we will add one more button called delta. The preceding
button will only
    # work like keyboard keys and will have only boolean values.

    # so we use delta button, which emulates a mouse device which will have
positive and negative values
    # and it will be useful in environment for exploring
    game.add_available_button(Button.TURN_LEFT_RIGHT_DELTA, 90)
    game.add_available_button(Button.LOOK_UP_DOWN_DELTA, 90)

    # initialize an array for actions
    actions = np.zeros((game.get_available_buttons_size(),
game.get_available_buttons_size()))
    count = 0
    for i in actions:
        i[count] = 1
        count += 1
    actions = actions.astype(int).tolist()


    # then we add the game variables, ammo, health, and killcount
    game.add_available_game_variable(GameVariable.AMMO0)
    game.add_available_game_variable(GameVariable.HEALTH)
    game.add_available_game_variable(GameVariable.KILLCOUNT)

    # we set episode_timeout to terminate the episode after some time step
    # we also set episode_start_time which is useful for skipping initial
events
    game.set_episode_timeout(6 * episode_length)
    game.set_episode_start_time(10)
    game.set_window_visible(render)
    # we can also enable sound by setting set_sound_enable to true
    game.set_sound_enabled(False)

    # we set living reward to 0, which rewards the agent for each move it
does even though the move is not useful
    game.set_living_reward(0)

    # doom has different modes such as player, spectator, asynchronous
player, and asynchronous spectator
    # in spectator mode humans will play and agent will learn from it.
```

```
    # in player mode, the agent actually plays the game, so we use player
mode.
    game.set_mode(Mode.PLAYER)

    # okay, So now we, initialize the game environment
    game.init()

    # now, let us create instance to our DRQN class and create our both
actor and target DRQN networks
    actionDRQN = DRQN((160, 256, 3), game.get_available_buttons_size() - 2,
learning_rate)
    targetDRQN = DRQN((160, 256, 3), game.get_available_buttons_size() - 2,
learning_rate)
    # we will also create an instance to the ExperienceReplay class with
the buffer size of 1000
    experiences = ExperienceReplay(1000)

    # for storing the models
    saver = tf.train.Saver({v.name: v for v in actionDRQN.parameters},
max_to_keep = 1)

    # now let us start the training process
    # we initialize variables for sampling and storing transitions from the
experience buffer
    sample = 5
    store = 50
    # start the tensorflow session
    with tf.Session() as sess:
        # initialize all tensorflow variables
        sess.run(tf.global_variables_initializer())
        for episode in range(num_episodes):
            # start the new episode
            game.new_episode()
            # play the episode till it reaches the episode length
            for frame in range(episode_length):
                # get the game state
                state = game.get_state()
                s = state.screen_buffer
                # select the action
                a = actionDRQN.prediction.eval(feed_dict =
{actionDRQN.input: s})[0]
                action = actions[a]
                # perform the action and store the reward
                reward = game.make_action(action)
                # update total reward
                total_reward += reward

                # if the episode is over then break
```

```
            if game.is_episode_finished():
                break
            # store the transition to our experience buffer
            if (frame % store) == 0:
                experiences.appendToBuffer((s, action, reward))

            # sample experience from the experience buffer
            if (frame % sample) == 0:
                memory = experiences.sample(1)
                mem_frame = memory[0][0]
                mem_reward = memory[0][2]
                # now, train the network
                Q1 = actionDRQN.output.eval(feed_dict =
{actionDRQN.input: mem_frame})
                Q2 = targetDRQN.output.eval(feed_dict =
{targetDRQN.input: mem_frame})

                # set learning rate
                learning_rate = actionDRQN.learning_rate.eval()

                # calculate Q value
                Qtarget = old_q_value + learning_rate * (mem_reward +
discount_factor * Q2 - old_q_value)
                # update old Q value
                old_q_value = Qtarget

                # compute Loss
                loss = actionDRQN.loss.eval(feed_dict =
{actionDRQN.target_vector: Qtarget, actionDRQN.input: mem_frame})
                # update total loss
                total_loss += loss

                # update both networks
                actionDRQN.update.run(feed_dict =
{actionDRQN.target_vector: Qtarget, actionDRQN.input: mem_frame})
                targetDRQN.update.run(feed_dict =
{targetDRQN.target_vector: Qtarget, targetDRQN.input: mem_frame})

        rewards.append((episode, total_reward))
        losses.append((episode, total_loss))

        print("Episode %d - Reward = %.3f, Loss = %.3f." % (episode,
total_reward, total_loss))

        total_reward = 0
        total_loss = 0
```

Let us train for 10000 episodes, where each episode has a length of 300:

```
train(num_episodes = 10000, episode_length = 300, learning_rate = 0.01,
render = True)
```

When you run the program, you can see the output shown as follows, and you can see how our agent is learning through episodes:

DARQN

We have improved our DQN architecture by adding a recurrent layer, which captures temporal dependency, and we called it DRQN. Do you think we can improve our DRQN architecture further? Yes. We can further improve our DRQN architecture by adding the attention layer on top of the convolutional layer. So, what is the function of the attention layer? Attention implies the literal meaning of the word. Attention mechanisms are widely used in image captioning, object detection, and so on. Consider the task of neural networks captioning the image; to understand what is in the image, the network has to give attention to the specific object in the image for generating the caption.

Similarly, when we add the attention layer to our DRQN, we can select and pay attention to small regions of the image, and ultimately this reduces the number of parameters in the network and also reduces the training and testing time. Unlike DRQN, LSTM layers in DARQN not only stored previous state information for taking the next optimal action; it also stores information for deciding which region of an image to focus on next.

Architecture of DARQN

The architecture of DARQN is shown as follows:

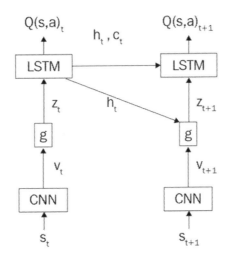

It consists of three layers; convolutional, attention, and LSTM recurrent layers. The game screen is fed as the image to the convolutional network. The convolutional network processes the image and produces the feature maps. The feature maps then feed into the attention layer. The attention layer transforms them into a vector and results in their linear combination, called context vectors. The context vectors, along with previous hidden states, are then passed to the LSTM layer. The LSTM layer gives two outputs; in one, it gives the Q value for deciding what action to perform in a state, and in the other, it helps the attention network decide what region of the image to focus on in the next time step so that better context vectors can be generated.

The attention is of two types:

- **Soft attention**: We know that feature maps produced by the convolutional layer are fed as an input to the attention layer, which then produces the context vector. With soft attention, these context vectors are simply the weighted average of all the output (feature maps) produced by the convolutional layer. Weights are chosen according to the relative importance of the features.
- **Hard attention**: With hard attention, we focus only on the particular location of an image at a time step t according to some location selection policy π. This policy is represented by a neural network whose weights are the policy parameters and the output of the network is the location selection probability. However, hard attentions are not much better than soft attentions.

Summary

In this chapter, we learned how DRQN is used to remember information about the previous states and how it overcomes the problem of partially observable MDP. We have seen how to train our agent to play the game Doom using a DRQN algorithm. We have also learned about DARQN as an improvement to DRQN, which adds an attention layer on top of the convolution layer. Following this, we saw the two types of attention mechanism; namely, soft and hard attention.

In the next chapter, Chapter 10, *Asynchronous Advantage Actor Critic Network*, we will learn about another interesting deep reinforcement learning algorithm called Asynchronous Advantage Actor Critic network.

Questions

The question list is as follows:

1. What is the difference between DQN and DRQN?
2. What are the shortcomings of DQN?
3. How do we set up an experience replay in DQN?
4. What is the difference between DRQN and DARQN?
5. Why do we need DARQN?
6. What are the different types of attention mechanism?
7. Why do we set a living reward in Doom?

Further reading

Consider the following to further your knowledge:

- **DRQN paper**: https://arxiv.org/pdf/1507.06527.pdf
- **Playing the FPS game using DRQN**: https://arxiv.org/pdf/1609.05521.pdf
- **DARQN paper**: https://arxiv.org/pdf/1512.01693.pdf

10
The Asynchronous Advantage Actor Critic Network

In the previous chapters, we have seen how cool a **Deep Q Network** (**DQN**) is and how it succeeded in generalizing its learning to play a series of Atari games with a human level performance. But the problem we faced is that it required a large amount of computation power and training time. So, Google's DeepMind introduced a new algorithm called the **Asynchronous Advantage Actor Critic** (**A3C**) algorithm, which dominates the other deep reinforcement learning algorithms, as it requires less computation power and training time. The main idea behind A3C is that it uses several agents for learning in parallel and aggregates their overall experience. In this chapter, we will see how A3C networks work. Following this, we will learn how to build an agent to drive up a mountain using A3C.

In this chapter, you will learn the following:

- The Asynchronous Advantage Actor Critic Algorithm
- The three As
- The architecture of A3C
- How A3C works
- Driving up a mountain with A3C
- Visualization in TensorBoard

The Asynchronous Advantage Actor Critic

The A3C network came as a storm and took over the DQN. Aside of the previously stated advantages, it also yields good accuracy compared to other algorithms. It works well in both continuous and discrete action spaces. It uses several agents, and each agent learns in parallel with a different exploration policy in copies of the actual environment. Then, the experience obtained from these agents is aggregated to the global agent. The global agent is also called a master network or global network and other agents are also called the workers. Now, we will see in detail how A3C works and how it differs from the DQN algorithm.

The three As

Before diving in, what does A3C mean? What do the three As signify?

In A3C, the first A, **Asynchronous**, implies how it works. Instead of having a single agent that tries to learn the optimal policy such as in DQN, here, we have multiple agents that interact with the environment. Since we have multiple agents interacting to the environment at the same time, we provide copies of the environment to every agent so that each agent can interact with its own copy of the environment. So, all these multiple agents are called worker agents and we have a separate agent called global network that all the agents report to. The global network aggregates the learning.

The second A is **Advantage**; we have seen what an advantage function is while discussing the dueling network architecture of DQN. The advantage function can be defined as the difference between the Q function and the value function. We know that the Q function specifies how good the action is in a state and the value function specifies how good the state is. Now, think intuitively; what does the difference between these two imply? It tells us how good it is for an agent to perform an action a in a state s compared to all other actions.

The third A is **Actor Critic**; the architecture has two types of network, actor and critic. The role of the actor is to learn a policy and the role of the critic is to evaluate how good the policy learned by the actor is.

The architecture of A3C

Now, let's look at the architecture of A3C. Look at the following diagram:

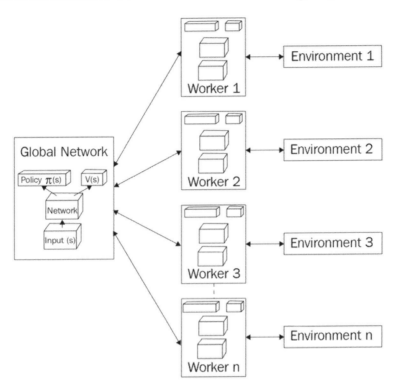

We can understand how A3C works by just looking at the preceding diagram. As we discussed, we can see there are multiple worker agents each interacting with its own copies of the environment. A worker then learns policy and calculates the gradient of the policy loss and updates the gradients to the global network. This global network is updated simultaneously by every agent. One of the advantages of A3C is that, unlike DQN, we don't use experience replay memory here. In fact, that it is one of the greatest advantages of an A3C network. Since we have multiple agents interacting with the environment and aggregating the information to the global network, there will be low to no correlation between the experience. Experience replay needs a lot of memory holding all of the experience. As A3C doesn't need that, our storage space and computation time will be reduced.

How A3C works

First, the worker agent resets the global network, and then they start interacting with the environment. Each worker follows a different exploration policy to learn an optimal policy. Following this, they compute value and policy loss and then they calculate the gradient of the loss and update the gradients to the global network. The cycle continues as the worker agent starts resetting the global network and repeats the same process. Before looking at the value and policy loss function, we will see how the advantage function is calculated. As we know, advantage is the difference between the Q function and the value function:

$$A(s,a) = Q(s,a) - V(s)$$

Since we don't actually calculate the Q value directly in A3C, we make use of discounted return as an estimate of the Q value. The discounted return R can be written as follows:

$$R = r_n + \gamma r_{n-1} + \gamma^2 r_{n-2}$$

We replace the Q function with the discounted return R as follows:

$$A(s,a) = R - V(s)$$

Now, we can write our value loss as the squared difference between the discounted return and the value of a state:

$$ValueLoss(L_v) = \sum (R - V(s))^2$$

And the policy loss can be defined as follows:

$$PolicyLoss(L_p) = Log(\pi(s)) * A(s) * \beta H(\pi)$$

Okay, what is that new term $H(\pi)$? It is the entropy term. It is used to ensure sufficient exploration of policy. Entropy tells us the spread of action probabilities. When the entropy value is high, every action's probability will be the same, so the agent will be unsure as to which action to perform, and when the entropy value is lowered, one action will have a higher probability than the others and the agent can pick up the action that has this high probability. Thus, adding entropy to the loss function encourages the agent to explore further and avoid getting stuck at the local optima.

Driving up a mountain with A3C

Let's understand A3C with a mountain car example. Our agent is the car and it is placed between two mountains. The goal of our agent is to drive up the mountain on the right. However, the car can't drive up the mountain in one pass; it has to drive up back and forth to build the momentum. A high reward will be assigned if our agent spends less energy on driving up. Credits for the code used in this section goes to Stefan Boschenriedter (`https:/
/github.com/stefanbo92/A3C-Continuous`). The environment is shown as follows:

Episode 1

Okay, let's get to the coding! The complete code is available as the Jupyter notebook with an explanation here (`https://github.com/sudharsan13296/Hands-On-Reinforcement-
Learning-With-Python/blob/master/10.
%20Aysnchronous%20Advantage%20Actor%20Critic%20Network/10.
5%20Drive%20up%20the%20Mountain%20Using%20A3C.ipynb`).

First, let's import the necessary libraries:

```
import gym
import multiprocessing
import threading
import numpy as np
import os
import shutil
import matplotlib.pyplot as plt
import tensorflow as tf
```

Now, we will initialize all our parameters:

```
# number of worker agents
no_of_workers = multiprocessing.cpu_count()

# maximum number of steps per episode
no_of_ep_steps = 200

# total number of episodes
no_of_episodes = 2000

global_net_scope = 'Global_Net'

# sets how often the global network should be updated
update_global = 10

# discount factor
gamma = 0.90

# entropy factor
entropy_beta = 0.01

# learning rate for actor
lr_a = 0.0001

# learning rate for critic
lr_c = 0.001

# boolean for rendering the environment
render=False

# directory for storing logs
log_dir = 'logs'
```

Initialize our MountainCar environment:

```
env = gym.make('MountainCarContinuous-v0')
env.reset()
```

Get the number of states and actions, and also the action_bound:

```
no_of_states = env.observation_space.shape[0]
no_of_actions = env.action_space.shape[0]
action_bound = [env.action_space.low, env.action_space.high]
```

We will define our Actor Critic network in an `ActorCritic` class. As usual, we first understand the code of every function in a class and see the final code as a whole at the end. Comments are added to each line of code for better understanding. We will look into the clean uncommented whole code at the end:

```
class ActorCritic(object):
    def __init__(self, scope, sess, globalAC=None):
        # first we initialize the session and RMS prop optimizer for both
        # our actor and critic networks
        self.sess=sess
        self.actor_optimizer = tf.train.RMSPropOptimizer(lr_a,
name='RMSPropA')
        self.critic_optimizer = tf.train.RMSPropOptimizer(lr_c,
name='RMSPropC')

        # now, if our network is global then,
        if scope == global_net_scope:
            with tf.variable_scope(scope):
                # initialize states and build actor and critic network
                self.s = tf.placeholder(tf.float32, [None, no_of_states],
'S')
                # get the parameters of actor and critic networks
                self.a_params, self.c_params = self._build_net(scope)[-2:]
        # if our network is local then,
        else:
            with tf.variable_scope(scope):
                # initialize state, action, and also target value
                # as v_target
                self.s = tf.placeholder(tf.float32, [None, no_of_states],
'S')
                self.a_his = tf.placeholder(tf.float32, [None,
no_of_actions], 'A')
                self.v_target = tf.placeholder(tf.float32, [None, 1],
'Vtarget')
                # since we are in continuous actions space,
                # we will calculate
                # mean and variance for choosing action
                mean, var, self.v, self.a_params, self.c_params =
self._build_net(scope)

                # then we calculate td error as the difference
                # between v_target - v
                td = tf.subtract(self.v_target, self.v, name='TD_error')

                # minimize the TD error
                with tf.name_scope('critic_loss'):
                    self.critic_loss = tf.reduce_mean(tf.square(td))
```

```
                        # update the mean and var value by multiplying mean
                        # with the action bound and adding var with 1e-4

                        with tf.name_scope('wrap_action'):
                            mean, var = mean * action_bound[1], var + 1e-4
                        # we can generate distribution using this updated
                        # mean and var
                        normal_dist = tf.contrib.distributions.Normal(mean, var)
                        # now we shall calculate the actor loss.
                        # Recall the loss function.
                        with tf.name_scope('actor_loss'):
                            # calculate first term of loss which is log(pi(s))
                            log_prob = normal_dist.log_prob(self.a_his)
                            exp_v = log_prob * td
                            # calculate entropy from our action distribution
                            # for ensuring exploration
                            entropy = normal_dist.entropy()
                            # we can define our final loss as
                            self.exp_v = exp_v + entropy_beta * entropy
                            # then, we try to minimize the loss
                            self.actor_loss = tf.reduce_mean(-self.exp_v)
                        # now, we choose an action by drawing from the
                        # distribution and clipping it between action bounds,
                        with tf.name_scope('choose_action'):
                          ˙ self.A =
tf.clip_by_value(tf.squeeze(normal_dist.sample(1), axis=0),
action_bound[0], action_bound[1])
                        # calculate gradients for both of our actor
                        # and critic networks,
                        with tf.name_scope('local_grad'):

                                self.a_grads = tf.gradients(self.actor_loss,
self.a_params)
                                self.c_grads = tf.gradients(self.critic_loss,
self.c_params)


                # now, we update our global network weights,
                with tf.name_scope('sync'):
                    # pull the global network weights to the local networks
                    with tf.name_scope('pull'):
                            self.pull_a_params_op = [l_p.assign(g_p) for l_p, g_p
in zip(self.a_params, globalAC.a_params)]
                            self.pull_c_params_op = [l_p.assign(g_p) for l_p, g_p
in zip(self.c_params, globalAC.c_params)]
                        # push the local gradients to the global network
                        with tf.name_scope('push'):
                            self.update_a_op =
self.actor_optimizer.apply_gradients(zip(self.a_grads, globalAC.a_params))
```

```
                        self.update_c_op =
self.critic_optimizer.apply_gradients(zip(self.c_grads, globalAC.c_params))


     # next, we define a function called _build_net for building
     # our actor and critic network
     def _build_net(self, scope):
     # initialize weights
        w_init = tf.random_normal_initializer(0., .1)
        with tf.variable_scope('actor'):
            l_a = tf.layers.dense(self.s, 200, tf.nn.relu6,
kernel_initializer=w_init, name='la')
            mean = tf.layers.dense(l_a, no_of_actions,
tf.nn.tanh,kernel_initializer=w_init, name='mean')
            var = tf.layers.dense(l_a, no_of_actions, tf.nn.softplus,
kernel_initializer=w_init, name='var')
        with tf.variable_scope('critic'):
            l_c = tf.layers.dense(self.s, 100, tf.nn.relu6,
kernel_initializer=w_init, name='lc')
            v = tf.layers.dense(l_c, 1, kernel_initializer=w_init,
name='v')
        a_params = tf.get_collection(tf.GraphKeys.TRAINABLE_VARIABLES,
scope=scope + '/actor')
        c_params = tf.get_collection(tf.GraphKeys.TRAINABLE_VARIABLES,
scope=scope + '/critic')
        return mean, var, v, a_params, c_params
     # update the local gradients to the global network
     def update_global(self, feed_dict):
        self.sess.run([self.update_a_op, self.update_c_op], feed_dict)
     # get the global parameters to the local networks
     def pull_global(self):
        self.sess.run([self.pull_a_params_op, self.pull_c_params_op])
     # select action
     def choose_action(self, s):
        s = s[np.newaxis, :]
        return self.sess.run(self.A, {self.s: s})[0]
```

Now, we will initialize the `Worker` class:

```
class Worker(object):
    def __init__(self, name, globalAC, sess):
        # initialize environment for each worker
        self.env = gym.make('MountainCarContinuous-v0').unwrapped
        self.name = name
        # create an ActorCritic agent for each worker
        self.AC = ActorCritic(name, sess, globalAC)
        self.sess=sess
    def work(self):
```

```
global global_rewards, global_episodes
total_step = 1

# store state, action, reward
buffer_s, buffer_a, buffer_r = [], [], []
# loop if the coordinator is active and the global
# episode is less than the maximum episode
while not coord.should_stop() and global_episodes < no_of_episodes:
    # initialize the environment by resetting
    s = self.env.reset()
    # store the episodic reward
    ep_r = 0
    for ep_t in range(no_of_ep_steps):
        # Render the environment for only worker 1
        if self.name == 'W_0' and render:
            self.env.render()
        # choose the action based on the policy
        a = self.AC.choose_action(s)

        # perform the action (a), receive reward (r),
        # and move to the next state (s_)
        s_, r, done, info = self.env.step(a)
        # set done as true if we reached maximum step per episode
        done = True if ep_t == no_of_ep_steps - 1 else False
        ep_r += r
        # store the state, action, and rewards in the buffer
        buffer_s.append(s)
        buffer_a.append(a)
        # normalize the reward
        buffer_r.append((r+8)/8)
        # we update the global network after a particular time step
        if total_step % update_global == 0 or done:
            if done:
                v_s_ = 0
            else:
                v_s_ = self.sess.run(self.AC.v, {self.AC.s:
s_[np.newaxis, :]})[0, 0]
            # buffer for target v
            buffer_v_target = []
            for r in buffer_r[::-1]:
                v_s_ = r + gamma * v_s_
                buffer_v_target.append(v_s_)
            buffer_v_target.reverse()
            buffer_s, buffer_a, buffer_v_target =
np.vstack(buffer_s), np.vstack(buffer_a), np.vstack(buffer_v_target)
            feed_dict = {
                    self.AC.s: buffer_s,
                    self.AC.a_his: buffer_a,
```

```
                               self.AC.v_target: buffer_v_target,
                               }
                     # update global network
                     self.AC.update_global(feed_dict)
                     buffer_s, buffer_a, buffer_r = [], [], []
                     # get global parameters to local ActorCritic
                     self.AC.pull_global()
               s = s_
               total_step += 1
               if done:
                   if len(global_rewards) < 5:
                       global_rewards.append(ep_r)
                   else:
                       global_rewards.append(ep_r)
                       global_rewards[-1] =(np.mean(global_rewards[-5:]))
                   global_episodes += 1
                   break
```

Now, let's start the TensorFlow session and run our model:

```
# create a list for string global rewards and episodes
global_rewards = []
global_episodes = 0

# start tensorflow session
sess = tf.Session()

with tf.device("/cpu:0"):
# create an instance to our ActorCritic Class
    global_ac = ActorCritic(global_net_scope,sess)
    workers = []
    # loop for each worker
    for i in range(no_of_workers):
        i_name = 'W_%i' % i
        workers.append(Worker(i_name, global_ac,sess))

coord = tf.train.Coordinator()
sess.run(tf.global_variables_initializer())

# log everything so that we can visualize the graph in tensorboard

if os.path.exists(log_dir):
    shutil.rmtree(log_dir)

tf.summary.FileWriter(log_dir, sess.graph)

worker_threads = []
```

```
#start workers

for worker in workers:

    job = lambda: worker.work()
    t = threading.Thread(target=job)
    t.start()
    worker_threads.append(t)
coord.join(worker_threads)
```

The output is shown as follows. If you run the program, you can see how our agent is learning to climb the mountain over several episodes:

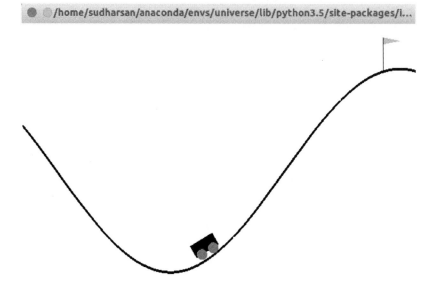

Visualization in TensorBoard

Let's visualize our network in TensorBoard. To launch TensorBoard, open your Terminal and type the following:

```
tensorboard --logdir=logs --port=6007 --host=127.0.0.1
```

This is our A3C network. We have one global network and four workers:

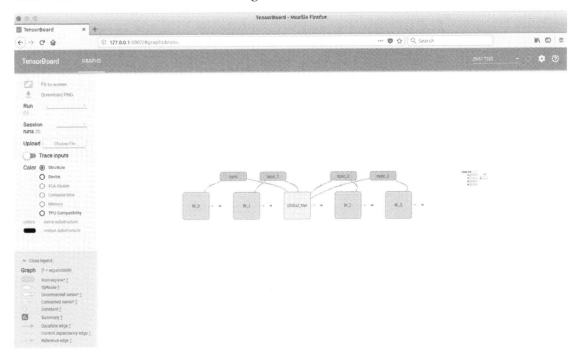

Let's expand our global network; you can see we have one actor and one critic:

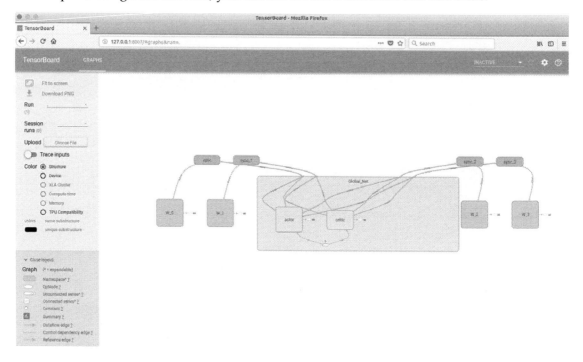

Okay, what is really going on in workers? Let's expand our worker network. You can see how the worker nodes are performing:

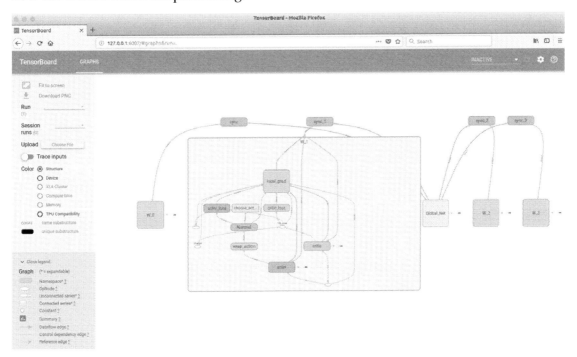

What about the sync node? What is that doing? The sync node pushes the local gradients from the local to the global network and pulls gradients from the global to the local network:

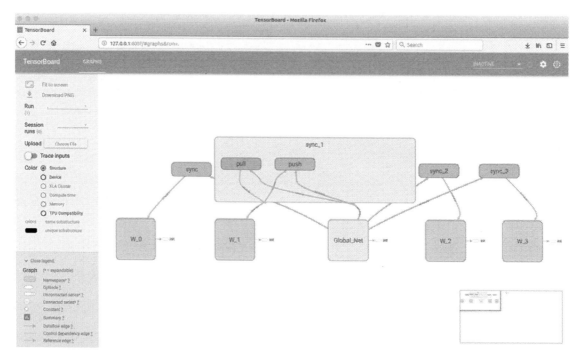

Summary

In this chapter, we learned how the A3C network works. In A3C, Asynchronous implies multiple agents working independently by interacting with multiple copies of the environment, Advantage implies the advantage function, which is the difference between the Q function and the value function, and Actor Critic refers to the Actor Critic network, where the actor network is responsible for generating a policy and the critic network evaluates the policy generated by the actor network. We have seen how A3C works, and saw how to solve a mountain car problem using the algorithm.

In the next chapter, Chapter 11, *Policy Gradients and Optimization*, we will see policy gradient methods that directly optimize the policy without requiring the Q function.

Questions

The question list is as follows:

1. What is A3C?
2. What do the three As signify?
3. Name one advantage of A3N over DQN
4. What is the difference between global and worker nodes?
5. Why do we entropy to our loss function?
6. Explain the workings of A3C.

Further reading

You can also refer to these papers:

- **A3C paper**: https://arxiv.org/pdf/1602.01783.pdf
- **Vision enhanced A3C**: http://cs231n.stanford.edu/reports/2017/pdfs/617.pdf

Now we will see how to train our agents to correctly land on the landing pad with policy gradients. Credit for the code used in this section goes to Gabriel (https://github.com/gabrielgarza/openai-gym-policy-gradient):

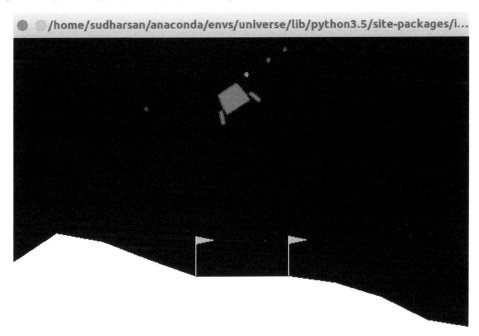

First, we import the necessary libraries:

```
import tensorflow as tf
import numpy as np
from tensorflow.python.framework import ops
import gym
import numpy as np
import time
```

Then we define the `PolicyGradient` class, which implements the policy gradient algorithm. Let's break down the class and see each function separately. You can look at the whole program as a Jupyter notebook (https://github.com/sudharsan13296/Hands-On-Reinforcement-Learning-With-Python/blob/master/11.%20Policy%20Gradients%20and%20Optimization/11.2%20Lunar%20Lander%20Using%20Policy%20Gradients.ipynb):

```
class PolicyGradient:
    # first we define the __init__ method where we initialize all variables
```

```
    def __init__(self, n_x,n_y,learning_rate=0.01, reward_decay=0.95):
        # number of states in the environment
        self.n_x = n_x
        # number of actions in the environment
        self.n_y = n_y
        # learning rate of the network
        self.lr = learning_rate
        # discount factor
        self.gamma = reward_decay
        # initialize the lists for storing observations,
        # actions and rewards
        self.episode_observations, self.episode_actions,
self.episode_rewards = [], [], []
        # we define a function called build_network for
        # building the neural network
        self.build_network()
        # stores the cost i.e loss
        self.cost_history = []
        # initialize tensorflow session
        self.sess = tf.Session()
        self.sess.run(tf.global_variables_initializer())
```

Next, we define a `store_transition` function which stores the transitions, that is, `state`, `action`, and `reward`. We can use this information for training the network:

```
    def store_transition(self, s, a, r):
        self.episode_observations.append(s)
        self.episode_rewards.append(r)

        # store actions as list of arrays
        action = np.zeros(self.n_y)
        action[a] = 1
        self.episode_actions.append(action)
```

We define the `choose_action` function for choosing the `action` given the `state`:

```
    def choose_action(self, observation):

        # reshape observation to (num_features, 1)
        observation = observation[:, np.newaxis]

        # run forward propagation to get softmax probabilities
        prob_weights = self.sess.run(self.outputs_softmax, feed_dict =
{self.X: observation})
```

```
        # select action using a biased sample this will return
        # the index of the action we have sampled
        action = np.random.choice(range(len(prob_weights.ravel())),
p=prob_weights.ravel())
        return action
```

We define the `build_network` function for building the neural network:

```
    def build_network(self):
        # placeholders for input x, and output y
        self.X = tf.placeholder(tf.float32, shape=(self.n_x, None),
name="X")
        self.Y = tf.placeholder(tf.float32, shape=(self.n_y, None),
name="Y")
        # placeholder for reward
        self.discounted_episode_rewards_norm = tf.placeholder(tf.float32,
[None, ], name="actions_value")

        # we build 3 layer neural network with 2 hidden layers and
        # 1 output layer
        # number of neurons in the hidden layer
        units_layer_1 = 10
        units_layer_2 = 10
        # number of neurons in the output layer
        units_output_layer = self.n_y
        # now let us initialize weights and bias value using
        # tensorflow's tf.contrib.layers.xavier_initializer
        W1 = tf.get_variable("W1", [units_layer_1, self.n_x], initializer =
tf.contrib.layers.xavier_initializer(seed=1))
        b1 = tf.get_variable("b1", [units_layer_1, 1], initializer =
tf.contrib.layers.xavier_initializer(seed=1))
        W2 = tf.get_variable("W2", [units_layer_2, units_layer_1],
initializer = tf.contrib.layers.xavier_initializer(seed=1))
        b2 = tf.get_variable("b2", [units_layer_2, 1], initializer =
tf.contrib.layers.xavier_initializer(seed=1))
        W3 = tf.get_variable("W3", [self.n_y, units_layer_2], initializer =
tf.contrib.layers.xavier_initializer(seed=1))
        b3 = tf.get_variable("b3", [self.n_y, 1], initializer =
tf.contrib.layers.xavier_initializer(seed=1))

        # and then, we perform forward propagation

        Z1 = tf.add(tf.matmul(W1,self.X), b1)
        A1 = tf.nn.relu(Z1)
        Z2 = tf.add(tf.matmul(W2, A1), b2)
        A2 = tf.nn.relu(Z2)
        Z3 = tf.add(tf.matmul(W3, A2), b3)
        A3 = tf.nn.softmax(Z3)
```

```
        # as we require, probabilities, we apply softmax activation
        # function in the output layer,
        logits = tf.transpose(Z3)
        labels = tf.transpose(self.Y)
        self.outputs_softmax = tf.nn.softmax(logits, name='A3')

        # next we define our loss function as cross entropy loss
        neg_log_prob =
tf.nn.softmax_cross_entropy_with_logits(logits=logits, labels=labels)
        # reward guided loss
        loss = tf.reduce_mean(neg_log_prob *
self.discounted_episode_rewards_norm)

        # we use adam optimizer for minimizing the loss
        self.train_op = tf.train.AdamOptimizer(self.lr).minimize(loss)
```

Next, we define the `discount_and_norm_rewards` function which will result in the discount and normalized reward:

```
    def discount_and_norm_rewards(self):
        discounted_episode_rewards = np.zeros_like(self.episode_rewards)
        cumulative = 0
        for t in reversed(range(len(self.episode_rewards))):
            cumulative = cumulative * self.gamma + self.episode_rewards[t]
            discounted_episode_rewards[t] = cumulative

        discounted_episode_rewards -= np.mean(discounted_episode_rewards)
        discounted_episode_rewards /= np.std(discounted_episode_rewards)
        return discounted_episode_rewards
```

Now we actually perform the learning:

```
    def learn(self):
        # discount and normalize episodic reward
        discounted_episode_rewards_norm = self.discount_and_norm_rewards()

        # train the network
        self.sess.run(self.train_op, feed_dict={
            self.X: np.vstack(self.episode_observations).T,
            self.Y: np.vstack(np.array(self.episode_actions)).T,
            self.discounted_episode_rewards_norm:
discounted_episode_rewards_norm,
        })
```

```
        # reset the episodic data
        self.episode_observations, self.episode_actions,
    self.episode_rewards = [], [], []

        return discounted_episode_rewards_norm
```

You can see the output as follows:

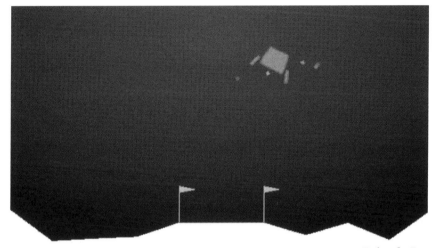

Episode 3

Deep deterministic policy gradient

In Chapter 8, *Atari Games with Deep Q Network*, we looked at how DQN works and we applied DQNs to play Atari games. However, those are discrete environments where we have a finite set of actions. Think of a continuous environment space like training a robot to walk; in those environments it is not feasible to apply Q learning because finding a greedy policy will require a lot of optimization at each and every step. Even if we make this continuous environment discrete, we might lose important features and end up with a huge set of action spaces. It is difficult to attain convergence when we have a huge action space.

So we use a new architecture called Actor Critic with two networks—Actor and Critic. The Actor Critic architecture combines the policy gradient and state action value functions. The role of the **Actor** network is to determine the best actions in the **state** by tuning the parameter θ, and the role of the **Critic** is to evaluate the action produced by the **Actor**. **Critic** evaluates the Actor's action by computing the temporal difference error. That is, we perform a policy gradient on an **Actor** network to select the actions and the **Critic** network evaluates the action produced by the **Actor** network using the TD error. The Actor Critic architecture is shown in the following diagram:

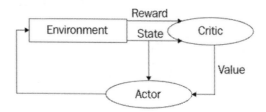

Similar to DQN, here we use an experience buffer, using which Actor and Critic networks are trained by sampling a mini batch of experiences. We also use a separate target Actor and Critic network for computing the loss.

For example, in a Pong game we will have different features of different scales such as position, velocity, and so on. So we scale the features in a way that all the features will be in the same scale. We use a method called batch normalization for scaling the features. It normalizes all the features to have unit mean and variance. How do we explore new actions? In a continuous environment, there will be n number of actions. To explore new actions we add some noise N to the action produced by the Actor network. We generate this noise using a process called the Ornstein-Uhlenbeck random process.

Now we will look at the DDPG algorithm in detail.

Let's say we have two networks: the Actor network and Critic network. We represent the Actor network with $\mu(s; \theta^{\mu})$ which takes input as a state and results in the action where θ^{μ} is the Actor network weights. We represent the Critic network as $Q(s, a; \theta^{Q})$, which takes an input as a state and action and returns the Q value where θ^{Q} is the Critic network weights.

Similarly, we define a target network for both the Actor network and Critic network as $\mu(s; \theta^{\mu'})$ and $Q(s, a; \theta^{Q'})$ respectively, where $\theta^{\mu'}$ and $\theta^{Q'}$ are the weights of the target Actor and Critic network.

We update Actor network weights with policy gradients and the Critic network weight with the gradients calculated from the TD error.

First, we select an action by adding the exploration noise N to the action produced by the Actor network, such as $\mu(s;\theta^\mu) + N$. We perform this action in a state, s, receive a reward, r and move to a new state, s'. We store this transition information in an experience replay buffer.

After some iterations, we sample transitions from the replay buffer and train the network, and then we calculate the target Q value $y_i = r_i + \gamma Q'(s_{i+1}, \mu'(s_{i+1}|\theta^{\mu'})|\theta^{Q'})$. We compute the TD error as:

$$L = \frac{1}{M}\sum_i (y_i - Q(s_i, a_i|\theta^Q)^2)$$

Where M is the number of samples from the replay buffer that are used for training. We update our Critic networks weights with gradients calculated from this loss L.

Similarly, we update our policy network weights using a policy gradient. Then we update the weights of Actor and Critic network in the target network. We update the weights of the target networks slowly, which promotes greater stability; it is called the soft replacement:

$$\theta' < -\tau\theta + (1-\tau)\theta'$$

Swinging a pendulum

We have a pendulum that starts in a random position, and the goal of our agent is to swing the pendulum up so it stays upright. We will see how to use DDPG here. Credit for the code used in this section goes to wshuail (https://github.com/wangshuailong/reinforcement_learning_with_Tensorflow/tree/master/DDPG).

First, let's import the necessary libraries:

```
import tensorflow as tf
import numpy as np
import gym
```

Next, we define the hyperparameters as follows:

```
# number of steps in each episode
epsiode_steps = 500

# learning rate for actor
lr_a = 0.001

# learning rate for critic
lr_c = 0.002

# discount factor
gamma = 0.9

# soft replacement
alpha = 0.01

# replay buffer size
memory = 10000

# batch size for training
batch_size = 32
render = False
```

We will implement the DDPG algorithm in the DDPG class. We break down the class to see each function. First, we initialize everything:

```
class DDPG(object):
    def __init__(self, no_of_actions, no_of_states, a_bound,):
        # initialize the memory with shape as no of actions, no of states
and our defined memory size
        self.memory = np.zeros((memory, no_of_states * 2 + no_of_actions +
1), dtype=np.float32)
        # initialize pointer to point to our experience buffer
        self.pointer = 0
        # initialize tensorflow session
        self.sess = tf.Session()
        # initialize the variance for OU process for exploring policies
        self.noise_variance = 3.0
        self.no_of_actions, self.no_of_states, self.a_bound =
no_of_actions, no_of_states, a_bound,
        # placeholder for current state, next state and rewards
        self.state = tf.placeholder(tf.float32, [None, no_of_states], 's')
        self.next_state = tf.placeholder(tf.float32, [None, no_of_states],
's_')
        self.reward = tf.placeholder(tf.float32, [None, 1], 'r')
        # build the actor network which has separate eval(primary)
```

```
        # and target network
        with tf.variable_scope('Actor'):
            self.a = self.build_actor_network(self.state, scope='eval',
trainable=True)
            a_ = self.build_actor_network(self.next_state, scope='target',
trainable=False)
        # build the critic network which has separate eval(primary)
        # and target network
        with tf.variable_scope('Critic'):
            q = self.build_crtic_network(self.state, self.a, scope='eval',
trainable=True)
            q_ = self.build_crtic_network(self.next_state, a_,
scope='target', trainable=False)


        # initialize the network parameters
        self.ae_params = tf.get_collection(tf.GraphKeys.GLOBAL_VARIABLES,
scope='Actor/eval')
        self.at_params = tf.get_collection(tf.GraphKeys.GLOBAL_VARIABLES,
scope='Actor/target')
        self.ce_params = tf.get_collection(tf.GraphKeys.GLOBAL_VARIABLES,
scope='Critic/eval')
        self.ct_params = tf.get_collection(tf.GraphKeys.GLOBAL_VARIABLES,
scope='Critic/target')


        # update target value
        self.soft_replace = [[tf.assign(at, (1-alpha)*at+alpha*ae),
tf.assign(ct, (1-alpha)*ct+alpha*ce)]
            for at, ae, ct, ce in zip(self.at_params, self.ae_params,
self.ct_params, self.ce_params)]
        # compute target Q value, we know that Q(s,a) = reward + gamma *
          Q'(s',a')
        q_target = self.reward + gamma * q_
        # compute TD error i.e actual - predicted values
        td_error = tf.losses.mean_squared_error(labels=(self.reward + gamma
* q_), predictions=q)
        # train the critic network with adam optimizer
        self.ctrain = tf.train.AdamOptimizer(lr_c).minimize(td_error,
name="adam-ink", var_list = self.ce_params)
        # compute the loss in actor network
        a_loss = - tf.reduce_mean(q)
        # train the actor network with adam optimizer for
        # minimizing the loss
        self.atrain = tf.train.AdamOptimizer(lr_a).minimize(a_loss,
var_list=self.ae_params)
```

```
# initialize summary writer to visualize our network in tensorboard
tf.summary.FileWriter("logs", self.sess.graph)
# initialize all variables
self.sess.run(tf.global_variables_initializer())
```

How do we select an action in DDPG? We select an action by adding noise to the action space. We use the Ornstein-Uhlenbeck random process for generating noise:

```
def choose_action(self, s):
    a = self.sess.run(self.a, {self.state: s[np.newaxis, :]})[0]
    a = np.clip(np.random.normal(a, self.noise_variance), -2, 2)
    return a
```

Then we define the `learn` function where the actual training happens. Here we select a batch of `states`, `actions`, `rewards`, and the next state from the experience buffer. We train Actor and Critic networks with that:

```
def learn(self):
    # soft target replacement
    self.sess.run(self.soft_replace)

    indices = np.random.choice(memory, size=batch_size)
    batch_transition = self.memory[indices, :]
    batch_states = batch_transition[:, :self.no_of_states]
    batch_actions = batch_transition[:, self.no_of_states:
self.no_of_states + self.no_of_actions]
    batch_rewards = batch_transition[:, -self.no_of_states - 1: -
self.no_of_states]
    batch_next_state = batch_transition[:, -self.no_of_states:]

    self.sess.run(self.atrain, {self.state: batch_states})
    self.sess.run(self.ctrain, {self.state: batch_states, self.a:
batch_actions, self.reward: batch_rewards, self.next_state:
batch_next_state})
```

We define a `store_transition` function, that stores all the information in the buffer and performs the learning:

```
def store_transition(self, s, a, r, s_):
    trans = np.hstack((s,a,[r],s_))
    index = self.pointer % memory
    self.memory[index, :] = trans
    self.pointer += 1

    if self.pointer > memory:
        self.noise_variance *= 0.99995
        self.learn()
```

We define the `build_actor_network` function for building our Actor network:

```
def build_actor_network(self, s, scope, trainable):
    # Actor DPG
    with tf.variable_scope(scope):
        l1 = tf.layers.dense(s, 30, activation = tf.nn.tanh, name =
'l1', trainable = trainable)
        a = tf.layers.dense(l1, self.no_of_actions, activation =
tf.nn.tanh, name = 'a', trainable = trainable)
        return tf.multiply(a, self.a_bound, name = "scaled_a")
```

We define the `build_ crtic_network` function:

```
def build_crtic_network(self, s, a, scope, trainable):
    # Critic Q-leaning
    with tf.variable_scope(scope):
        n_l1 = 30
        w1_s = tf.get_variable('w1_s', [self.no_of_states, n_l1],
trainable = trainable)
        w1_a = tf.get_variable('w1_a', [self.no_of_actions, n_l1],
trainable = trainable)
        b1 = tf.get_variable('b1', [1, n_l1], trainable = trainable)
        net = tf.nn.tanh( tf.matmul(s, w1_s) + tf.matmul(a, w1_a) + b1
)

        q = tf.layers.dense(net, 1, trainable = trainable)
        return q
```

Now, we initialize our `gym` environment using the `make` function:

```
env = gym.make("Pendulum-v0")
env = env.unwrapped
env.seed(1)
```

We get the number of states:

```
no_of_states = env.observation_space.shape[0]
```

We get the number of actions:

```
no_of_actions = env.action_space.shape[0]
```

Also, higher bound of the action:

```
a_bound = env.action_space.high
```

Now, we create an object for our DDPG class:

```
ddpg = DDPG(no_of_actions, no_of_states, a_bound)
```

We initialize the list to store the total rewards:

```
total_reward = []
```

Set the number of episodes:

```
no_of_episodes = 300
```

Now, let's begin training:

```
# for each episodes
for i in range(no_of_episodes):
    # initialize the environment
    s = env.reset()
    # episodic reward
    ep_reward = 0
    for j in range(epsiode_steps):
        env.render()

        # select action by adding noise through OU process
        a = ddpg.choose_action(s)
        # perform the action and move to the next state s
        s_, r, done, info = env.step(a)
        # store the the transition to our experience buffer
        # sample some minibatch of experience and train the network
        ddpg.store_transition(s, a, r, s_)
        # update current state as next state
        s = s_
        # add episodic rewards
        ep_reward += r
        if j == epsiode_steps-1:
            # store the total rewards
            total_reward.append(ep_reward)
            # print rewards obtained per each episode
            print('Episode:', i, ' Reward: %i' % int(ep_reward))
            break
```

You will see the output as follows:

Episode 1

We can see the computation graph in TensorBoard:

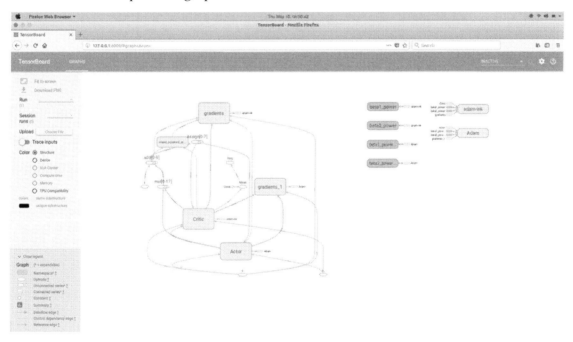

Trust Region Policy Optimization

Before understanding **Trust Region Policy Optimization** (TRPO), we need to understand constrained policy optimization. We know that in RL agents learn by trial and error to maximize the reward. To find the best policy, our agents will explore all different actions and choose the one that gives a good reward. While exploring different actions there is a very good chance that our agents will explore bad actions as well. But the biggest challenge is when we allow our agents to learn in the real world and when the reward functions are not properly designed. For example, consider an agent learning to walk without hitting any obstacles. The agent will receive a negative reward if it gets hit by any obstacle and a positive reward for not getting hit by any obstacle. To figure out the best policy, the agent explores different actions. The agent also takes action, such as hitting an obstacle to check whether it gives a good reward. But that is not safe for our agent; it is particularly unsafe when an agent is learning in a real-world environment. So we introduce constraint-based learning. We set a threshold and if the probability of hitting the obstacle is less than this threshold, then we consider our agent safe, or else we consider our agent unsafe. A constraint is added to make sure that our agent is in a safe region.

In TRPO, we iteratively improve the policy and we impose a constraint such that the **Kullback–Leibler** (**KL**) divergence between an old policy and a new policy is to be less than some constant δ. This constraint is called the trust region constraint.

So what is KL divergence? KL divergence tells us how two probability distributions are different from each other. Since our policies are probability distribution over actions, KL divergence tells us how far a new policy is from the old policy. Why do we have to keep the distance between the old policy and new policy less than some constant δ? Because we don't want our new policy to drift apart from the old policy. So we impose a constraint to keep the new policy near to the old policy. Again, why do we have to stay near the old policy? When the new policy is far away from the old policy, then it will affect our agent's learning performance and also lead to a completely different learning behavior. In a nutshell, in TRPO, we take a step toward the direction that improves our policy, that is, maximizes the reward, but we should also be sure that the trust region constraint is satisfied. It uses conjugate gradient descent (`http://www.idi.ntnu.no/~elster/tdt24/tdt24-f09/cg.pdf`) to optimize the network parameter θ while satisfying the constraint. The algorithm guarantees monotonic policy improvement and has also achieved excellent results in various continuous environments.

Now we will see how TRPO works mathematically; you can skip this section if you are not interested in math.

Get ready for some cool math.

Let 's specify the total expected discounted reward $\eta(\pi)$, as follows:

$$\eta(\pi) = \mathbf{E}_{s_0,a_0,..}[\sum_{t=0}^{\infty} \gamma^t r(s_t)]$$

Now let's consider the new policy as π'; it can be defined as the expected return of policy π' in terms of advantages over our old policy π, as follows:

$$\eta(\pi') = \eta(\pi) + \mathbf{E}_{s_0,a_0,..\ \pi'}[\sum_{t=0}^{\infty} \gamma^t A_\pi(s_t, a_t)]$$

Okay, why are we using the advantages of the old policy? Because we are measuring how good the new policy π' is with respect to the average performance of the old policy π. We can rewrite the preceding equation with a sum over states instead of timesteps as follows:

$$
\begin{aligned}
\eta(\pi') =& \eta(\pi) + \mathbf{E}_{s_0,a_0,..\ \pi'}[\sum_{t=0}^{\infty} \gamma^t A_\pi(s_t, a_t)] \\
=& \eta(\pi) + \sum_{t=0}^{\infty} \sum_{s} P(s_t = s|\pi') \sum_{a} \pi'(a|s)\gamma^t A_\pi(s, a) \\
=& \eta(\pi) + \sum_{s} \sum_{t=0}^{\infty} P(s_t = s|\pi') \sum_{a} \pi'(a|s)\gamma^t A_{\pi_0}(s, a) \\
=& \eta(\pi) + \sum_{s} \rho_{\pi'}(s) \sum_{a} \pi'(a|s) A_\pi(s, a)
\end{aligned}
$$

ρ is the discounted visitation frequencies, that is:

$$\rho_\pi(s) = P(s_0 = s) + \gamma P(s_1 = s) + \gamma^2 P(s_2 = s) + \ldots$$

If you see the preceding equation $\eta(\pi')$ there is a complex dependency of $\rho_{\pi'}(s)$ on π' and so it is difficult to optimize the equation. So we will introduce the local approximation $L_\pi(\pi')$ to $\eta(\pi')$ as follows:

$$L_\pi(\pi') = \eta(\pi) + \sum_s \rho_\pi(s) \sum_a \pi'(a|s) A_\pi(s,a)$$

L_π uses the visitation frequency ρ_π rather than $\rho_{\pi'}$, that is, we ignore the changes in state visitation frequency due to the change in policy. To put it in simple terms, we assume that the state visitation frequency is not different for both the new and old policy. When we are calculating the gradient of L_π, which will also improve η with respect to some parameter θ we can't be sure how much big of a step to take.

Kakade and Langford proposed a new policy update method called conservative policy iteration, shown as follows:

$$\pi_{new}(a|s) = (1 - \alpha)\pi_{old}(a|s) + \alpha\pi'(a|s) \quad \text{---- (1)}$$

π_{new} is the new policy. π_{old} is the old policy.

$\pi' = argmax_{\pi'} L_{\pi_{old}}(\pi')$, that is, π', is the policy which maximizes $L_{\pi_{old}}$.

Kakade and Langford derived the following equation from (1) as follows:

$$\eta(\pi') \geq L_\pi(\pi') - CD_{KL}^{max}(\pi, \pi') \quad \text{---- (2)}$$

C is the penalty coefficient and it is equal to $\dfrac{4\epsilon\gamma}{(1 - \alpha)^2}$, and $D_{KL}^{max}(\pi, \pi')$ denotes the KL divergence between the old policy and the new policy.

If we look at the preceding equation (2) closely, we notice that our expected long-term reward η increases monotonically as long as the right-hand side is maximized.

Let's define this right-hand side term as $M_i(\pi)$, as follows:

$$M_i(\pi) = L_{\pi_i}(\pi) - CD_{KL}^{max}(\pi_i, \pi) \quad \text{---- (3)}$$

Substituting equation (3) in (2), we get:

$$\eta(\pi_i + 1) \geq M_i(\pi_i + 1) \quad \text{---- (4)}$$

Since we know that the KL divergence between the two same policies will be *0*, we can write:

$$\eta(\pi) = M_i(\pi_i) \quad \text{----(5)}$$

Combining equations (4) and (5), we can write:

$$\eta(\pi_{i+1}) - \eta(\pi) \geq M_i(\pi_{i+1}) - M(\pi_i)$$

In the preceding equation, we can understand that maximizing M_i guarantees the maximization of our expected reward. So now our goal is to maximize M_i which in turn maximizes our expected reward. Since we use parameterized policies, we replace π with θ in our previous equation and we use θ_{old} to represent a policy that we want to improve, as shown next:

$$\text{maximize}_\theta \quad [L_{\theta_{old}}(\theta) - CD_{KL}^{max}(\theta_{old}, \theta)]$$

But having a penalty coefficient *C* in the preceding equation will cause the step size to be very small, which in turn slows down the updates. So, we impose a constraint on the KL divergence's old policy and new policy, which is the trust region constraint, and it will help us to find the optimal step size:

$$\text{maximize}_\theta \quad L_{\theta_0}(\theta)$$
$$\text{subject to} \quad D_{KL}^{max}(\theta_{old}, \theta) \leq \delta$$

Now, the problem is KL divergence is imposed on every point in the state space and it is really not feasible to solve when we have a high dimensional state space. So we use a heuristic approximation which takes the average KL divergence as:

$$\bar{D}_{KL}^\rho(\theta_{old}, \theta) := \mathbf{E}_{s \sim \rho}[D_{KL}(\pi_{\theta_1}(.|s)\|\pi_{\theta_2}(.|s))]$$

So now, we can rewrite our preceding objective function with the average KL divergence constraint as:

$$\text{maximize}_\theta \qquad L_{\theta_{old}}(\theta)$$

$$\text{subject to} \qquad \bar{D}_{KL}^{\rho\theta_{old}}(\theta_{old}, \theta) \leq \delta$$

Expanding the value of *L*, we get the following:

$$\text{maximize}_\theta \qquad \sum_s \rho\theta_{old}(S) \sum_a \pi_\theta(a|s) A_{\theta_{old}}(s, a)$$

$$\text{subject to} \qquad \bar{D}_{KL}^{\rho\theta_{old}}(\theta_{old}, \theta) \leq \delta$$

In the preceding equation, we replace sum over states $\sum_s \rho\theta_{old}$ as expectation $E_{s \sim \rho\theta_{old}}$ and we replace sum over actions by importance sampling estimator as:

$$\sum_a \pi_\theta(a|s_n) A_{\theta_{old}}(s_n, a) = E_{a \sim q}\left[\frac{\pi_\theta(a|s_n)}{q(a|s_n)} A_{\theta_{old}}(s_n, a)\right]$$

Then, we substitute advantage target values $A_{\theta_{old}}$ with Q values $Q_{\theta_{old}}$.

So, our final objective function will become:

$$\text{maximize}_\theta \qquad E_s \pi_{\theta_{old}}, a\pi_{\theta_{old}}\left[\frac{\pi_\theta(a|s)}{\pi_{\theta_{old}}(a|s)} A_{\theta_{old}}(s, a)\right]$$

$$\text{subject to} \qquad E_{s, \pi_{\theta_{old}}}\left[DKL(\pi_{\theta_{old}}(\cdot|s)\|\pi_{\theta_{old}}(\cdot|s))\right] \leq \delta$$

Optimizing the preceding mentioned objective function, which has a constraint, is called constrained optimization. Our constraint is to keep the average KL divergence between the old policy and new policy less than δ. We use conjugate gradient descent for optimizing the preceding function.

Proximal Policy Optimization

Now we will look at another policy optimization algorithm called **Proximal Policy Optimization (PPO)**. It acts as an improvement to TRPO and has become the default RL algorithm of choice in solving many complex RL problems due to its performance. It was proposed by researchers at OpenAI for overcoming the shortcomings of TRPO. Recall the surrogate objective function of TRPO. It is a constraint optimization problem where we impose a constraint—that average KL divergence between the old and new policy should be less than δ. But the problem with TRPO is that it requires a lot of computing power for computing conjugate gradients to perform constrained optimization.

So, PPO modifies the objective function of TRPO by changing the constraint to a penalty term so that we don't want to perform conjugate gradient. Now let's see how PPO works. We define $r_t(\theta)$ as a probability ratio between new and old policy. So, we can write our objective function as:

$$
\begin{aligned}
L^{CPI}(\theta) &= \hat{E}_t\Big[\frac{\pi_\theta(a_t|s_t)}{\pi_{\theta_{old}}(a_t|s_t)}\hat{A}_t\Big] \\
&= \hat{E}_t\big[r_t(\theta)\hat{A}_t\big]
\end{aligned}
$$

L^{CPI} denotes the conservative policy iteration. But maximizing L would lead to a large policy update without constraint. So, we redefine our objective function by adding the penalty term which penalizes a large policy update. Now the objective function becomes:

$$
L^{CLIP}(\theta) = \hat{E}_t\big[minr_t(\theta)\hat{A}_t, clip(r_t(\theta), 1-\epsilon, 1+\epsilon)\hat{A}_t\big]
$$

We have just added a new term, $clip(r_t(\theta), 1-\epsilon, 1+\epsilon)\hat{A}_t$, to the actual equation. What does this mean? It actually clips the value of $r_t(\theta)$ between the interval $[1-\epsilon, 1+\epsilon]$, that is, if the value of $r_t(\theta)$ causes the objective function to increase, heavily clipping the value between an interval will reduce its effects.

We clip the probability ratio either at $1 - \epsilon$ or ϵ based on two cases:

- **Case 1**: $\hat{A}_t > 0$

  When the advantage is positive, which means that the corresponding action should be preferred over the average of all other actions. We will increase the value of $r_t(\theta)$ for that action, so it will have a greater chance of being selected. As we are performing a clipping value of $r_t(\theta)$, will not exceed greater than $1 + \epsilon$:

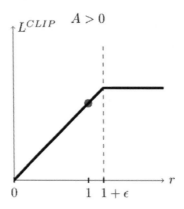

- **Case 2**: $\hat{A}_t$

  When the value of the advantage is negative, this means that the action has no significance and it should not be adopted. So, in this case, we will reduce the value of $r_t(\theta)$ for that action so that it will have a lower chance of being selected. Similarly, as we are performing clipping, a value of $r_t(\theta)$ will not decrease to less than $1 - \epsilon$:

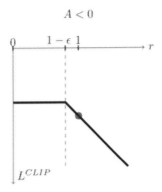

When we are using neural network architectures, we must define the loss function which includes the value function error for our objective function. We will also add entropy loss to ensure enough exploration, as we did in A3C. So our final objective function becomes:

$$L_t^{CLIP+VP+S}(\theta) = \hat{E}_t[L_t^{CLIP}(\theta) - c1 L_t^{VF}(\theta) + c_2 S[\pi_\theta](s_t)]$$

c_1 and c_2 are the coefficients, L_t^{VP} is the squared error loss between the actual and target value function, that is, $(V_\theta(s_t) - V_t^{target})^2$, and S is the entropy bonus.

Summary

We started off with policy gradient methods which directly optimized the policy without requiring the Q function. We learned about policy gradients by solving a Lunar Lander game, and we looked at DDPG, which has the benefits of both policy gradients and Q functions.

Then we looked at policy optimization algorithms such as TRPO, which ensure monotonic policy improvements by enforcing a constraint on KL divergence between the old and new policy is not greater than δ.

We also looked at proximal policy optimization, which changed the constraint to a penalty by penalizing the large policy update. In the next chapter, Chapter 12, *Capstone Project – Car Racing Using DQN*, we will see how to build an agent to win a car racing game.

Questions

The question list is as follows:

1. What are policy gradients?
2. Why are policy gradients effective?
3. What is the use of the Actor Critic network in DDPG?
4. What is the constraint optimization problem?
5. What is the trust region?
6. How does PPO overcome the drawbacks of TRPO?

Further reading

You can further refer to the following papers:

- **DDPG paper**: https://arxiv.org/pdf/1509.02971.pdf
- **TRPO paper**: https://arxiv.org/pdf/1502.05477.pdf
- **PPO paper**: https://arxiv.org/pdf/1707.06347.pdf

Capstone Project – Car Racing Using DQN

12

In the last few chapters, we have learned how Deep Q learning works by approximating the q function with a neural network. Following this, we have seen various improvements to **Deep Q Network (DQN)** such as Double Q learning, dueling network architectures, and the Deep Recurrent Q Network. We have seen how DQN makes use of a replay buffer to store the agent's experience and trains the network with the mini-batch of samples from the buffer. We have also implemented DQNs for playing Atari games and a **Deep Recurrent Q Network (DRQN)** for playing the Doom game. In this chapter, let's get into the detailed implementation of a dueling DQN, which is essentially the same as a regular DQN, except the final fully connected layer will be broken down into two streams, namely a value stream and an advantage stream, and these two streams will be clubbed together to compute the Q function. We will see how to train an agent for winning the car racing game with a dueling DQN.

In this chapter, you will learn how to implement the following:

- Environment wrapper functions
- A dueling network
- Replay buffer
- Training the network
- Car racing

Environment wrapper functions

The credit for the code used in this chapter goes to Giacomo Spigler's GitHub repository (`https://github.com/spiglerg/DQN_DDQN_Dueling_and_DDPG_Tensorflow`). Throughout this chapter, the code is explained at each and every line. For a complete structured code, check the above GitHub repository.

First, we import all the necessary libraries:

```
import numpy as np
import tensorflow as tf
import gym
from gym.spaces import Box
from scipy.misc import imresize
import random
import cv2
import time
import logging
import os
import sys
```

We define the `EnvWrapper` class and define some of the environment wrapper functions:

```
class EnvWrapper:
```

We define the `__init__` method and initialize variables:

```
    def __init__(self, env_name, debug=False):
```

Initialize the `gym` environment:

```
        self.env = gym.make(env_name)
```

Get the `action_space`:

```
        self.action_space = self.env.action_space
```

Get the `observation_space`:

```
        self.observation_space = Box(low=0, high=255, shape=(84, 84, 4))
```

Initialize `frame_num` for storing the frame count:

```
self.frame_num = 0
```

Initialize `monitor` for recording the game screen:

```
self.monitor = self.env.monitor
```

Initialize `frames`:

```
self.frames = np.zeros((84, 84, 4), dtype=np.uint8)
```

Initialize a Boolean called `debug`, which, when set to `true` displays the last few frames:

```
self.debug = debug

if self.debug:
    cv2.startWindowThread()
    cv2.namedWindow("Game")
```

Next, we define a function called `step`, which takes the current state as input and returns the preprocessed next state's frame:

```
def step(self, a):
    ob, reward, done, xx = self.env.step(a)
  return self.process_frame(ob), reward, done, xx
```

We define a function called `reset` for resetting the environment; after resetting, it will return the preprocessed game screen:

```
def reset(self):
    self.frame_num = 0
    return self.process_frame(self.env.reset())
```

Next, we define another function for rendering the environment:

```
def render(self):
    return self.env.render()
```

Now, we define the `process_frame` function for preprocessing the frame:

```
def process_frame(self, frame):


    # convert the image to gray
    state_gray = cv2.cvtColor(frame, cv2.COLOR_BGR2GRAY)

    # change the size
```

```
state_resized = cv2.resize(state_gray,(84,110))
#resize
gray_final = state_resized[16:100,:]


if self.frame_num == 0:
    self.frames[:, :, 0] = gray_final
    self.frames[:, :, 1] = gray_final
    self.frames[:, :, 2] = gray_final
    self.frames[:, :, 3] = gray_final

else:
    self.frames[:, :, 3] = self.frames[:, :, 2]
    self.frames[:, :, 2] = self.frames[:, :, 1]
    self.frames[:, :, 1] = self.frames[:, :, 0]
    self.frames[:, :, 0] = gray_final

# Next we increment the frame_num counter

self.frame_num += 1

if self.debug:
    cv2.imshow('Game', gray_final)

return self.frames.copy()
```

After preprocessing, our game screen looks like the following screenshot:

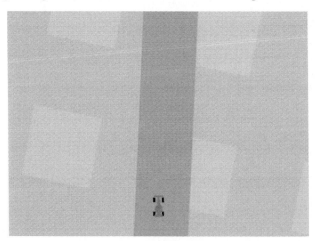

Dueling network

Now, we build our dueling DQN; we build three convolutional layers followed by two fully connected layers, and the final fully connected layer will be split into two separate layers for value stream and advantage stream. We will use the aggregate layer, which combines both the value stream and the advantage stream, to compute the q value. The dimensions of these layers are given as follows:

- **Layer 1**: 32 8x8 filters with stride 4 + RELU
- **Layer 2**: 64 4x4 filters with stride 2 + RELU
- **Layer 3**: 64 3x3 filters with stride 1 + RELU
- **Layer 4a**: 512 unit fully-connected layer + RELU
- **Layer 4b**: 512 unit fully-connected layer + RELU
- **Layer 5a**: 1 unit FC + RELU (state value)
- **Layer 5b**: Actions FC + RELU (advantage value)
- **Layer6**: Aggregate $V(s)+A(s,a)$

```
class QNetworkDueling(QNetwork):
```

We define the __init__ method to initialize all layers:

```
def __init__(self, input_size, output_size, name):
        self.name = name
        self.input_size = input_size
        self.output_size = output_size
        with tf.variable_scope(self.name):

            # Three convolutional Layers
            self.W_conv1 = self.weight_variable([8, 8, 4, 32])
            self.B_conv1 = self.bias_variable([32])
            self.stride1 = 4

            self.W_conv2 = self.weight_variable([4, 4, 32, 64])
            self.B_conv2 = self.bias_variable([64])
            self.stride2 = 2

            self.W_conv3 = self.weight_variable([3, 3, 64, 64])
            self.B_conv3 = self.bias_variable([64])
            self.stride3 = 1


            # Two fully connected layer
            self.W_fc4a = self.weight_variable([7*7*64, 512])
            self.B_fc4a = self.bias_variable([512])
```

```
        self.W_fc4b = self.weight_variable([7*7*64, 512])
        self.B_fc4b = self.bias_variable([512])

        # Value stream
        self.W_fc5a = self.weight_variable([512, 1])
        self.B_fc5a = self.bias_variable([1])

        # Advantage stream
        self.W_fc5b = self.weight_variable([512, self.output_size])
        self.B_fc5b = self.bias_variable([self.output_size])
```

We define the __call__ method and perform the convolutional operation:

```
    def __call__(self, input_tensor):
        if type(input_tensor) == list:
            input_tensor = tf.concat(1, input_tensor)

        with tf.variable_scope(self.name):
            # Perform convolutional on three layers

            self.h_conv1 = tf.nn.relu( tf.nn.conv2d(input_tensor,
self.W_conv1, strides=[1, self.stride1, self.stride1, 1], padding='VALID')
+ self.B_conv1 )

            self.h_conv2 = tf.nn.relu( tf.nn.conv2d(self.h_conv1,
self.W_conv2, strides=[1, self.stride2, self.stride2, 1], padding='VALID')
+ self.B_conv2 )

            self.h_conv3 = tf.nn.relu( tf.nn.conv2d(self.h_conv2,
self.W_conv3, strides=[1, self.stride3, self.stride3, 1], padding='VALID')
+ self.B_conv3 )


            # Flatten the convolutional output
            self.h_conv3_flat = tf.reshape(self.h_conv3, [-1, 7*7*64])
            # Fully connected layer
            self.h_fc4a = tf.nn.relu(tf.matmul(self.h_conv3_flat,
self.W_fc4a) + self.B_fc4a)

            self.h_fc4b = tf.nn.relu(tf.matmul(self.h_conv3_flat,
self.W_fc4b) + self.B_fc4b)


            # Compute value stream and advantage stream
            self.h_fc5a_value = tf.identity(tf.matmul(self.h_fc4a,
self.W_fc5a) + self.B_fc5a)
```

```
        self.h_fc5b_advantage = tf.identity(tf.matmul(self.h_fc4b,
self.W_fc5b) + self.B_fc5b)

        # Club both the value and advantage stream
        self.h_fc6 = self.h_fc5a_value + ( self.h_fc5b_advantage -
tf.reduce_mean(self.h_fc5b_advantage, reduction_indices=[1,],
keep_dims=True) )


        return self.h_fc6
```

Replay memory

Now, we build the experience replay buffer, which is used for storing all the agent's experience. We sample a minibatch of experience from the replay buffer for training the network:

```
class ReplayMemoryFast:
```

First, we define the __init__ method and initiate the buffer size:

```
    def __init__(self, memory_size, minibatch_size):

        # max number of samples to store
        self.memory_size = memory_size

        # minibatch size
        self.minibatch_size = minibatch_size
        self.experience = [None]*self.memory_size
        self.current_index = 0
        self.size = 0
```

Next, we define the store function for storing the experiences:

```
    def store(self, observation, action, reward, newobservation, is_terminal):
```

Store the experience as a tuple (current state, action, reward, next state, is it a terminal state):

```
        self.experience[self.current_index] = (observation, action, reward,
newobservation, is_terminal)
        self.current_index += 1
        self.size = min(self.size+1, self.memory_size)
```

If the index is greater than the memory, then we flush the index by subtracting it with memory size:

```
if self.current_index >= self.memory_size:
    self.current_index -= self.memory_size
```

Next, we define a `sample` function for sampling a minibatch of experience:

```
def sample(self):
    if self.size < self.minibatch_size:
        return []

    # First we randomly sample some indices
    samples_index =
np.floor(np.random.random((self.minibatch_size,))*self.size)

    # select the experience from the sampled indexed
    samples = [self.experience[int(i)] for i in samples_index]

    return samples
```

Training the network

Now, we will see how to train the network.

First, we define the DQN class and initialize all variables in the __init__ method:

```
class DQN(object):
    def __init__(self, state_size,
                       action_size,
                       session,
                       summary_writer = None,
                       exploration_period = 1000,
                       minibatch_size = 32,
                       discount_factor = 0.99,
                       experience_replay_buffer = 10000,
                       target_qnet_update_frequency = 10000,
                       initial_exploration_epsilon = 1.0,
                       final_exploration_epsilon = 0.05,
                       reward_clipping = -1,
                        ):
```

Initialize all variables:

```
self.state_size = state_size
self.action_size = action_size


self.session = session
self.exploration_period = float(exploration_period)
self.minibatch_size = minibatch_size
self.discount_factor = tf.constant(discount_factor)
self.experience_replay_buffer = experience_replay_buffer
self.summary_writer = summary_writer
self.reward_clipping = reward_clipping


self.target_qnet_update_frequency = target_qnet_update_frequency
self.initial_exploration_epsilon = initial_exploration_epsilon
self.final_exploration_epsilon = final_exploration_epsilon
self.num_training_steps = 0
```

Initialize the primary dueling DQN by creating an instance to our QNetworkDueling class:

```
self.qnet = QNetworkDueling(self.state_size, self.action_size,
"qnet")
```

Similarly, initialize the target dueling DQN:

```
self.target_qnet = QNetworkDueling(self.state_size,
self.action_size, "target_qnet")
```

Next, initialize the optimizer as an RMSPropOptimizer:

```
self.qnet_optimizer =
tf.train.RMSPropOptimizer(learning_rate=0.00025, decay=0.99, epsilon=0.01)
```

Now, initialize experience_replay_buffer by creating the instance to our ReplayMemoryFast class:

```
self.experience_replay =
ReplayMemoryFast(self.experience_replay_buffer, self.minibatch_size)
        # Setup the computational graph
        self.create_graph()
```

Next, we define the `copy_to_target_network` function for copying weights from the primary network to our target network:

```
def copy_to_target_network(source_network, target_network):
    target_network_update = []

    for v_source, v_target in zip(source_network.variables(),
target_network.variables()):

        # update target network
        update_op = v_target.assign(v_source)
        target_network_update.append(update_op)

    return tf.group(*target_network_update)
```

Now, we define the `create_graph` function and build our computational graph:

```
def create_graph(self):
```

We calculate the `q_values` and select the action that has the maximum q value:

```
with tf.name_scope("pick_action"):

    # placeholder for state
    self.state = tf.placeholder(tf.float32, (None,)+self.state_size
, name="state")

    # placeholder for q values
    self.q_values = tf.identity(self.qnet(self.state) ,
name="q_values")

    # placeholder for predicted actions
    self.predicted_actions = tf.argmax(self.q_values, dimension=1 ,
name="predicted_actions")

    # plot histogram to track max q values
    tf.histogram_summary("Q values",
tf.reduce_mean(tf.reduce_max(self.q_values, 1))) # save max q-values to
track learning
```

Next, we calculate the target future reward:

```
with tf.name_scope("estimating_future_rewards"):
    self.next_state = tf.placeholder(tf.float32,
(None,)+self.state_size , name="next_state")

    self.next_state_mask = tf.placeholder(tf.float32, (None,) ,
name="next_state_mask")
```

```
        self.rewards = tf.placeholder(tf.float32, (None,) ,
name="rewards")

        self.next_q_values_targetqnet =
tf.stop_gradient(self.target_qnet(self.next_state),
name="next_q_values_targetqnet")
        self.next_q_values_qnet =
tf.stop_gradient(self.qnet(self.next_state), name="next_q_values_qnet")

        self.next_selected_actions = tf.argmax(self.next_q_values_qnet,
dimension=1)

        self.next_selected_actions_onehot =
tf.one_hot(indices=self.next_selected_actions, depth=self.action_size)

        self.next_max_q_values = tf.stop_gradient( tf.reduce_sum(
tf.mul( self.next_q_values_targetqnet, self.next_selected_actions_onehot )
, reduction_indices=[1,] ) * self.next_state_mask )

        self.target_q_values = self.rewards +
self.discount_factor*self.next_max_q_values
```

Next, we perform the optimization using RMS prop optimizer:

```
        with tf.name_scope("optimization_step"):
        self.action_mask = tf.placeholder(tf.float32, (None,
self.action_size) , name="action_mask")

        self.y = tf.reduce_sum( self.q_values * self.action_mask ,
reduction_indices=[1,])

        ## ERROR CLIPPING
        self.error = tf.abs(self.y - self.target_q_values)

        quadratic_part = tf.clip_by_value(self.error, 0.0, 1.0)
        linear_part = self.error - quadratic_part

        self.loss = tf.reduce_mean( 0.5*tf.square(quadratic_part) +
linear_part )

        # optimize the gradients

        qnet_gradients =
self.qnet_optimizer.compute_gradients(self.loss, self.qnet.variables())

        for i, (grad, var) in enumerate(qnet_gradients):
            if grad is not None:
```

```
                        qnet_gradients[i] = (tf.clip_by_norm(grad, 10), var)

            self.qnet_optimize =
    self.qnet_optimizer.apply_gradients(qnet_gradients)
```

Copy the primary network weights to the target network:

```
            with tf.name_scope("target_network_update"):
                self.hard_copy_to_target =
    DQN.copy_to_target_network(self.qnet, self.target_qnet)
```

We define the `store` function for storing all the experience in the
`experience_replay_buffer`:

```
        def store(self, state, action, reward, next_state, is_terminal):
            # rewards clipping
            if self.reward_clipping > 0.0:
                reward = np.clip(reward, -self.reward_clipping,
    self.reward_clipping)

            self.experience_replay.store(state, action, reward, next_state,
    is_terminal)
```

We define an `action` function for selecting actions using a decaying epsilon-greedy policy:

```
        def action(self, state, training = False):
            if self.num_training_steps > self.exploration_period:
                epsilon = self.final_exploration_epsilon
            else:
                epsilon = self.initial_exploration_epsilon -
    float(self.num_training_steps) * (self.initial_exploration_epsilon -
    self.final_exploration_epsilon) / self.exploration_period

            if not training:
                epsilon = 0.05

            if random.random() <= epsilon:
                action = random.randint(0, self.action_size-1)
            else:
                action = self.session.run(self.predicted_actions,
    {self.state:[state] } )[0]

            return action
```

Now, we define a `train` function for training our network:

```
def train(self):
```

Copy the primary network weights to the target network:

```
if self.num_training_steps == 0:
    print "Training starts..."
    self.qnet.copy_to(self.target_qnet)
```

Sample experiences from the replay memory:

```
minibatch = self.experience_replay.sample()
```

Get the states, actions, rewards, and next states from the `minibatch`:

```
batch_states = np.asarray( [d[0] for d in minibatch] )
actions = [d[1] for d in minibatch]
batch_actions = np.zeros( (self.minibatch_size, self.action_size) )
for i in xrange(self.minibatch_size):
    batch_actions[i, actions[i]] = 1

batch_rewards = np.asarray( [d[2] for d in minibatch] )
batch_newstates = np.asarray( [d[3] for d in minibatch] )

batch_newstates_mask = np.asarray( [not d[4] for d in minibatch] )
```

Perform the training operation:

```
scores, _, = self.session.run([self.q_values, self.qnet_optimize],
                        { self.state: batch_states,
                          self.next_state: batch_newstates,
                          self.next_state_mask:
batch_newstates_mask,

                          self.rewards: batch_rewards,
                          self.action_mask: batch_actions} )
```

Update the target network weights:

```
if self.num_training_steps % self.target_qnet_update_frequency ==
0:
        self.session.run( self.hard_copy_to_target )

        print 'mean maxQ in minibatch: ',np.mean(np.max(scores,1))

        str_ = self.session.run(self.summarize, { self.state:
batch_states,
                                self.next_state: batch_newstates,
```

```
                                                    self.next_state_mask:
    batch_newstates_mask,

                                                    self.rewards: batch_rewards,
                                                    self.action_mask: batch_actions})

            self.summary_writer.add_summary(str_, self.num_training_steps)

        self.num_training_steps += 1
```

Car racing

So far, we have seen how to build a dueling DQN. Now, we will see how to make use of our dueling DQN when playing the car racing game.

First, let's import our necessary libraries:

```
import gym
import time
import logging
import os
import sys
import tensorflow as tf
```

Initialize all of the necessary variables:

```
ENV_NAME = 'Seaquest-v0'
TOTAL_FRAMES = 20000000
MAX_TRAINING_STEPS = 20*60*60/3
TESTING_GAMES = 30
MAX_TESTING_STEPS = 5*60*60/3
TRAIN_AFTER_FRAMES = 50000
epoch_size = 50000
MAX_NOOP_START = 30
LOG_DIR = 'logs'
outdir = 'results'
logger = tf.train.SummaryWriter(LOG_DIR)
# Intialize tensorflow session
session = tf.InteractiveSession()
```

Build the agent:

```
agent = DQN(state_size=env.observation_space.shape,
 action_size=env.action_space.n,
 session=session,
 summary_writer = logger,
 exploration_period = 1000000,
 minibatch_size = 32,
 discount_factor = 0.99,
 experience_replay_buffer = 1000000,
 target_qnet_update_frequency = 20000,
 initial_exploration_epsilon = 1.0,
 final_exploration_epsilon = 0.1,
 reward_clipping = 1.0,
)
session.run(tf.initialize_all_variables())
logger.add_graph(session.graph)
saver = tf.train.Saver(tf.all_variables())
```

Store the recording:

```
env.monitor.start(outdir+'/'+ENV_NAME,force = True,
video_callable=multiples_video_schedule)
num_frames = 0
num_games = 0
current_game_frames = 0
init_no_ops = np.random.randint(MAX_NOOP_START+1)
last_time = time.time()
last_frame_count = 0.0
state = env.reset()
```

Now, let's start the training:

```
while num_frames <= TOTAL_FRAMES+1:
    if test_mode:
        env.render()
    num_frames += 1
    current_game_frames += 1
```

Select the action, given the current state:

```
action = agent.action(state, training = True)
```

Perform the action on the environment, receive the reward, and move to the next_state:

```
next_state,reward,done,_ = env.step(action)
```

Store this transitional information in the `experience_replay_buffer`:

```
if current_game_frames >= init_no_ops:
    agent.store(state,action,reward,next_state,done)
state = next_state
```

Train the agent:

```
if num_frames>=TRAIN_AFTER_FRAMES:
    agent.train()

if done or current_game_frames > MAX_TRAINING_STEPS:
    state = env.reset()
    current_game_frames = 0
    num_games += 1
    init_no_ops = np.random.randint(MAX_NOOP_START+1)
```

Save the network's parameters after every epoch:

```
if num_frames % epoch_size == 0 and num_frames > TRAIN_AFTER_FRAMES:
    saver.save(session,
outdir+"/"+ENV_NAME+"/model_"+str(num_frames/1000)+"k.ckpt")
    print "epoch: frames=",num_frames," games=",num_games
```

We test the performance for every two epochs:

```
if num_frames % (2*epoch_size) == 0 and num_frames > TRAIN_AFTER_FRAMES:
    total_reward = 0
    avg_steps = 0
    for i in xrange(TESTING_GAMES):
        state = env.reset()
        init_no_ops = np.random.randint(MAX_NOOP_START+1)
        frm = 0

        while frm < MAX_TESTING_STEPS:
            frm += 1
            env.render()
            action = agent.action(state, training = False)
            if current_game_frames < init_no_ops:
                action = 0
            state,reward,done,_ = env.step(action)
            total_reward += reward

            if done:
                break

        avg_steps += frm
    avg_reward = float(total_reward)/TESTING_GAMES
```

```
        str_ = session.run( tf.scalar_summary('test reward
('+str(epoch_size/1000)+'k)', avg_reward) )
        logger.add_summary(str_, num_frames)
        state = env.reset()


env.monitor.close()
```

We can see how the agent is learning to win the car racing game, as shown in the following screenshot:

Summary

In this chapter, we have learned how to implement a dueling DQN in detail. We started off with the basic environment wrapper functions for preprocessing our game screens and then we defined the QNetworkDueling class. Here, we implemented a dueling Q Network, which splits the final fully connected layer of DQN into a value stream and an advantage stream and then combines these two streams to compute the q value. Following this, we saw how to create a replay buffer, which is used to store the experience and samples a minibatch of experience for training the network, and finally, we initialized our car racing environment using OpenAI's Gym and trained our agent. In the next chapter, Chapter 13, *Recent Advancements and Next Steps*, we will see some of the recent advancements in RL.

Questions

The question list is as follows:

1. What is the difference between a DQN and a dueling DQN?
2. Write the Python code for a replay buffer.
3. What is a target network?
4. Write the Python code for a prioritized experience replay buffer.
5. Create a Python function to decay an epsilon-greedy policy.
6. How does a dueling DQN differ from a double DQN?
7. Create a Python function for updating primary network weights to the target network.

Further reading

The following links will help expand your knowledge:

- **Flappy Bird using DQN**: `https://github.com/yenchenlin/DeepLearningFlappyBird`
- **Super Mario using DQN**: `https://github.com/JSDanielPark/tensorflow_dqn_supermario`

13
Recent Advancements and Next Steps

Congratulations! You have made it to the final chapter. We have come a long way! We started off with the very basics of RL, such as MDP, Monte Carlo methods, and TD learning and moved on to advanced deep reinforcement learning algorithms such as DQN, DRQN, and A3C. We have also learned about interesting state-of-the-art policy gradient methods such as DDPG, PPO, and TRPO, and we built a car-racing agent as our final project. But RL still has a lot more for us to explore, with increasing advancements each and every day. In this chapter, we will learn about some of the advancement in RL followed by hierarchical and inverse RL.

In this chapter, you will learn the following:

- **Imagination augmented agents (I2A)**
- Learning from human preference
- Deep Q learning from demonstrations
- Hindsight experience replay
- Hierarchical reinforcement learning
- Inverse reinforcement learning

Imagination augmented agents

Are you a fan of the game chess? If I asked you to play chess, how would you play the game? Before moving any pieces on the chessboard, you might imagine the consequences of moving any piece and move the piece you think would help you to win. So, basically, before taking any action, you imagine the consequence and, if it is favorable, you proceed with that action, or else you refrain from performing that action.

Similarly, imagination augmented agents are augmented with imagination; before taking any action in an environment they imagine the consequences of taking the action and, if they think the action will provide a good reward, they will perform the action. They also imagine the consequences of taking a different action. Augmenting agents with imaginations is the next big step towards general artificial intelligence.

Now we will see how imagination augmented agents works in brief; I2A takes advantage of both model-based and model-free learning.

The architecture of I2A is as follows:

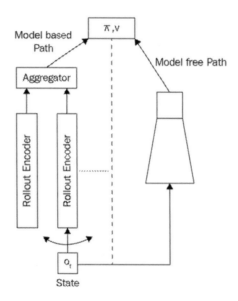

I2A architecture

The action the agent takes is the result of both the model-based and model-free path. In the model-based path, we have something called rollout encoders; these rollout encoders are where the agent performs imagination tasks. Let's take a closer look at rollout encoders. A rollout encoder is shown as follows:

Single Imagination Rollout

Rollout encoders have two layers: imagine future and encoder. Imagine future is where the imagination happens. Look at the preceding diagram; the imagine future consists of the imagination core. When feeding in the state, o_t, to the imagination core, we get the new state $\hat{o}_{t+1}$ and the reward $\hat{r}_{t+1}$, and when we feed this new state $\hat{o}_{t+1}$ to the next imagination core we get the next new state $\hat{o}_{t+2}$ and reward $\hat{r}_{t+2}$. When we repeat these for some *n* steps we get a rollout which is basically a pair of states and rewards, and then we use encoders such as LSTM for encoding this rollout. As a result we get rollout encoding. These rollout encodings are actually the embeddings describing the future imagined path. We will have multiple rollout encoders for different future imagined paths and we use an aggregator for aggregating this rollout encoder.

Wait. How does the imagination happen in the **imagination core**? What is actually in the **imagination core**? A single **imagination core** is shown in the following diagram:

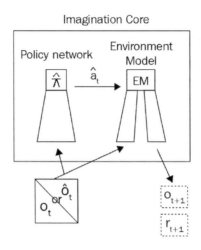

The **imagination core** consists of a **policy network** and **environment model**. The **environment model** is actually where everything happens. The **environment model** learns from all the actions that the agent has performed so far. It takes the information about the state $\hat{O}_t$ and imagines all the possible futures considering the experience and chooses the action $\hat{a}_t$ which gives a high reward.

The architecture of I2A with all components expanded is shown as follows:

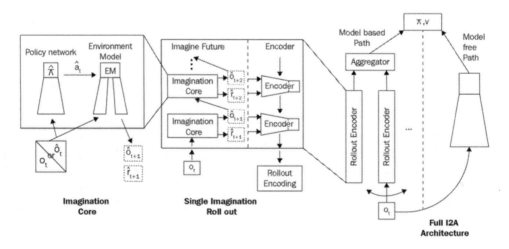

Have you played Sokoban before? Sokoban is a classic puzzle game where the player has to push boxes to a target location. The rules of the game are very simple: boxes can only be pushed and cannot be pulled. If we push a box in the wrong direction then the puzzle becomes unsolvable:

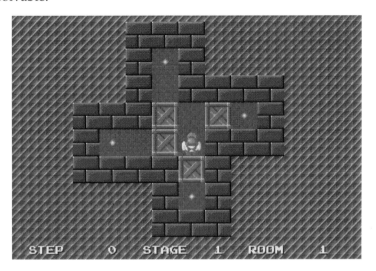

If we were asked to play Sokoban, then we imagine and plan before making any moves as bad moves lead to the end of the game. The I2A architecture will provide good results in these kinds of environments, where the agent has to plan in advance before taking any action. The authors of this paper tested I2A performance on Sokoban and achieved significant results.

Learning from human preference

Learning from human preference is a major breakthrough in RL. The algorithm was proposed by researchers at OpenAI and DeepMind. The idea behind the algorithm is to make the agent learn according to human feedback. Initially, the agents act randomly and then two video clips of the agent performing an action are given to a human. The human can inspect the video clips and tell the agent which video clip is better, that is, in which video the agent is performing the task better and will lead it to achieving the goal. Once this feedback is given, the agent will try to do the actions preferred by the human and set the reward accordingly. Designing reward functions is one of the major challenges in RL, so having human interaction with the agent directly helps us to overcome the challenge and also helps us to minimize the writing of complex goal functions.

The training process is shown in the following diagram:

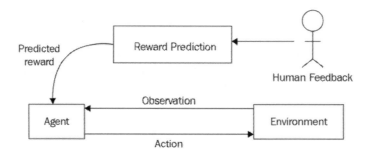

Let's have a look at the following steps:

1. First, our **agent** interacts with the **environment** through a random policy.
2. The behavior of the agent's interaction with the **environment** will be captured in a pair of two to three seconds of video clips and given to the human.
3. The human will inspect the video clips and understand in which video clip the agent is performing better. They will send the result to the reward predictor.
4. Now the agent will receive these signals from the reward predicted and set its goal and reward functions in line with the human's feedback.

A trajectory is a sequence of observations and actions. We can denote the trajectory segment as σ, so $\sigma = ((o_0, a_0), (o_1, a_1), (o_2, a_2)\ldots(o_{k-1}, a_{k-1}))$, where o is the observation and a is the action. The agents receive an observation from the environment and perform some action. Let's say we will store this sequence of interactions in two σ_1 trajectory segments, and σ_2. Now, these two trajectories are shown to the human. If the human prefers σ_2 to σ_1, then the agent's goal is to produce the trajectories preferred by the human, and the reward function will be set accordingly. These trajectory segments are stored in a database as $(\sigma_1, \sigma_2, \mu)$; if the human prefers σ_2 to σ_1 then the μ is set to prefer σ_2. If none of the trajectories are preferred, then both will be removed from the database. If both are preferred, then the μ is set to a uniform.

You can check out the video at `https://youtu.be/oC7Cw3fu3gU` to see how the algorithm works.

Deep Q learning from demonstrations

We have learned a lot about DQN. We started off with vanilla DQN and then we saw various improvements such as double DQN, dueling network architecture, and prioritized experience replay. We have also learned to build DQN to play Atari games. We stored the agent's interactions with the environment in the experience buffer and made the agent learn from those experiences. But the problem was, it took us a lot of training time to improve performance. For learning in simulated environments, it is fine, but when we make our agent learn in a real-world environment it causes a lot of problems. To overcome this, a researcher from Google's DeepMind introduced an improvement on DQN called **deep Q learning from demonstrations (DQfd)**.

If we already have some demonstration data, then we can directly add those demonstrations to the experience replay buffer. For example, consider an agent learning to play Atari games. If we already have some demonstration data that tells our agent which state is better and which action provides a good reward in a state, then the agent can directly make use of this data for learning. Even a small amount of demonstration will increase the agent's performance and also minimizes the training time. Since the demonstrated data will be added directly to the prioritized experience replay buffer, the amount of data the agent can use from the demonstration data and the amount of data the agent can use from its own interaction for learning will be controlled by the prioritized experience replay buffer, as the experience will be prioritized.

Loss functions in DQfd will be the sum of various losses. In order to prevent our agent from overfitting to the demonstration data, we compute L2 regularization loss over the network weights. We compute TD loss as usual and also supervised loss to see how our agent is learning from the demonstration data. Authors of this paper experimented with DQfd and various environments, and the performance of DQfd was better and faster than prioritized dueling Double DQN.

You can check out this video to see how DQfd learned to play the Private Eye game: https://youtu.be/4IFZvqBHsFY.

Hindsight experience replay

We have seen how experience replay is used in DQN to avoid a correlated experience. Also, we learned that prioritized experience replay is an improvement to the vanilla experience replay as it prioritizes each experience with the TD error. Now we will look at a new technique called **hindsight experience replay (HER)**, proposed by OpenAI researchers for dealing with sparse rewards. Do you remember how you learned to ride a bike? On your first try, you wouldn't have balanced the bike properly. You would have failed several times to balance correctly. But all those failures don't mean you didn't learn anything. The failures would have taught you how not to balance a bike. Even though you did not learn to ride the bike (goal), you learned a different goal, that is, you learned how not to balance a bike. This is how we humans learn, right? We learn from failure, and this is the idea behind hindsight experience replay.

Let's consider the same example given in the paper. Look at the FetchSlide environment as shown in the diagram; the goal in this environment is to move the robotic arm and slide a puck across the table to hit the target, a small red circle (diagram from `https://blog.openai.com/ingredients-for-robotics-research/`):

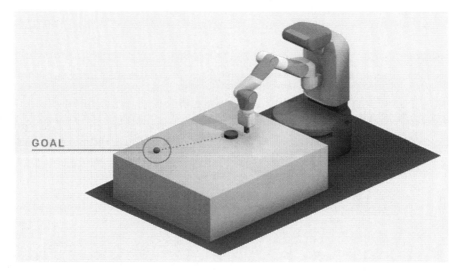

In few first trails, the agent could not definitely achieve the goal. So the agent only received -1 as the reward, which told the agent it was doing wrong and that it did not achieve the goal:

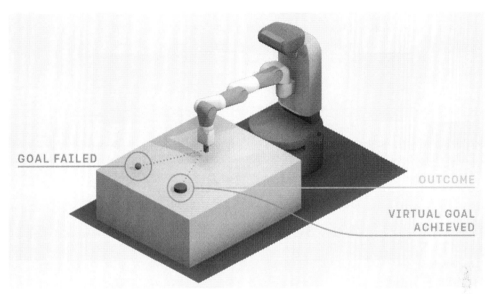

But this doesn't mean that agent has not learned anything. The agent has achieved a different goal, that is, it has learned to move closer to the actual goal. So instead of considering it a failure, we consider that it has a different goal. If we repeat this process over several iterations, the agent will learn to achieve our actual goal. HER can be applied to any off-policy algorithms. The performance of HER is compared by DDPG without HER and vice versa and it is seen that DDPG with HER converge quicker than DDPG without HER. You can see the performance of HER in this video: `https://youtu.be/Dz_HuzgMxzo`.

Hierarchical reinforcement learning

The problem with RL is that it cannot scale well with a large number of state spaces and actions, which ultimately leads to the curse of dimensionality. **Hierarchical reinforcement learning (HRL)** is proposed to solve the curse of dimensionality where we decompress large problems into small subproblems in a hierarchy. Let's say the agent's goal is to reach its home from school. Here the problem is split into a set of subgoals such as going out of the school gate, booking a cab, and so on.

There are different methods used in HRL such as state-space decomposition, state abstraction, and temporal abstraction. In state-space decomposition, we decompose the state space into different subspaces and try to solve the problem in a smaller subspace. Breaking down the state space also allows faster exploration as the agent does not want to explore the entire state space. In state abstraction, the agent ignores the variables, that are irrelevant in achieving the current subtasks in the current state space. In temporal abstraction, the action sequence and action sets are grouped, which divides the single step into multiple steps.

We can now look into one of the most commonly used algorithms in HRL, called MAXQ Value Function Decomposition.

MAXQ Value Function Decomposition

MAXQ Value Function Decomposition is one of the frequently used algorithms in HRL; let's see how MAXQ works. In MAXQ Value Function Decomposition, we decompose the value function into a set of value functions for each of the subtasks. Let's take the same example given in the paper. Remember the taxi problem we solved using Q learning and SARSA?

There are four locations in total, and the agent has to pick up a passenger at one location and drop them off at another location. The agent will receive +20 points as a reward for a successful drop off and -1 point for every time step it takes. The agent will also lose -10 points for illegal pickups and drops. So the goal of our agent is to learn to pick up and drop off passengers at the correct location in a short time without adding illegal passengers.

The environment is shown next, where the letters (**R, G, Y, B**) represent the different locations and a tiny, yellow-colored rectangle is the taxi driven by our agent:

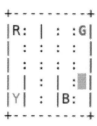

Now we break our goal into four subtasks as follows:

- **Navigate**: Here the goal is to drive the taxi from the current location to one of the target locations. The Navigate(t) subtask should use the four primitive actions north, south, east, and west.
- **Get**: Here the goal is to drive the taxi from its current location to the passenger's location and pick up the passenger.
- **Put**: Here the goal is to drive the taxi from its current location to the passenger's destination location and drop off the passenger.
- **Root**: Root is the whole task.

We can represent all these subtasks in a directed acyclic graph called a task graph, shown as follows:

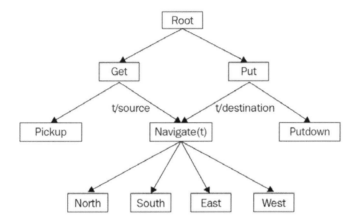

You can see in the preceding figure that all the subtasks are arranged hierarchically. Each node represents the subtask or primitive action and each edge connects the way in which one subtask can call its child subtask.

The **Navigate(t)** subtask has four primitive actions: **east**, **west**, **north**, and **south**. The **Get** subtask has a **pickup** primitive action and a navigate subtask; similarly **Put** subtask, has a **putdown** (drop) primitive action and navigate subtask.

In MAXQ decomposition, MDP M will be divided into a set of tasks such as $(M_0, M_1, M_2 \ldots M_n)$

M_0 is the root task and $M_1, M_2 \ldots M_n$ is the subtasks.

A subtask M_i defines the semi MDP with states S_i, actions A_i, probability transition function $P_i^\pi(s', N|s, a)$, and expected reward function $\bar{R}(s, a) = V^\pi(a, s)$, where $V^\pi(a, s)$ is the projected value function for the child task M_a in state s.

If the action a is a primitive action, then we can define $V^\pi(a, s)$ as an expected immediate reward of executing action a in the state s:

$$V^\pi(a, s) = \sum_{s'} P(s'|s, a). R(s'|s, a)$$

Now, we can rewrite the preceding value function in the Bellman equation form as follows:

$$V^\pi(i, s) = V^\pi(\pi_i(s), s) + \sum_{s', N} P_i^\pi(s', N|s, \pi_i(s))\gamma^N V^\pi(i, s')$$

--(1)

We will denote the state-action value function Q as follows:

$$Q^\pi(i, s, a) = V^\pi(a, s) + \sum_{s', N} P_i^\pi(s', N|s, a)\gamma^N Q^\pi(i, s', \pi(s'))$$

-- (2)

Now, we define one more function called a completion function, which is the expected discounted cumulative reward of completing a subtask M_i:

$$C^\pi(i, s, a) = \sum_{s', N} P_i^\pi(s', N|s, a)\gamma^N Q^\pi(i, s', \pi(s'))$$

-- (3)

For equations (2) and (3), we can write the Q function as:

$$Q^\pi(i, s, a) = V^\pi(a, s) + C^\pi(i, s, a)$$

Finally we can redefine the value function as:

$$V^\pi(i,s) = \begin{cases} Q^\pi(i,s,\pi_i(s)) & \text{if i is composite} \\ \sum_{s'} P(s'|s,i)R(s'|s,i) & \text{if i is primitive} \end{cases}$$

The previous equations will decompose the value function of the root task into value functions of the individual subtask tasks.

For efficient designing and debugging of MAXQ decompositions, we can redraw our task graphs as follows:

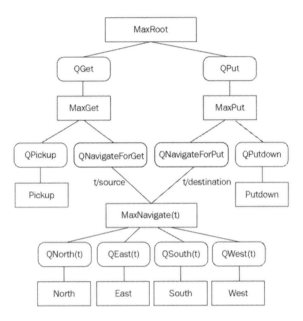

Our redesigned graph contains two special types of nodes: max node and Q nodes. The max nodes define the subtasks in the task decomposition and the Q nodes define the actions that are available for each subtask.

Inverse reinforcement learning

So, what did we do in RL? We tried to find the optimal policy given the reward function. Inverse reinforcement learning is just the inverse of reinforcement learning, that is, the optimal policy is given and we need to find the reward function. But why is inverse reinforcement learning helpful? Designing a reward function is not a simple task and a poor reward function will lead to the bad behavior of an agent. We do not always know the proper reward function but we know the right policy, that is, the right action in each state. So this optimal policy is fed to the agent by human experts and the agents try to learn the reward function. For example, consider an agent learning to walk in a real-world environment; it is difficult to design the reward function for all the actions it will do. Instead, we can feed in to the agents the demonstrations (optimal policy) from the human expert and the agents will try to learn the reward function.

There are various improvements and advancements happening around RL. Now that you have finished reading the book, you can start exploring various advancements in reinforcement learning and start experimenting with various projects. Learn and reinforce!

Summary

In this chapter, we have learned about several recent advancements in RL. We saw how I2A architecture uses the imagination core for forward planning followed by how agents can be trained according to human preference. We also learned about DQfd, which boosts the performance and reduces the training time of DQN by learning from demonstrations. Then we looked at hindsight experience replay where we learned how agents learn from failures.

Next, we learned about hierarchical RL, where the goal is decompressed into a hierarchy of sub-goals. We learned about inverse RL where the agents try to learn the reward function given the policy. RL is evolving each and every day with interesting advancements; now that you have understood various reinforcement learning algorithms, you can build agents to perform various tasks and contribute to RL research.

Questions

The question list is as follows:

1. What is imagination in an agent?
2. What is the imagination core?
3. How do the agents learn from human preference?
4. How is DQfd different from DQN?
5. What is hindsight experience replay?
6. What is the need for hierarchical reinforcement learning?
7. How does inverse reinforcement learning differ from reinforcement learning?

Further reading

You can further refer to these papers:

- **I2A paper**: https://arxiv.org/pdf/1707.06203.pdf
- **DRL from human preference paper**: https://arxiv.org/pdf/1706.03741.pdf
- **HER paper**: https://arxiv.org/pdf/1707.01495.pdf
- **AI safety via debate**: https://arxiv.org/pdf/1805.00899.pdf

Assessments

Chapter 1

1. **Reinforcement learning (RL)** is a branch of machine learning where the learning occurs via interacting with an environment.
2. RL works by train and error method, unlike other ML paradigms.
3. Agents are the software programs that make intelligent decisions and they are basically learners in RL.
4. Policy function specifies what action to take in each state and value function specifies the value of each state.
5. In model-based agent use the previous experience whereas in model-free learning there won't be any previous experience.
6. Deterministic, stochastic, fully observable, partially observable, discrete continuous, episodic and non-episodic.
7. OpenAI Universe provides rich environments for training RL agents.
8. Refer section *Applications of RL*.

Chapter 2

1. `conda create --name universe python=3.6 anaconda`
2. With Docker, we can pack our application with its dependencies, which is called container, and we can simply run our applications on the server without using any external dependency with our packed Docker container.
3. `gym.make(env_name)`
4. ```
   from gym import envs
   print(envs.registry.all())
   ```
5. OpenAI Universe is an extension of OpenAI Gym and it also provides various rich environments.
6. Placeholder is used for feeding external data whereas variable is used for holding values.
   ```

7. Everything in TensorFlow will be represented as a computational graph that consists of nodes and edges, where nodes are the mathematical operations, say addition, multiplication and so on, and edges are the tensors.

8. Computation graphs will only be defined; in order to execute the computation graph, we use TensorFlow sessions.

Chapter 3

1. The Markov property states that the future depends only on the present and not on the past.

2. MDP is an extension of the Markov chain. It provides a mathematical framework for modeling decision-making situations. Almost all RL problems can be modeled as MDP.

3. Refer section *Discount factor*.

4. The discount factor decides how much importance we give to the future rewards and immediate rewards.

5. We use Bellman function for solving the MDP.

6. Refer section *Deriving the Bellman equation for value and Q functions*.

7. Value function specifies goodness of a state and Q function specifies goodness of an action in that state.

8. Refer section *Value iteration* and *Policy iteration*.

Chapter 4

1. The Monte Carlo algorithm is used in RL when the model of the environment is not known.

2. Refer section *Estimating the value of pi using Monte Carlo*.

3. In Monte Carlo prediction, we approximate the value function by taking the mean return instead of the expected return.

4. In every visit Monte Carlo, we average the return every time the state is visited in an episode. But in the first visit MC method, we average the return only the first time the state is visited in an episode.

5. Refer section *Monte Carlo control.*
6. Refer section *On-policy Monte Carlo control* and *Off-policy Monte Carlo control*
7. Refer section *Let's play Blackjack with Monte Carlo.*

Chapter 5

1. Monte Carlo methods are applied only for episodic tasks whereas TD learning can be applied to both episodic and nonepisodic tasks
2. The difference between the actual value and the predicted value is called TD error
3. Refer section *TD prediction* and *TD control*
4. Refer section *Solving taxi problem using Q learning*
5. In Q learning, we take action using an epsilon-greedy policy and, while updating the Q value, we simply pick up the maximum action. In SARSA, we take the action using the epsilon-greedy policy and also, while updating the Q value, we pick up the action using the epsilon-greedy policy.

Chapter 6

1. An MAB is actually a slot machine, a gambling game played in a casino where you pull the arm (lever) and get a payout (reward) based on a randomly generated probability distribution. A single slot machine is called a one-armed bandit and, when there are multiple slot machines it is called multi-armed bandits or k-armed bandits.
2. An explore-exploit dilemma arises when the agent is not sure whether to explore new actions or exploit the best action using the previous experience.
3. The epsilon is used to for deciding whether the agent should explore or exploit actions with 1-epsilon we choose best action and with epsilon we explore new action.
4. We can solve explore-exploit dilemma using a various algorithm such epsilon-greedy policy, softmax exploration, UCB, Thompson sampling.
5. The UCB algorithm helps us in selecting the best arm based on a confidence interval.
6. In Thomson sampling, we estimate using prior distribution and in UCB we estimate using a confidence interval.

Chapter 7

1. In neurons, we introduce non-linearity to the result, z, by applying a function $f()$ called the activation or transfer function. Refer section *Artificial neurons*.
2. Activation functions are used for introducing nonlinearity.
3. We calculate the gradient of the cost function with respect to the weights to minimize the error.
4. RNN predicts the output not only based on the current input but also on the previous hidden state.
5. While backpropagating the network if the gradient value becomes smaller and smaller it is called vanishing gradient problem if the gradient value becomes bigger then it is exploding gradient problem.
6. Gates are special structures in LSTM used to decide what information to keep, discard and update.
7. The pooling layer is used to reduce the dimensions of the feature maps and keeps only necessary details so that the amount of computation can be reduced.

Chapter 8

1. **Deep Q Network (DQN)** is a neural network used for approximating the Q function.
2. Experience replay is used to remove the correlations between the agent's experience.
3. When we use the same network for predicting target value and predicted value there will lot of divergence so we use separate target network.
4. Because of the max operator DQN overestimates Q value.
5. By having two separate Q functions each learning independently double DQN avoids overestimating Q values.
6. Experiences are priorities based on TD error in prioritized experience replay.
7. Dueling DQN estimating the Q value precisely by breaking the Q function computation into value function and advantage function.

Chapter 9

1. DRQN makes use of **recurrent neural network (RNN)** where DQN makes use of vanilla neural network.
2. DQN is not used applied when the MDP is partially observable.
3. Refer section *Doom with DRQN*.
4. DARQN makes use of attention mechanism unlike DRQN.
5. DARQN is used to understand and focus on particular area of game screen which is more important.
6. Soft and hard attention.
7. We set living reward to 0 which the agent does for each move, even though the move is not useful.

Chapter 10

1. A3C is the Asynchronous Advantage Actor Critic network which uses several agents to learn parallel.
2. Three A's are Asynchronous, Advantage, Actor Critic.
3. A3C requires less computation power and training time than DQN.
4. All agents (workers) works in copies of the environment and then global network aggregate their experience.
5. Entropy is used to ensure enough exploration.
6. Refer section *How A3C works*.

Chapter 11

1. The policy gradient is one of the amazing algorithms in RL where we directly optimize the policy parameterized by some parameter.
2. Policy gradients are effective as we don't need to compute Q function to find the optimal policy.
3. The role of the Actor network is to determine the best actions in the state by tuning the parameter, and the role of the Critic is to evaluate the action produced by the Actor.

4. Refer section *Trust region policy optimization*
5. We iteratively improve the policy and we impose a constraint that **Kullback–Leibler (KL)** divergence between old policy and a new policy is to be less than some constant. This constraint is called the trust region constraint.
6. PPO modifies the objective function of TRPO by changing the constraint to a penalty a term so that we don't want to perform conjugate gradient.

Chapter 12

1. DQN computes the Q value directly whereas Dueling DQN breaks down the Q value computation into value function and advantage function.
2. Refer section *Replay memory*.
3. When we use the same network for predicting target value and predicted value there will lot of divergence so we use separate target network.
4. Refer section *Replay memory*.
5. Refer section *Dueling network*.
6. Dueling DQN breaks down the Q value computation into value function and advantage function whereas double DQN uses two Q function to avoid overestimation.
7. Refer section Dueling *network*.

Chapter 13

1. Imagination in an agent specifies visualizing and planning before taking any action.
2. Imagination core consists of policy network and environmental model for performing imagination.
3. Agents repeatedly take feedback from the human and change its goal according to the human preference.
4. DQfd uses some demonstration data for training where as DQN doesn't use any demonstrations data upfront.
5. Refer section **Hindsight Experience Replay (HER)**.

6. **Hierarchical reinforcement learning (HRL)** is proposed to solve the curse of dimensionality where we decompress large problems into small subproblems in a hierarchy
7. We tried to find the optimal policy given the reward function in RL whereas in inverse reinforcement learning, the optimal policy is given and we find the reward function

Other Books You May Enjoy

If you enjoyed this book, you may be interested in these other books by Packt:

Artificial Intelligence with Python
Prateek Joshi

ISBN: 978-1-78646-439-2

- Realize different classification and regression techniques
- Understand the concept of clustering and how to use it to automatically segment data
- See how to build an intelligent recommender system
- Understand logic programming and how to use it
- Build automatic speech recognition systems
- Understand the basics of heuristic search and genetic programming
- Develop games using Artificial Intelligence
- Learn how reinforcement learning works
- Discover how to build intelligent applications centered on images, text, and time series data
- See how to use deep learning algorithms and build applications based on it

Statistics for Machine Learning
Pratap Dangeti

ISBN: 978-1-78829-575-8

- Understand the Statistical and Machine Learning fundamentals necessary to build models
- Understand the major differences and parallels between the statistical way and the Machine Learning way to solve problems
- Learn how to prepare data and feed models by using the appropriate Machine Learning algorithms from the more-than-adequate R and Python packages
- Analyze the results and tune the model appropriately to your own predictive goals
- Understand the concepts of required statistics for Machine Learning
- Introduce yourself to necessary fundamentals required for building supervised & unsupervised deep learning models
- Learn reinforcement learning and its application in the field of artificial intelligence domain

Leave a review - let other readers know what you think

Please share your thoughts on this book with others by leaving a review on the site that you bought it from. If you purchased the book from Amazon, please leave us an honest review on this book's Amazon page. This is vital so that other potential readers can see and use your unbiased opinion to make purchasing decisions, we can understand what our customers think about our products, and our authors can see your feedback on the title that they have worked with Packt to create. It will only take a few minutes of your time, but is valuable to other potential customers, our authors, and Packt. Thank you!

Index

optimal value 49

P

partially observable environment 14
partially observable Markov Decision Process
    (POMDP) 194
pi value
    estimating, with Monte Carlo method 72, 75
placeholders 35
policy function 11, 31, 47
policy gradient
    about 232
    URL 233
    using, for Lunar Lander 232
prioritized experience replay 189, 190
Project Malmo 16
proportional prioritization 190
Proximal Policy Optimization (PPO) 251, 252

Q

Q learning, TD control
    about 97, 99
    and SARSA algorithm, differentiating 112
    used, for solving taxi problem 102, 104

R

recurrent neural network (RNN)
    about 131, 148, 150, 193
    backpropagation through time (BPTT) 151
    Long Short-Term Memory RNN 152
    unrolled version 149
reinforcement learning (RL)
    about 7, 9, 173, 232
    algorithm 9
    comparing, with ML paradigms 10
    elements 10
replay buffer
    building 261
RL environments
    continuous environment 14
    deterministic environment 13
    discrete environment 14
    episodic and non-episodic environment 14
    fully observable environment 13

partially observable environment 14
single and multi-agent environment 14
stochastic environment 13
types 13
RL platforms
    about 15
    DeepMind Lab 15
    OpenAI Gym 15
    OpenAI Universe 15
    Project Malmo 16
    RL-Glue 15
    ViZDoom 16

S

SARSA algorithm, TD control
    about 105, 108
    and Q learning, differentiating 112
    used, for solving taxi problem 109
sequential environment 14
single-agent environment 14
soft attention 210
softmax exploration algorithm 119
state value function 48
state-action value function (Q function) 48
stochastic environment 13
subtasks, hierarchical reinforcement learning (HRL)
    get 283
    navigate 283
    put 283
    root 283
system, setting up
    about 19
    Anaconda, installing 20
    Docker, installing 21
    OpenAI Gym, installing 22
    OpenAI Universe, installing 22

T

TD control
    about 96
    off-policy learning algorithm 96
    on-policy learning algorithm 96
    Q learning 97, 99, 100
    State-Action-Reward-State-Action (SARSA)

Printed in Great Britain
by Amazon

47870589R00181